CRITICAL RACE NARRATIVES

CRITICAL AMERICA

Richard Delgado and Jean Stefancic

GENERAL EDITORS

CRITICAL RACE NARRATIVES

A Study of Race, Rhetoric, and Injury

CARL GUTIÉRREZ-JONES

NEW YORK UNIVERSITY PRESS

New York and London

NEW YORK UNIVERSITY PRESS
New York and London

Library of Congress Cataloging-in-Publication Data
Gutiérrez-Jones, Carl Scott.
Critical race narratives : a study of race, rhetoric, and injury /
Carl Gutiérrez-Jones.
p.   cm. — (Critical America)
Includes bibliographical references and index.
ISBN 0-8147-3144-9 (cloth : alk. paper) —
ISBN 0-8147-3145-7 (pbk. : alk. paper)
1. Racism—United States. 2. United States—Race relations.
3. Minorities—United States—Social conditions. 4. Racism—United
States—Historiography. 5. United States—Race relations—
Historiography. 6. Minorities—United States—Social
conditions—Historiography. 7. Narration (Rhetoric) 8. Discourse
analysis, Narrative. 9. Hate speech—United States.   I. Title.
II. Series.
E184.A1 G98 2001
305.8'00973—dc21   2001002344

New York University Press books are printed on acid-free paper,
and their binding materials are chosen for strength and durability.

Manufactured in the United States of America
10 9 8 7 6 5 4 3 2 1

CONTENTS

ACKNOWLEDGMENTS

As the product of many conversations, this book has been, from start to finish, a collective endeavor. Foremost, I convey my deep gratitude to my partner, Leslie Gutiérrez-Jones, who has offered rich insights, fruitful suggestions, and unflagging support. A number of people have also given very generously of their time by commenting on draft versions of this work. In particular, I would like to thank Donald E. Pease, Robyn Wiegman, Dominick LaCapra, Ramón Gutiérrez, Aranye Fradenburg, Debra Castillo, Richard Delgado, Jean Stefancic, Julie Carlson, Charles Bazerman, Giles Gunn, Forrest Robinson, and Abdul JanMohamed. To work with such fine colleagues has been a joy in itself. This project has also benefited from the labors of exceptional graduate student research assistants, including Fatima Mujcinovic, Marc Coronado, Samara Paysse, Rita Raley, and Parker Douglas.

The writing process has been supported by a number of awards, including grants from the Interdisciplinary Humanities Center and the Center for Chicano Studies at the University of California, Santa Barbara. Funding and writing time have also been provided by the California State Legislature (SCR-43 Program) and the University of California's Humanities Fellowship Program. Dartmouth College's Summer Institute on American Studies and the School for Criticism and Theory have been tremendous resources and I thank the organizers and participants alike for their helpful comments and suggestions. In addition, the students attending my graduate seminars have significantly shaped the arguments offered here; I highly value all that these students have taught me during our exchanges.

Parts of this book have appeared elsewhere in somewhat different form; these essays include: "Colorblindness and Acting Out" (in *The*

Futures of American Studies, edited by Donald E. Pease and Robyn Wiegman, Duke University Press); "Injury by Design" (*Cultural Critique* 40 [Fall 1998]: 73–102); and "Haunting Presences and the New Western History: Reading Repetition, Negotiating Trauma" (reprinted from *Arizona Quarterly* 53:2 [Summer 1997]: 135–153, by permission of the Regents of the University of Arizona). My thanks to the respective editors for their comments and for permission to reproduce these materials.

Invaluable research assistance has been provided by the staff at both the University of California, Santa Barbara and the Dartmouth College libraries; in particular, I extend my appreciation to Patrick José Dawson, Head of UCSB's Colección Tloque Nahuaque, and to Salvador Güereña, Director of the California Ethnic and Multicultural Archive. Finally, my thanks to the editors at New York University Press, who have contributed diligent work and very helpful advice.

INTRODUCTION

Almost four decades after embarking on fundamental reforms that would guarantee formal equality to all of its citizens, the United States still finds itself telling very different stories about race and about the prevalence of racism. In a general yet significant sense, people of different racial and ethnic backgrounds tend to read race and racism in ways that are crucially at odds. The O. J. Simpson criminal and civil cases have become one key barometer of this interpretive conflict.[1] One nationwide poll conducted by the *Los Angeles Times* in 1997 found that 76 percent of whites agreed with the civil case verdict that found Simpson liable for the killings of Nicole Brown Simpson and Ronald Lyle Goldman (with 16 percent of whites disagreeing).[2] By contrast, the same poll revealed that only 25 percent of blacks nationwide agreed with the verdict; 67 percent of blacks disagreed. Underscoring the conflict, the poll also demonstrated that most respondents held their views "strongly."[3] Such differences have been apparent as well in responses to police brutality cases, including the beating of Rodney King and the killing of Amadou Diallo.[4] These racially marked results are also consistent with polls measuring general assessments of large urban police departments; the willingness to identify a culture of racism in such police departments is linked in a significant fashion to the respondent's race.[5] Changes of venue in high profile cases only highlight these disparities, as was the case when judges moved the trial of the officers who beat Rodney King from Los Angeles to the "white-flight" suburb of Simi Valley, and shifted the trial of the officers who killed Amadou Diallo from the Bronx (30 percent black, 48 percent latino, and 18.6 percent white) to Albany (9.2 percent black, 86 percent white).[6] In sum, comparable responses to various cases suggest a pattern of competing literacies as regards race issues: To an important extent, minorities and whites are reading race as well as racism differently.

Given this pattern, minority faith in the formal equality of the law may be strained if not broken: In an important sense, the riots that followed the King beating verdict were a statement about the racially defined failure of the criminal justice system. With a few exceptions, that statement was lost as minority protesters were rewoven into narratives that understood them first and foremost as intrinsically dangerous criminals.[7] In this way, the riots could be used to confirm what defense lawyers for the police officers had been suggesting throughout their frame-by-frame analysis of the videotape that captured King's beating: A minority body, in any position, is a threat.[8] In fact, the defense was so persuasive that one juror announced in a post-trial interview that Rodney King had actually been in complete control of the officers throughout the entire beating.[9]

A similar underlying assumption legitimates the practice of racial profiling by police; in this case, the minority threat is worked into formal and informal institutional practices via "official" narratives justifying particular behaviors toward always-incipient offenders.[10] Such institutionalized notions of threat have fundamentally shaped the New York Police Department's Street Crime Unit (associated with the Diallo killing) and the Los Angeles Police Department's Community Resources Against Street Hoodlums (CRASH) units (associated with the Rampart Division scandal). New York's "Stop and Frisk" policy, initiated as part of Mayor Rudolph Giuliani's war on crime, builds on a similar tactic of "aggressive policing," a tactic that would identify racialized offenders before they act. Of a total of 27,000 Stop and Frisk incidents recorded by NYPD officers, 83 percent have targeted black suspects; of those black suspects, only one in sixteen was arrested, and of all suspects arrested on gun possession charges (the primary objective of the unit), only approximately 50 percent were convicted.[11] Stop and Frisk has likely contributed to a decline in certain kinds of crime in New York City, but as numerous observers ask, at what cost?[12] At what point does such racial profiling create the criminality it narrates as well as perpetuate the civil abuses that themselves constitute a form of crime? Similar scrutiny should be applied to the relationship between racial profiling and the exponential growth of prison populations that are increasingly defined by their minority demographics.[13]

The stories that people tell, and how they tell them, as they respond to these issues and questions is the subject of this book. In contrast to philosophically grounded calls for race-blindness, calls that assume formal equality before the law has effectively corrected previous racism, I argue that greater attention to competing narrative and interpretive practices offers the best opportunity for addressing the legacy of racism in the United States. If the divergent polls that I have cited reveal anything, it is not that minorities and whites form different opinions simply because they are minorities or whites; rather, these groups are reaching different conclusions because they read institutions and events in distinct fashions.

In order to clarify the kinds of narrative practices that are in conflict, as well as the stakes that attend the interpretive struggles, let us consider the killing of Amadou Diallo and the subsequent trial of the NYPD officers involved.[14] On February 4, 1999, four civilian-clothed members of the NYPD Street Crimes Unit left their unmarked car to approach Diallo, a West African male, because they believed he was acting suspiciously and was possibly part of a robbery. Diallo had been standing in the entranceway of his home, glancing repeatedly up and down the street. According to the officers, they identified themselves, then shouted orders at Diallo instructing him to make his hands visible. Witnesses at the trial, neighbors of Diallo, testified that no shouts from the police were audible.[15] Diallo apparently hesitated, then reached for his wallet. Whether he had identified the men as police officers or as robbers we will never know because the officers reacted to Diallo's gesture by firing at him 41 times. During their trial, the officers, charged with second-degree murder, justified the shooting, and the number of shots, by emphasizing the apparent threat posed by Diallo.[16] They noted the way in which their own gunfire echoed in the entranceway of Diallo's home, yielding the impression that shots were being returned by him. They also testified that Diallo was slow to react to their shots, that his standing body gave the impression of continuing threat. This position was opened to question when the coroner who examined Diallo's body determined that

3

most of the 19 bullets that struck Diallo did so as he was falling or on the ground.[17]

For its part, the prosecution claimed that we can only fully understand Diallo's shooting by approaching critically the assumptions that the officers carried with them as they confronted Diallo.[18] In this interpretation, Diallo's presumed guilt set in motion a chain of events that had little if any basis in evidence and certainly took no account of the fact that Diallo may himself have been fearful of four burly, civilian-dressed men who aggressively approached at him. The defense lawyers worked to censor these sorts of considerations altogether, arguing that the only way to judge the officers was to view their actions as a split-second, life-or-death decision.[19] This tactic effectively evacuated Diallo as a person; as understood by the defense lawyers, he was significant only in terms of the officers' projection of him as a threat.[20] In this way, Diallo became a vessel for the "white paranoia" identified by Judith Butler in the trial of the LAPD officers who beat Rodney King.[21]

In both contexts, lawyers for the accused officers defended police violence by reconstituting narratives around singular moments; once freed from the constraints of what preceded and followed, these moments could be recycled to tell whatever stories the defenses wanted about the incipient threat of the racial body. In the King beating case, this meant breaking up the videotape of the assault into individual photographic stills so that each still could be reinterpreted by police experts as evidence of King's continuing menace, even when he appeared to be unconscious.[22] The notion that King somehow maintained control over the scene was premised on this technique.[23] In the trial of the officers who killed Diallo, the shift of focus to the split second of the shooting eliminated troubling questions about the events leading to the killing, including the effects of racial profiling by the NYPD; it also deferred any meaning that might be ascribed to the actual duration of the shooting itself. The time it takes to execute 41 shots is thus compressed into a moment that appears to equate the first bullet with all of the rest.

Ultimately, the jurors in the NYPD case accepted the defense's version because they could identify with the police officers' vision of Diallo as a threat. In fact, the judge ordered the jurors to make this leap, instructing them to put themselves in the officers' shoes and view the world as they viewed it.[24] In this manner, the acquittal of the NYPD officers, like the verdict in the King beating case, depended on a strategic narrative reconstruction that excluded all but the defendants' perspectives, and focused on particular, isolated moments. These moments became the foundations for stories which validate the preexisting assumptions and fantasies of officers who were, in effect, out of control during the use of force. In an important sense, Diallo or King as actual threats had little to do with the jury's final judgment about the officers' actions; in this arena, the difference between a gun and a wallet simply does not matter. A defense lawyer in the Diallo case highlighted this point when he told the jurors that Diallo being at home and without a gun was beside the point, and constituted "Monday morning quarterbacking."[25] In closing arguments, the defense added that "Justification [of the officers' actions] is like a knife going through the middle of this indictment. If you find justification, it's over."[26]

In the context of racial profiling, one might well wonder when justification is not implicitly present, especially if one considers the time prior to the "split second" of the shooting, the time when the officers were deciding that Diallo's glances constituted a reason to confront him with deadly force. Former New York Mayor David Dinkins argued something similar as he was arrested among those who were protesting Diallo's killing and the NYPD's profiling practices.[27] However, jurors in Albany are relatively removed from firsthand experience with NYPD profiling. Change of venue in this sense is not so much about how many minorities end up in the jurors' box, but rather about the receptiveness that jurors have for certain kinds of narrative tactics, and the caution they might exercise toward other kinds. Even seemingly obvious evidence, like the videotape of the King beating, is open to mediation through narrative, and if the reactions to the various verdicts reveal anything, it is that whites and minorities tend to read these narrative practices differently, with minorities recognizing in some of them racially vexed material which taints the justice system.

～

> Whoever chases monsters should see to it that in the process he does not become a monster himself.
>
> —Former LAPD Officer Rafael Perez's statement to the Court during his sentencing

The same day that the jury in the Diallo case handed down its verdict, a Los Angeles judge was sentencing former LAPD CRASH unit member Rafael Perez to five years in prison for stealing eight pounds of cocaine from a police storage facility.[28] Perez, who will be eligible for parole after serving only 16 months, received the reduced punishment after pleading for forgiveness and cooperating with investigators in order to reveal the worst corruption scandal in the modern history of the LAPD;[29] at least 70 officers have been placed under investigation for more than 100 incidents of misconduct, including framing suspects, wrongful shootings of innocent people, brutality, theft, falsified police reports, and perjury.[30] Thirty of these officers, including three sergeants, have been suspended, fired, or have quit in response to the probe.[31] Three officers have been convicted of framing innocent people, and the LAPD has acknowledged that at least 99 convictions have been tainted by police corruption (and that number is likely to increase significantly).[32] Although only 85 convictions have been overturned, investigators anticipate that many more will be affected. Altogether, Perez provided 3,242 pages of transcribed interviews to investigators—material that is being collaborated as the inquiry continues.[33] Evidence of corruption and mismanagement has spread beyond the confines of Perez's anti-gang CRASH unit and even beyond the Rampart Division that oversaw it. In fact, an LAPD Board of Inquiry Report released in March 2000 found fault across the entire LAPD, including the department's interactions with the District Attorney's office.[34] Federal Immigration Services also appear to be involved inasmuch as false gang-related charges may have been used to round up potential immigration violators; overall, officials estimate that the total cost to the city in terms of Rampart-related lawsuits (about 200 in all) will run about $200 million.[35]

Perez's interviews reveal the systematic terrorization by his CRASH unit of a poor, largely minority community. In his apology offered in court, Perez cited a pernicious "us versus them" mentality that was fostered by his fellow CRASH unit members, as well as by his superiors.[36] This outlook, combined with an ethic of results by any means, led to moral confusion, according to Perez. Further, Perez claimed that he "succumbed to the seductress of power."[37] One can certainly wonder about the sincerity of Perez's apology; although some less-than-sympathetic observers from the LAPD credited the apology as a truthful reflection of Perez's feelings, he was a highly skilled liar who exploited his talents regularly in the courtroom.[38] All the same, there is much that is telling in his construction of his actions; deceptive or sincere, the apology reads as if it were a medieval romance detailing the acts of knights, sirens, and dragons.

The final line of the apology, cited above, is a rather remarkable bid for sympathy, one that works to the extent that it reminds readers of the mission that the CRASH unit professed: to maintain a thin blue line between the public and the "monsters," in this case racialized gangs. The gesture is deft because it displaces many of Perez's actual targets—innocent minorities—and supplants them with an image of imminent threat, the same sort of threat that ultimately swayed the juries in the King and Diallo cases.[39] Completely lost is the sense held by many community members that the police as a group were as dangerous as the gangs.[40] The romance framing also conveniently abstracts "power" as the real evil, then feminizes it (by naming it "seductress"), thereby revivifying the very macho, "kick butt" ethic that reached one of its more horrid homosocial expressions in the rape of Abner Louima by NYPD officers.[41] Even in his apology, Perez appears to reconstitute self-aggrandizing macho assumptions that were basic to the functioning of the CRASH units and to its policy of aggressive policing.[42]

The extent of the Rampart scandal forced Los Angeles Police Chief Bernard Parks to discontinue the CRASH units.[43] However, it remains to be seen if policing policy will be seriously affected, since new anti-gang units with the same mission replaced the CRASH units shortly after their departure.[44] Supervision has increased as the new units have physically joined existing divisional headquarters, but as is abundantly apparent in the LAPD Board of Inquiry Report, the supervisory ranks have themselves been seriously negligent.[45] Chief Parks has also announced that membership in the units will be limited to three years and that selection into the units will no longer be determined by existing members.[46] Among other things, experience in the field will become a key criterion.[47] Although these efforts may help to change the CRASH unit culture described by Perez, it is not clear that the additional experience will solve a problem that may have a great deal to do with the racial profiling at the heart of the aggressive policing policy.

This is not to say that lack of experience and training is not a problem in itself. Richard Riordan's 1993 Los Angeles mayoral campaign was built on a promise to dramatically increase the police force by thousands of officers during his first term, and he did so despite warnings from then Police Chief Willie Williams that the department simply did not have the capacity to train officers as quickly as they were being hired, nor to conduct proper background checks on new hires.[48] It is also worthwhile to remember that Perez was an experienced officer who had joined the LAPD in 1989 and who had conducted himself well enough until entry into the CRASH unit.[49] For all of the efforts to identify personnel and training problems, then, there remain fundamental issues that are not being sufficiently addressed by the LAPD self-critiques: Why these particular victims? Why have CRASH units in particular been the hub of misconduct?

Public reactions to the Rampart scandal, as indicated by *Los Angeles Times* polls, convey distinctly different readings of the LAPD's woes.[50] These polls show that "white respondents hold the now-departed Captain of the Rampart Division largely responsible for the problems in that division"; by contrast, black respondents "overwhelmingly pointed to the LAPD's culture and climate as the underlying cause of the scandal."[51] While the scope of the scandal has inspired broad-based condemnation of the LAPD not seen since the Rodney King beating (75 percent of the Los Angeles residents polled support the creation of an independent commission to investigate Rampart), the reasoning for this negative assessment varies greatly among whites and minorities.[52] Whites appear more willing to disassociate the scandal from the rest of the department by focusing on individuals.[53] Blacks and Latinos, by contrast, tend to interpret the scandal as exposure of racism that they already believe exists broadly within the police department. While 61 percent of whites described themselves as "very upset" by the misconduct, only 26 percent of blacks held the same opinion: Rampart did not seem to be news to minorities.[54] The extent of the distinction is also revealed in opinions about the LAPD's use of brutality: 83 percent of blacks and 72 percent of Latinos polled in Los Angeles think that LAPD officers *commonly* commit acts of brutality; only 43 percent of white respondents shared that belief.[55]

At first, Mayor Riordan and Chief Parks attempted to ride the sentiments held by many whites, claiming that the Rampart scandal represented an aberration in an otherwise healthy institution.[56] After 70 officers were implicated, the mayor and chief were forced to change their approach and to focus instead on managerial shortcomings and inadequate supervision.[57] However, none of the LAPD's self-analysis offered a viable treatment of racism in the department, and this is one reason why the real battle over the Rampart scandal comes down to oversight, particularly civilian oversight of the LAPD.[58] With such oversight comes the opportunity not just to affect individual cases of misconduct, but also to impact the overall culture and policymaking of the department.[59] Oversight is an especially appealing prospect for many minority community members who have experienced firsthand the negative effects of aggressive policing and racial profiling. At stake in such oversight is the ability to legitimate different narratives about the police's reaction to, and construction of, different communities. In a very real sense, this debate has everything to do with challenging the projection of the "monsters" alluded to by Perez.

Battles regarding oversight tend to elicit conflicting assumptions about law enforcement when race and racism are at issue.[60] Minority critics of aggressive policing have argued that crime itself is a social construct, and that this construct has been used implicitly and explicitly to discriminate against minority communities.[61] Problematic definitions of crime are understood as a means for some whites to justify actions and policies that cement minorities (and particularly poor minorities) into second-class citizenship.[62] In this interpretation, bias in the criminal justice system falsely amplifies and/or distorts what minorities would define as criminal behavior. As I have noted, New York City's Stop and Frisk policy is one example of how minorities are disproportionately drawn into criminal justice processing. Such processing can also train minorities for further conflict with the law, especially when the subjects are juveniles.[63] Outright bias remains a question in the penalties assessed to like crimes; minority critics, for instance, ask why the cheap crack cocaine used by impoverished minorities should carry significantly greater penalties than those applied to the largely white, affluent users of powder cocaine.[64] Extending the argument further, critics of the war on drugs ask why this national policy, aimed squarely at inner-city minorities, came to be an overwhelming focus of national attention when corporate crime and violence was so seriously damaging peoples' lives.[65] Consider for instance that "the total loss from street robbery in the United States in 1989 was $405 million, but a single price-fixing conspiracy by oil companies cost the nation's consumers $432 million; 3.2 million burglaries accounted for a $3.4 billion loss, yet the S&L scandal cost this nation from $300 to $500 billion."[66]

These factors, among others, lead minority analysts to a cautious appraisal of formal equality's value, precisely because the doctrine of equality has been marshaled to argue that racism in the law is a thing of the past.[67] If formal equality exists, as the 1960s anti-discrimination laws would seem to guarantee, then it would not matter who maintains oversight of the police because the rule of law does not allow the expression of racism. The changes of venue in the King beating and the Diallo killing trials are ultimately protected by a similar logic: If the law is color-blind, it should not matter where a trial takes place or what the racial makeup of the jury might be. In the wake of Diallo's killing and the Rampart scandal, both the NYPD and the LAPD have strongly resisted reforms that would entail greater civilian oversight; however, in the case of the LAPD, the federal government was able to convince the city to sign a consent decree that mandates, among other things, data collection regarding racial profiling and a stronger civilian police commission.[68] In both cases, the institutions are defending their autonomy and power by capitalizing on the supposed guarantees associated with formal equality.

This book explores the relations between the formal equality argument and the minority critique by focusing on the narrative and interpretive dynamics that the approaches both share and contest. In part, the goal is to better understand why the criminalization (and imprisonment) of minorities has developed as it has during a period celebrated for its formal equality reforms. The project builds on the work of Critical Race scholars who have led the way in demonstrating how power and ideology are mediated through the stories that legal actors tell; in the process, I expand the purview of the Critical Race Studies (a legal-based discipline also known as Critical Race Theory, or CRT) and query the resistant as well as remediary qualities that a number of Critical Race scholars attribute to their narrative interventions.[69] Among other goals, I want to suggest that the CRT interventions may be enhanced by testing their limits as legal gestures even more. For instance, as valuable as the debates about hate crime have been, the CRT positions have been open to critique by analysts who question both the ways such laws may reproduce racism as well as the ways such laws may leave the deeper culture of racism untouched precisely by offering a bureaucratic remedy.[70] Critical Race scholars see a greater potential for the hate crime laws,[71] but I believe that tapping that potential will require a more compelling articulation of their project in relation to the various forms of race literacy circulating in the United States.

This book contributes to this project by focusing on the construction of racial injury as played out in diverse disciplinary and institutional settings; in the process, I engage sociology, history, law, cultural studies, and sociobiology as well as popular culture. The book addresses practitioners of the specific fields considered, especially those interested in testing disciplinary conventions; it is also oriented toward scholars of American studies, a field that has long demonstrated a commitment to interdisciplinary race analysis. The ambitious scope of the project speaks to my belief that race and racism as concepts will remain analytically viable to the extent that they are grounded in specific contexts and intellectual histories. I have chosen the disciplines that I focus on according to two principal criteria. First, I have sought out fields that have played important roles in terms of negotiating public policy, as well as state and nation formation, in relation to race issues. The fields in question have all contributed in significant ways to race-oriented policymaking and/or the construction of ideas about race, not just by lending finished research to the race debates, but also by adding field-specific assumptions about what counts as evidence of racial injury to public dialogues.

Second, I have selected fields that offer rich examples of experimental, narrative-oriented race analysis (examples of which are explored in Chapters 3 through 6). This variously positioned work with race and narrative acts as a thread drawing the case studies together.

Looking to how racial injuries are differently construed by these disciplines, this book resists a contemporary tendency to flatten out distinctions in arguments about race. This flattening is particularly apparent when participants in the debates adopt a narrow philosophical register that equates the acknowledgment of race with the practice of racism (a phenomenon treated in Chapters 1 and 2). As was apparent during California's anti-affirmative action campaign, close rhetorical and linguistic fighting (debate in which opponents read the same language, evidence, and historical figures in radically different ways) can strategically contribute to this "flattening" of race and racism by dislodging these terms from specific contexts and thereby making them all the more available for abstraction. Responding to this confusion, voters can become skeptical of distinctions between race and racism, a situation that makes pro–color-blind legislation all the more appealing for some.

By contrast, an analysis across disciplines may confirm the ways in which the concepts of race and racism have deep analytical value. Studying these concepts as developed in specific fields tells us a great deal about the definition of social problems. Analyzing these fields' negotiation of race and racism also yields a more nuanced picture of racial culture in the United States. Only with this more nuanced picture may we fully appreciate the stakes of the critical narrative interventions being advocated by a host of scholars exploring new avenues for studying race and racism.

Critical Race Narratives moves between specialized academic work, popular academic work, media, literature, and popular culture, including film. The book therefore examines the ways race rhetoric plays through different spheres of activity so that we might better analyze how ideas about race change over time, as well as better assess the effectiveness of interventions like race hate laws and reparations for racial injuries. To these ends, the readings offered here mine the term "injury," a word whose etymological roots demonstrate a fundamental sensitivity to rhetorical dynamics.[72] To injure is in a basic way to transgress accepted conventions of communicating: to violate the rules and laws that govern language use. Approaching the race debates in terms of competing notions of racial injury, therefore, presents an important challenge to the philosophically grounded censorship of race analysis at the core of the color-blindness movement.

The approach to racial injury pursued in the following chapters invites participants in the race debates to rethink commonly held assumptions that may effectively limit the working through of racism.[73] In the first part of this book, "Working Through Racial Injury," I argue that the success of such a project depends upon complicating the notion that racial injury is primarily a matter of inclusion and exclusion; such a notion must be supplemented with analyses that highlight more varied methods of interpreting race dynamics. Here, I suggest that the focus on racial inclusion as a remedy for discrimination (a particularly strong part of the 1980s "culture wars") has displaced questions of what happens when inclusion is achieved. In this vein, the book overall speaks to the question of what changes when people excluded for reasons of race do gain a chance to participate, whether the issue on the table is civilian oversight of police departments or genetic propensities toward intelligence.

This question of what changes with inclusion points critics toward competing modes of cultural literacy—as John Guillory has demonstrated, possibly the most significant stakes of the culture wars.[74] In addition to whatever symbolic value such instances of inclusion provide, a more forceful impact may well grow out of the included party's critical shaping of the interpretive practices and disciplinary literacies of a given institution, school, or profession: practices and literacies at work each time a person teaches a neophyte to think like a police officer, a sociologist, an historian, or a lawyer.

In an effort to chart the literacy struggles within the selected disciplines, the second part of the book, "Narrative Interventions," examines specific debates over how to "read" racial injuries. What one discovers are conflicting stories that attempt to make sense of racial injury by weaving such injury into relationship with the analytical expectations of a given field or institution. Even in instances where race and racism are approached through the lens of "raw" or "hard" data (as with certain forms of sociology or genetics), the significance of such data is always determined by stories (by the process of contextualizing and narrating) that researchers offer as they try to convince their peers to embrace their findings. As important as "hard" data may be, this evidence simply does not have meaning without such stories, for instance the DNA mystique that has been built up around the Human Genome Project as it has justified anticipated costs of $3 billion over 15 years.[75]

The effort to persuade, whether in the interests of funding or of policy, frequently entails either explicit presentation or implicit assumption of arguments regarding how most appropriately to read social and/or cultural variables.[76] For example, disproportionate poverty among minorities is devoid of racist implications if one assumes that such poverty is simply a matter of bad life choices made by discrete individuals. Within this context, a number of the scholars considered in these chapters posit narrative analysis as a crucial tool in the process of understanding and working through racial injuries. Among other things, narrative analysis is credited with best accommodating the wide range of social and cultural variables that inevitably crosscut any phenomenon as complex as racism.[77] It is therefore no accident that when one considers Patricia Limerick's use of anecdote to rethink Western history, or Patricia Williams's mobilization of autobiography to reconstitute the raced legal subject, or Jerome Miller's impassioned argument for the incorporation of narrative analysis during criminal justice processing, one finds a pattern emerging: Narrative intervention itself has become a crucial feature of U.S. race studies. The "promise" of storytelling surfaces in my comparative analysis both as a problem (how does one define the advantages of the narrative intervention?) and as a point of methodological debate (opponents of storytelling frequently brand it as a violation of disciplinary practices that presumably guarantee objectivity).

In key respects, these struggles over literacy and narrative have drawn me, as a scholar trained in literary and historical analysis, to the project. As a beneficiary of affirmative action policies, a beneficiary intimately aware of their limitations as well as their advantages, I am also keenly interested in how best to address the effects of past and present racism. Inasmuch as this is an interdisciplinary project, I engage diverse methods and expectations; however, this book does not try to develop an interdisciplinary *esperanto*. Rather than perpetuating the standards of sociological, historical, sociobiological, and legal analysis throughout, I draw out points of comparison and contrast among particular texts while also exploring how these texts have affected public discussions of racial injury. In this vein, I am curious about how disciplinary treatments of racial injury are adjusted for, and received by, general audiences. Stephen and Abigail Thernstrom's *America in Black and White*, Patricia Limerick's *Legacy of Conquest*, as well as Richard Herrnstein and Charles Murray's *The Bell Curve* may not be the most professionally rigorous examples of sociology, history, or sociobiology, but they are profoundly influential books in terms of reinforcing certain public means of arguing about race: means that gain validity because of the sociological, historical, and scientific validation upon which these texts capitalize. These books are in this sense noteworthy precisely because they use, to differing degrees, discipline-based methods to persuade a general readership.

Critical Race Narratives, in turn, stages a juxtaposition between books that would reinforce discipline-based approaches to race, and books that experimentally rewrite disciplinary conventions. In terms of the latter, Patricia Williams's *Alchemy of Race and Rights*, Jerome Miller's *Search and Destroy*, and Stephen J. Gould's *The Mismeasure of Man* analyze the limitations of discipline-bound approaches to race, and argue that innovative engagements with narrative, both as a form of analytical practice and as a subject of inquiry, lead to a better, more democratic understanding of race dynamics.

Implicit in these experimental texts is the notion that narrative practice in general cannibalizes various disciplinary and professional languages and so allows for a critical reprocessing that, in turn, affords readers a better purchase on how knowledge about race and racism is made. To date, very little work has been undertaken that bridges the race-focused narrative experiment in academic writing and the critical engagement of disciplinary discourses in novels and film. The narrative works that I incorporate in the coming chapters explore interpretive problems engaged by academic narrativists in their treatments of race. For example, Louise Erdrich's *Tracks* is taken up in conjunction with

Limerick's *Legacy of Conquest* in order to reframe ideas about property, ideas that expose a misreading of racial injury by Limerick as she tries to subordinate race conflicts to a "common ground" of economic struggle. In a similar vein, an analysis of John Rechy's *The Miraculous Day of Amalia Gómez* contributes to a reassessment of liberal individualism and the free exercise of choice, ideas that are invoked by Stephen and Abigail Thernstrom as they criticize race-conscious social programs. In addition, I draw the film *Gattaca* into my discussion regarding sociobiology because the work focuses attention on the interplay of altruism and genetics in a way that is only liminally apparent in works like Gould's *The Mismeasure of Man*.

All of these artistic narratives present critiques of disciplinary and institutional discourses, and therefore exemplify my critique of the academic writers experimenting with narrative. I have chosen these narratives because they contribute in very specific ways to certain arguments about racism, but as the Russian literary critic Mikhail Bakhtin has demonstrated, novelistic discourse in general is a cannibalistic medium in which authors combine various discourses (legal, medical, scientific, religious, etc.) in order to develop a critical sense of how people produce knowledge.[78] For Bakhtin, novelistic discourse generates a complicated, conflictual, flexible dialogue, a dialogue that forces readers to reassess the illusion that linguistic meaning is somehow transparent, a simple matter of "common sense." As described by Bakhtin, novelistic discourse is inherently interdisciplinary; this propensity helps explain why certain art forms constitute a valuable resource as we assess academic experiments with critical narratives.

Interdisciplinary work is usually celebrated only as long as one's own discipline is not significantly encroached upon; the risk becomes greater if the interdisciplinary work at hand actively resists disciplinary norms. Disciplines have, of course, developed in such a way as to validate certain field-defining questions at the expense of others. In a setting in which concerns about white supremacy and racism have usurped critical examinations of race, it is to be expected that race studies scholars would benefit by experimenting with unconventional tools.[79] In building on this assumption, I join a number of scholars who have written at length about the problematic shaping of the disciplines vis-à-vis race issues, including John Guillory, Henry Louis Gates, Jr., Vine Deloria, Jr., and Jerome Miller.[80] Disciplinary logics are comfortable to those trained in them in part because these logics add a sense of certainty to the work of the practitioners. Interdisciplinary work at its best leads practitioners out of this comfort zone and into speculation. In turn, this speculation can invite a critique of assumptions that are considered foundational for specific fields. In my experience, if interdisciplinary work does not partake of this speculation, it is usually because a certain disciplinary logic is ruling the day, and because the engagement of other fields is largely a matter of scholarly pastiche. In attempting to chart a different course, this book employs speculation in the hope that it may lead to a better understanding of the diverse experiments with narrative produced by academic writers and artists as they have wrestled with complicated racial dynamics. Without this sort of rethinking, there may be little prospect for mediating among the strongly divergent impressions regarding racism that are held by minorities and whites. The Los Angeles riots, the polarized reactions to O. J. Simpson's trials, the divisions over the acquittal of Amadou Diallo's killers, and the conflicting assessments of the LAPD's Rampart crisis all stand out as dramatic measures of this gap in how Americans read and narrate racial dynamics. The experimental narratives explored in this study speak to this gap by speculating about new ways to approach racial injury.

PART ONE

WORKING THROUGH RACIAL INJURY

CHAPTER ONE

THE CONTOURS OF THE CONTEMPORARY RACE DEBATE

The historic argument for inclusion has always been set within the overarching sign of "America": equal rights equals the achievement of America's democratic ideals. In the contemporary era, we are witnessing how this idea of rights can be turned into a means for garnering protection for the historically privileged, so that whites, men and heterosexuals can claim—and have been winning their claims in court—their right to exclude and discriminate.

—Robyn Wiegman, *American Anatomies*, 133

If recent decades in American studies will be recalled for a pervasive concern regarding the inclusion of previously disenfranchised communities, it may well be that the movement of American studies into the twenty-first century will be remembered for a pronounced skepticism toward the promise of inclusion. This is not to say that the inclusion-oriented debates—over curriculum, hiring policies, conference participation, and structure—that have animated the pages of the various professional journals and bulletins devoted to American studies are likely to evaporate. Instead, I mean to register a probable transformation in the political possibilities tied to inclusion as a form of remedy (for racism, for sexism, etc.). Though the skepticism explored here is not unique to American studies, it does speak in very pointed ways to the implicit and explicit ethical concerns that have exercised considerable influence over the shape and direction of American studies. Much of the skepticism I refer to focuses on the exaggerated nature of the remedy attributed to processes of inclusion in themselves. As posed by Robyn Wiegman in *American Anatomies: Theorizing Race and Gender,* the recent politics of visual representation in popular culture, a politics which might be read as a sign of America's movement toward integration, in fact reveals extremely troubling reinscriptions of social and cultural hierarchies, an indicator that white supremacy has deflected earlier criticisms by simply finding more sophisticated ways of disseminating its messages. Although Wiegman's argument is one of the most systematic critiques in this vein, scholars working within a variety of disciplines within American studies have begun voicing, more and more forcefully, their dissatisfactions with inclusion- and exclusion-oriented political claims.[1] For most, the result has been a desire not to discount the importance of inclusion, but rather to rethink the nature of the injury supposedly ameliorated by inclusion. The frequently implicit assumption, then, is that by refining notions of the injury previously equated in a blanket form with "exclusion," scholars might avoid some of the pitfalls that ensue when rights discourse in particular too quickly yields to a mythology of American consensus, when inclusion too quickly glosses the nature of injury.

Although the point is rarely made in debates about race and racism, most, if not all, of the key terms at issue—including merit, fairness, equality—draw directly on a highly complex discourse of injury which has notable contours that mark it as a product of U.S. cultures, and "Western" culture generally. Patricia Limerick's *Legacy of Conquest: The Unbroken Past of the American West* and the New Western History enterprise as a whole is but one example of how American studies has tried to reshape itself around a project which would complicate notions of injury. In the New Western History approach, the imaginative centrality of the frontier yields to a focus on the consequences of conquest itself. In this regard, Limerick and her cohorts are in fact elaborating a concern with the contours of injury which stretches back through lodestar texts like Richard Slotkin's *Regeneration through Violence,* and Henry Nash Smith's *Virgin Land.* This interest in injury has of course served varied political purposes. One might even argue that Frederick Jackson Turner's frontier thesis, a cornerstone of American history, is itself built upon a notion of injury

wrought by the closing of the West itself, an injury that helped transform the colonization of the West into a larger imperial project of
global dimensions by securing a basic ideological nostalgia for America's own subdued natives.

Whether our focus is the United States or abroad, ample evidence
suggests that current debates regarding injury, including debates over
discrimination and reverse discrimination, are far from exceptional.
Contemporary argument about the "efficacy" of official apologies for
racial injuries, including the Tuskegee experiments and slavery itself,
tended to produce struggles regarding claims of injury that are very similar to those found in the wake of civil and international wars.[2] A recent
measure in the California State Assembly offers an example of the difficult rhetorical terrain; here lawmakers asked Japan to apologize to U.S.
veterans who were forced into slave labor, to sex slaves from Korea, and
to the victims of the "rape of Nanking." Debate about the measure, in
turn, focused on the injuries caused to Japanese civilians by U.S. atom
bombs, on the internment of Japanese Americans during the war, and
on the injuries that may be received by Asian Americans if the bill enhances lingering racial resentments. Not surprisingly, divisions over the
measure extended to the Asian American members of the Assembly,
prompting U.S. Senator Daniel Inouye (Hawaii) to quell tensions by
sharing his own wartime experiences in Europe and emphasizing that
"in war, no party is blameless."[3]

As newspapers across the country have taken up U.S. race debates,
readers have been drawn through repeated examples of our tremendous differences, particularly in terms of our basic understandings of
what defines race and racism. Very rarely have these defining differences been laid out in an analytical fashion, and most often the func-
tional definitions in arguments are left implicit, if not simply vague. A
good part of the popular skepticism that filters through such articles
and op-ed pieces is bound up with the notion—sometimes explicitly
stated—that the "discussion" on race has run its course, or at least
stalled, and that there might not be anything gained in further efforts
that have no shared understandings.[4] As if to reenact this very impasse, media of all sorts have profiled a gambit of politically bal-
kanized, academically credentialed pundits, virtually none of whom

were asked to critically engage questions about what constitutes race, or what the defining dynamics of racism might be. Given the difficulties in both the popular and academic venues that I have been describing, American studies—at least to the extent that it has been invested in questions of race, class, and gender—appears to be at a crossroads of sorts. However we understand the vexed choices this crossroads represents, I would argue there is a significant value in rethinking the ways we are articulating the notions of injury which ground presumed engagements with politics.

A RHETORIC OF INJURY

Like most concepts that end up at the center of debate, "injury" seems to call forth a definition based in common sense. But as is the case with most such terms, closer inspection reveals a lot of baggage to unpack. In one sense, the term is resoundingly rhetorical in nature, a creature animated by the arts of persuasion. Like the verb form "to injure," injury marks an act against "jur," against the law, rights, and accepted privilege. There is also, woven into the term's history, an aspect of oral responsibility. The predominant definition of injury emphasizes its association with a verbal act, with calumny and the like. As suggested by terms like juror, jurat, jury, the law violated by injury is sustained with verbal practices and allegiances, by oaths of filiation to established authority. Injury is also a bit fickle as regards questions of agency. While one definition for the term emphasizes a willful action of hurt, and therefore a resulting blame, another definition treats injury as an effect without focus on the agent.[5] In this sense, injury marks a dichotomy in legal thought that establishes distinct poles as adjudication works through either the perpetrator's or the victim's perspectives. Extending the implications of this dichotomy, one might well argue that the competing basis for arguments about both reverse discrimination and institutional racism are bound up in this slippage. While the former claim assumes that group remedies have insufficiently identified racist agents and therefore enact racist remedies (affirmative action policies and the like), the latter assumes that injuries identified by effects are sufficient to merit judicial action. In sum, injury is continually rearticulated and jostled as it is employed in a rhetorical battle that is legally oriented from the start.

In recent scholarship, injury has also been rethought in terms of the psychoanalytic notion of "trauma," a term that has been particularly important in Holocaust studies and historical inquiries regarding the difficulty, if not impossibility, of representing extreme injury, or "limit events."[6] As I am using the term, injury is distinguished from trauma for a variety of reasons, but among them trauma as a notion is often more singularly oriented toward addressing the victim's experience of loss or hurt. By contrast, injury helps contextualize a larger rhetorical economy based on perpetrator/victim interplay. Obviously great caution is required as we move between study of the Holocaust and study of race dynamics in the United States. At the same time, there is much to be gained by comparing these critical projects as they wrestle with ethical dynamics that tend in these different contexts to be both impoverished and naturalized (or somehow trapped in a field of "common sense"). It is exactly this common-sense field of assumptions about injury which enables such distinct positions—reverse racism versus institutional racism—to be described in what seems to be a relatively consistent set of rhetorical gestures. Exploring these gestures can clarify their limits, and how they in fact contribute to the sense of impasse that national discussions on race continue to face.

When certain authors argue that affirmative action-oriented definitions of racism are "overextended," compromising essentially autonomous realms—threatening, that is, our embrace of merit, or fairness—they do so not only by limiting what counts as injuries to minorities, but also by reframing how the concept of injury may be legitimately used. In other words, what is at issue is not simply a dynamics of exclusion—critics of affirmative action claiming that minority injuries do not count—but rather a fight over the proper ways to read injury. In what follows, I argue that the best readers of racism do not simply respond by demanding inclusion per se; their interventions are directed toward complicating the rhetorical uses of racial injury. This self-consciousness about injury in turn reframes current calls to color-blindness, showing them to be an extension of a certain political consensus that dates back at least to the 1960s when mainstream politicians aligned right-wing white supremacists (including the KKK) with the black power movement, calling both "racist." Ultimately, the collapse of these groups into the same "racist" project enabled mainstream politicians to avoid questions regarding these groups' location relative to dynamics of social power; in turn, whatever might have been distinguished as social critique in the discourse of the black power movement or other minority nationalisms was vilified and thoroughly discounted.[7]

By turning to an analysis of injury in its shifting uses, my hope is to create a critical space for complicating the interpretive and ethical dimensions of racial injury. Like Dominick LaCapra's efforts regarding Holocaust representations, this labor will involve diversifying our attentions and probing the roles played by, and the responsibilities attached to, bystanders, collaborators, and resistors, which, for instance, is happening as Swiss banks are being held accountable for their part in hiding the resources due Holocaust survivors and their families. At issue in terms of racism in the United States are questions about the privileges and benefits afforded nonminority bystanders and collaborators in racism, participants who stand outside the law's definition of intentional actors guilty of discrimination. The undertaking I describe also requires us to consider specifically why these diverse positions (bystanders, collaborators, etc.) have not received treatment, a problem which brings us with some force to questions of moral equivalences in American and Western culture, and the shaping by these equivalences of perpetrator/victim paradigms.

Elaborating a version of the skepticism Robyn Wiegman advocates, I turn now to a set of examples that offers a limited map of current rhetorical gestures regarding racial injury. In one sense, this inquiry elaborates upon the supposition of political appropriation argued by Wiegman in my epigraph: It demonstrates the ways in which addressing racism has become a vehicle for furthering white privilege. Beyond this, however, the inquiry questions what might lie beyond the current limits of injury rhetoric and its particular economies. One way to think of this goal is to ask, are there alternative means of treating claims of injury? are there in fact alternative forms of injury "literacy" that challenge existing practice? It is with these questions in mind that we now take up arguments offered by four prominent voices in current debates about race. Although the citations are not exhaustive, nor are they necessarily fully representative of the range of the debates taking place, they do offer explicit engagements with the rhetoric of injury and therefore a means to explore what I argue is a crucial discursive moment in these debates.

My process of selection has been guided by the following interests: Each of these four authors is markedly explicit in defining racism, something that unfortunately cannot be taken for granted in treatises on the topic; each articulates a reasonably clear notion of injury; each situates his/her claims within a historically deep context (they are attuned to the rhetorical qualities of these debates); and finally, each tends, in varying degrees, to replicate a tendency in U.S. race discourse to pose black/white dynamics as the defining characteristic, a problem that we will consider as it speaks to certain "normalizing" tendencies articulated by and through the rhetoric of injury generally.

Although the persistence—and unfortunate success—of books on race and racism that refuse to define or even index these concepts is startling, I would not suggest that some blazing solution awaits the chosen one who supposedly surmounts once and for all these fundamental, though undervalued, efforts at definition.[8] The processes of defining race and racism must themselves be ongoing and incomplete because these terms have complex rhetorical lives. At the same time, this understanding of the complicated, socially constructed nature of the terms does not free us from recognizing that at any particular time and place, competing definitions may exercise tremendous influence, and not just in explicitly political or rhetorical spheres of activity. In an attempt to address the responsibilities that ensue, and with an eye toward the apparent impasse of current race "dialogues," I read the four selections offered here as windows into a consistent set of rhetorical gestures regarding racial injury. In keeping with my emphasis on the dynamic process of race and racism definition, I will also suggest ways in which two of the authors attempt to rethink the articulation of injury by incorporating techniques that may be aligned with the psychoanalytic notion of transference.

RETHINKING INCLUSION
AND EXCLUSION

Racism is an ideology of intellectual or moral superiority based upon the biological characteristics of race. . . . Racism began in the West as a biological explanation for a large gap of civilizational development separating blacks from whites. Today racism is reinforced and made plausible by the reemergence of that gap within the United States. For many whites the criminal and irresponsible black underclass represents a revival of barbarism in the midst of western civilization. If this is true, the best way to eradicate beliefs in black inferiority is to remove their empirical basis.

—Dinesh D'Souza, *The End of Racism*, 27, 527

Why is it so difficult for many white folks to understand that racism is oppressive not because white folks have prejudicial feelings about blacks (they could have such feelings and leave us alone) but because it is a system that promotes domination and subjugation? The prejudicial feelings some blacks may express about whites are in no way linked to a system of domination that affords us any power to coercively control the lives and well being of white folks. That needs to be understood.

—bell hooks, *Black Looks*, 15

Racial hostilities are engendered by racial unfairness. The reason is this: race is a category having absolutely nothing to do with merit, or with genuine entitlement; its use in the distribution of goods is therefore odious and by a good society repudiated. Racial favoritism first breeds resentment; resentment breeds distrust. . . . In those special circumstances in which we can ascertain that race was the ground of an earlier injury, and it is known by whom and to whom that racial injury was done, racial classifications can serve in the design of a fitting remedy. Such cases are very few. . . . With rare exceptions therefore, race-based measures cannot do justice.

—Carl Cohen, *Naked Racial Preference*, 213

The continuing struggle for racial justice is tied up with the degree to which segregation and the outright denial of black humanity have been naturalized in our civilization. . . . We must get beyond the halting conversations filled with the superficialities of hurt feelings and those "my maid says blacks are happy" or "whites are devils" moments. If we could press on to a conversation that takes into account the devastating legacy of slavery that lives on as a social crisis that needs generations more of us working to repair—if we could just get to the enormity of that unhappy acknowledgment, then that alone might be the source of a genuinely revivifying, rather than a false, optimism.

—Patricia Williams, *The Rooster's Egg*, 20, 24

Dinesh D'Souza traces the spread of racial categorization and the advent of Western racism to European expansion during the Enlightenment. In the course of his book, *The End of Racism*, D'Souza suggests that the same sort of racist dynamics operant at the height of European global expansion are controlling our current responses to blacks in the United States. At the core of this argument one finds an assumption that, at quite different historical and cultural moments, there exists a continuous (and essentially unquestioned) need for societies to rationalize perceived differences among people in terms of "civilizational" achievement. Race and racism—all but collapsed in this account—therefore constitute an ideological injury that may be remedied neither by reshaping or dismantling the apparent "needs" of a given society, nor by assuming a stance of cultural relativism. Instead, according to D'Souza, the answer lies in removing the "empirical" basis upon which the larger society projects its "rough justice."

D'Souza's text is more interesting than many of those produced by his conservative peers precisely because his arguments do try to engage an historical depth; unlike many proponents of "color-blindness," he does not craft a narrow philosophical stance. His results, however, are fairly consistent with this camp. First, race and racism are assumed to constitute a pathology that is ultimately ancillary to the development of Western civilization and thought. In this sense, race and racism are, conceptually speaking, accidents of history that do not call on D'Souza to challenge at all terms like "civilization," "barbarism," or the "empirical" for the ways they may have been affected by race dynamics (or "ideologies"). Second, the key factor of racial injury is not the larger, more advanced segment of society, but rather the black underclass which, according to D'Souza, chooses to partake in a social regression which ultimately injures the society as a whole. Race (and racism) here are written into a kind of social and cultural Darwinism; although not justified in biological terms, there is a clear sense here that race comes into being in order to mark a thoroughly naturalized difference in development. In this scenario, racial claims of any sort ultimately constitute an injury, inasmuch as the claims themselves defy the naturalized order which is crystallized in the presumably nonracial, superior portion of humanity.

Although the D'Souza example is not specifically focused on questions of "reverse racism," the mechanics of his argument do work in concert with these sorts of claims. In the reverse racism approach, perpetrators of color-consciousness constitute injurious agents as the "neutral" bulwarks of society—particularly notions involving measures of "merit"—are trammeled upon by any number of policies (including affirmative action) and by racialized crimes of the sort that are so fascinating to our culture industry (consider, for example, movies such as *Boyz N the Hood* and *American Me*).

Taking up this cultural obsession, bell hooks's *Black Looks* intervenes in debates about racism in order to think through the kinds of "representational" questions posed by media images of, and their reception by, blacks. Here again the stakes of the argument run quickly to the nature of the injuries claimed. For hooks, contemporary arguments about race, racism, and reverse racism must be read in conjunction with a critical analysis of the ways audiences in the United States are acculturated to certain highly problematic notions about black people.[9] Although the history of slavery remains a crucial base of hooks's analysis, *Black Looks* reads this legacy through the particular institutional frame of the U.S. media and in this sense this media becomes a key site for articulating injury. In turn, hooks challenges arguments of reverse racism for their failure to engage more specifically the dynamics of representational power with which blacks must contend.[10] One consequence of hooks's approach is that injuries assume more differentiated forms and impacts. As is highlighted in the epigraph, expressions of prejudice make up a realm of injury which hooks would distinguish from acts and practices that constitute racism as such. The latter may only be undertaken by people, groups, or institutions that are plugged into "the system of domination" established by and for white supremacy. As such, hooks's understanding of racism is in line with other institutional racism approaches first brought to prominence by Stokely Carmichael and Charles Hamilton in *Black Power: The Politics of Liberation in America*.[11] However, hooks is also keenly aware of the cultural stakes of the stories these institutions maintain, narratives that disseminate particular assumptions about injury.

Even though the media, the schools, and other sites have been the focus of much attention as regards claims of institutional racism, no recent battleground has been quite as animated as that provided by the courts. Legal cases define racial injuries and remedies with the backing of state force, a process that weaves together specific findings to construct particular rules about how we should interpret and decide such struggles. The Critical Legal Studies and Critical Race Studies movements have of course done much to elaborate the rhetorical and historiographic stakes of the courts' decisions. In so doing, these movements have emphasized not only the impacts of particular cases, but also, and perhaps more importantly, the methodological implications of decisions that redefine what will be construed as legitimate claims of injury and awards of remedy according to distinct argumentative styles.[12]

It is into this legal dynamic that Carl Cohen and Patricia Williams insert themselves as they rework notions of racial injury. The epigraph drawn from Cohen's *Naked Racial Preference* is representative of the more sophisticated versions of the "color-blindness" argument, inasmuch as Cohen, like D'Souza, brings together both philosophical and historical modes of analysis to argue finally that race and racism are for the most part synonymous, and that race-consciousness itself constitutes the ultimate injury. Working a bit more explicitly than D'Souza, Cohen positions race as totally disconnected from the tools by which we judge each other's actions, in the courtroom or in myriad other practices. In the process, Cohen treats Justice Harlan's dissent in *Plessy v. Ferguson*—the case which established segregation as federal law—as a lodestar moment, an example of a reasoned voice of pessimism regarding race-consciousness and social engineering emanating from within long-established tradition.

Slightly modifying the absolutism of this moral stance, Cohen does describe a very limited exception to race-blindness, one that acknowledges historical contingency and the potential applicability of race categories in defining discrimination. However, Cohen carefully situates this acknowledgment that discrimination exists within some basic presumptions of legal methodology that effectively foreclose any attempt to link the development of the law to racialized dynamics. This foreclosure is accomplished by accentuating those ways in which the law conventionally reduces the universe of "legitimate" injuries to a very circumscribed field of recognizable—and judgeable actions. In this field, only "transparent" and distinct interactions between isolated individuals who express obvious intentions are acknowledged, and all such actions must fall within a narrowly defined span of time.[13] As has been the tendency with the law until the advent of affirmative action policies, instances of racism that might be recognized within such legal parameters are assumed to be "irrational" and in an important sense accidental with regard to the larger movements of the institution and society. Inasmuch as the law has been one key venue for shaping the rhetoric of injury, then, these various rules have been instrumental in regulating the "common-sense" ground rules of our debates.

As the etymological breakdown of the word suggests, "in-jury" cannot be critically rethought without a concomitant reevaluation of the rhetorical field animated by the law itself. With a subtle understanding of this sensitive relationship, Cohen registers the possibility of continuing racism while at the same time arguing that such limited injuries in no way outstrip the more serious injuries fostered by diverse policies that make race a factor for consideration during regular decision making, including hiring, promotion, and admission. Hence, the recognition of race is ultimately integrated into a larger instance of injury in which the ultimate victim is the law itself: The law is race-blindness, and in this case, sight is harm.

Coming to wholly different conclusions, but likewise vying to define "legitimate" injuries and remedies in a specifically legal context, Patricia Williams offers a mapping of progress toward racial justice that places the United States "generations" from repair. Williams, like hooks, weaves together readings of individual and group dynamics, as well as legal and cultural interpretations drawn from a variety of sources. Again like hooks, Williams pursues an autobiographical style rich with biting humor and irony. Although there is also much to distinguish these authors, the two depart perhaps most obviously in their respective positions regarding notions of remedy; hooks's cast is openly militant and oriented toward black cultural, social, and political autonomy. Williams, on the other hand, is less inclined to advocate for a particular political program and instead pursues strategically placed meditations most frequently oriented toward examining legal method and its cultural implications. As suggested by the epigraph, what readers find moving across Williams's writings is a consistent concern with the complex, often "naturalized" legacy of slavery, not as an isolated force, but rather as an enduring injury shaping many ongoing social interactions, and interactions beyond the limited confines of victims and perpetrators.

Williams has taken her experiments with autobiography beyond an initial challenge to the presumably neutral stances of academic and legal scholarship in order to draw out her own subtle negotiation with the naturalization of racism she describes. Put in psychoanalytic terms, she is committed to thinking through the "transferential" aspects of her writing, or those ways in which the problems embedded in her objects of study may come to replicate themselves in unselfconscious ways within her analysis.[14] Williams thus explores methodological questions very much akin to those animating recent trends in intellectual history. These projects have been exploring, among other things, transferential dynamics as they affect writings about the Holocaust and its representation as a highly charged, "limit" historical event. Of particular interest for contributors like Dominick LaCapra has been the relative dearth of ethical tools or protocols for treating the complex positions assumed by people who lived through the Holocaust, as well as by those who have attempted to record it.[15] As I have noted, the value in comparing these critical projects is that it brings into relief a concern with ethical dynamics that appear to be both impoverished as well as naturalized in a field of "common sense." At stake in both endeavors are questions about how to engage injuries without uncritically repeating their damage.

The field of common sense regarding injury makes it possible for highly diverse critiques—including those cited here—to find expression in what appears to be a relatively consistent set of rhetorical moves. In fact, the "sense of impasse" in U.S. race debates that is currently being recorded in the media and academia alike is a predictable by-product of certain limits built into the rhetoric of injury. When D'Souza and Cohen conclude that overly broad and ultimately illegitimate definitions of institutional racism compromise notions of merit, or even civilization itself, they do so by invoking a claim of injurious exclusion that for many people bears a certain similarity to the claims made by D'Souza and Cohen's color-conscious opponents when they define the effects of institutional racism. In this sort of situation, when the rhetoric of injury seems so easily transferable, it becomes understandable why the public might become increasingly skeptical about race recognition and claims of racism altogether.[16] However, for many observers there has been a sense that something more than a skeptical bewilderment is at play in the backlash against affirmative action; the anger of the "angry white male" that led to national discussions of displaced white workers and to films like *Falling Down* taps a sense of violation and, more pointedly, resentment that seems to outstrip evidence of, or even formal claims to, reverse discrimination.[17]

As William Connolly suggests, it may be that the prevalence of resentment at different moments in U.S. political history is related to an ongoing pattern of injury rhetoric—a pattern which perpetuates an expectation of "moral equivalence" between injured and injuring parties. This model of moral equivalences is of course at the core of our legal system, which regulates both judgment and punishment in a context defined by the image of justice's balancing scales (rehabilitation in this setting is in many ways an afterthought if not a public relations gesture—a fact that helps explain the ease with which the recent gutting of prison reform programs has taken place).

Resentment may thus be considered as one predictable by-product of injury scenarios that do not find resolution in the ostensible economy of moral equivalences: In this context, it makes sense that poor whites do not understand why they in particular should bear the brunt of programs addressing racism. Certainly there have been particular political motives that have led some people actively to foster resentments—against immigrants, against colonized populations in the Southwest and elsewhere, against members of different classes—just as there have been moments in U.S. history when it has been crucial for some actors to contain and sublimate potential resentments, as for instance was the case in early colonial times when settlers were confronted by devastating losses and conditions that invited criticism of the religious leadership and its decisions.[18] And yet, whatever particular investments in resentment these distinct moments represent, there is also an ongoing manner in which resentment constitutes a fundamental aspect of American political identity and its perpetuation. Because the desire for, and realization of, moral equivalences can never be fully satisfied, the history of American political identity is also a history of resentment—its production, its containment, its manipulation.

With this interplay of resentment and the rhetoric of injury in mind, I will focus now on two recent studies of American political identity. Among other things, these studies contextualize a logic of equivalence that frequently attends notions of injury. Recalling that injury may be defined as an act intentionally inflicted on another by one who may be properly blamed, I will argue that claims of injury tend to play a crucial role in a larger political economy that is inescapably tied to the production of resentment. Teasing out such speculations, we will then inquire into the possibilities of structuring notions of injury around something other than a logic of equivalences, an alternative that I will align with certain aspects of hooks's and Williams's efforts and, specifically, with the "transferential" qualities of their writings.

INJURY, RESENTMENT, AND THE POLITICS OF IDENTITY

William E. Connolly's *Identity/Difference: Democratic Negotiations of Political Paradox* combines an interest in the modern liberal state, the relations of such states in the global environment, the contingent nature of liberal individualism, and the ultimately paradoxical nature of ethical discourse. Methodologically shaped by Nietzsche, Foucault, and Derrida, Connolly's work pursues the theory of *ressentiment* in order to rethink the origins and continuing basis of the liberal state as a project dramatically shaped by a constitutive focus on injury. Combining U.S. racial dynamics and Nietzschean analysis, Connolly suggests that liberal philosophy—particularly liberal individualism—necessarily produces ressentiment. Thinking about the way minority-conscious programs of the 1960s affected the white working class, Connolly emphasizes how justifications for these programs implied that only one group "deserved" to be stuck in the lousy jobs available to it—white working class males. In this scenario, it is perhaps inevitable that the liberal glorification of self-responsibility would come into conflict with welfare rationales, thereby accentuating the resentment felt by those whose status and apparent well-being seemed most threatened by the ameliorative programs (78).

This situation—which otherwise might be taken to represent a unique flaw in the dynamics of the otherwise healthy liberal state—is reframed by Connolly as he tries to come to terms with the apparently excessive nature of the backlash. Asking why subsequent resentment is "so virulent and volatile" leads to speculation about the structure of liberal individualism in general.

> From a Nietzschean perspective, the self constituted as a unified, self-responsible agent contains resentment within its very formation. The basic idea behind this formation is that for every evil there must be a responsible agent who deserves to be punished and that for every quotient of evil there must be a corollary quotient of assignable responsibility. No evil without responsibility. No responsibility without reward or punishment according to desert. No suffering without injustice, and no injustice unless there is a juridical recipe for redressing it in life or afterlife. (Connolly, 78)

Far from being a natural or necessary state, this submission to equivalences promotes a world view oriented by a particular economics of injury and suffering. Again building on Nietzsche, Connolly locates this demand for equivalences in the Christian "slave revolt in morality," an attempt by "sufferers held in human bondage to invent a god to hold the masters responsible for their cruelty and indifference" (79). Connolly further complicates this liberal resentment by suggesting that modern liberal identity formation is thoroughly invested in pervasive dynamics of "discipline and punish."[19]

> The modern normal, responsible individual can redirect resentment against the human condition into the self, first, by treating the rational, self-interested, free, and principled individual as morally responsible for willful deviations from normal identity and, second, by treating that in itself and other selves which falls below the threshold of responsibility as a natural defect in need of conquest or conversion, punishment or love. The modern individual, in short, contains resentment against the human condition in its own identity, and this comes out most clearly in the intensity of the resentment it expresses against any others who deviate significantly from that identity. . . . Resentment against injuries to oneself flowing from the standard of self-responsibility becomes translated into rancor against those whom one construes as escaping the dictates of that standard. (Connolly, 80)

In the project to fashion an "ethical life without paradox," then, there exists a concomitant submission to a politics of normalization. Here, injury rhetoric, modeling as it does a balance of moral equivalences, legitimates notions of harm and remedy that only make sense in reference to the norm itself—to injure may thereby be equated with displacement from the norm, and working within this assumption we end up with a racial politics and identity that is defined by inclusion and exclusion. The catch-22 is that this racial politics and identity may only fully address injury so understood by conforming to the norm through assimilation.

Wendy Brown has responded to Connolly's argument by undertaking a study which would, among other things, "historicize politicized identity itself" (165). In her essay, "Injury, Identity, Politics," Brown considers the ways in which the resentment typical of liberal political philosophy shapes contemporary U.S. "identity politics" in particular. Brown begins with the notion that identity politics has built itself around a concept of injury defined precisely in terms of a purported exclusion from a liberal ideal. In turn, remedies in this scenario entail a normalizing of the differences that were taken to be the basis of exclusionary and discriminatory acts. Brown's opening question, then, is why "radical" political efforts settle for registering injury in this way—why, in other words, would such efforts settle for assimilating injuries into an unscathed liberal political dynamic frequently oriented to gobble up differences in the structure of a bureaucratic regime?

Taking identity politics as a species of liberal identity, Brown likewise builds on Nietzsche's theory of ressentiment and the notion that "slave morality produces identity in reaction to power" (160). Identity politics is here understood to sustain itself through a "moralizing reproach to power" that purposefully maintains a posture of impotence. Reaction, in this context, becomes a substitute for creative, future-oriented action, and "redemptive" historical study becomes complicit in a resentful project inasmuch as previous events supply the basis for revenge caught in a closed circle; as such, uncritical reactions to distant experiences—rather than present wants and desires—dictate interpretive and political outcomes. Although Brown distances herself from a thoroughly Nietzschean reading—she refuses to call on race scholars and activists to "forget" the past as Nietzsche would presumably demand—she does argue that the rhetoric of injury which has formed multiculturalism's intellectual foundation needs to be rethought, and that identity politics in its current form is at best a reprieve (163). The question remains: Would it be possible to formulate an alternative rhetoric of injury which could embrace a complex recognition of harm, and advance a radically democratic political culture, while not allowing a political slide into the normalizing imperatives of established liberal practices? Given the tremendous energies that are going into bolstering the weak enforcement of existing "hate crime" laws, it is perhaps predictable that such a rethinking may take a back seat; this situation, however, leaves important issues of strategy and efficacy unattended.[20]

As Brown addresses this problem, her concern falls to the "therapeutic discourses" that have been brought to the discussion of injuries by some advocates of identity politics, discourses that may ensure a return to the processes of normalization and resentment she critiques. The "therapeutic" practices to which she alludes draw on, as well as perpetuate, essentially arbitrary "standards" that in turn ground the division of healthy from pathological behaviors.[21] In terms of race hate speech codes, for instance, this entails defining certain forms of censorship, an approach that has provoked animated debate.[22] Inasmuch as Brown leaves the notion of "therapeutic" fairly open-ended, her essay concludes with an invitation to imagine a form of historical engagement more conducive to an open conflict of wills and desires aimed at "forging an alternative future"(164). Williams and hooks, I will argue, offer a map of sorts to an alternative engagement of injury, an engagement more open to the conflict of wills and desires precisely because of its "transferential" self-consciousness. With this step to acknowledging transferential dynamics, readings of injury may no longer be held securely at arm's length, and the presumption of easily identifiable moral equivalences gives way to a more complicated, nuanced sense of responsibilities: responsibilities that pertain to, yet also transcend, the discreet injurers and injuries so zealously maintained by legal practice in particular.

RESENTMENT AND RACISM

To what extent do normalizing impulses come into play in the arguments about racism we have been considering, and how might resentment expressed in these dialogues demonstrate processes like those identified by Connolly and Brown? Among the four authors cited, those advocating a step away from race-consciousness invoke particular standards—fairness, merit—as part of a blaming structure. Here, proponents of race-conscious programs are credited with harming society as a whole by abusing universal measures and ideals. Cohen, for example, is particularly adept at drawing out the injustice afforded the white male working class in Supreme Court decisions like *United Steelworkers of America v. Weber* (1979).[23] Cohen's argument is thoroughly committed to a notion of moral equivalences, guaranteed in this case by recourse to particular legal principles that are fundamentally blind to race issues.[24] The notion of racial "preferences" here becomes central, acting as a lightning rod that would gather outrage against those citizens who have not been able to "make the grade" in the first place (California's Anti-Affirmative Action Proposition 209 and Washington State's I 200 are testaments to the success of such resentment-oriented rhetoric).

Failure to live up to standards is of course at the heart of D'Souza's critique as well, and hence his focus on the empirical evidence of minority inferiority. For all the stress on empirical evidence, the strength of the response to "ameliorative" programs in these authors does not appear to be bound to any statistically grounded evidence of reverse discrimination. This situation, combined with some fairly damaging exposés of conservative pundits who have tried to claim themselves as victims of reverse racism, invites readers to look for deeper running sources of resentment.[25] I would like to suggest that, to a certain extent, the deeper offense of race-conscious advocates like hooks and Williams is their very experimentation with the rhetoric of injury itself, including their efforts to think beyond legally limited victim/perpetrator scenarios and their willingness to challenge a belief in strictly held moral equivalences. In this sense, hooks and Williams's work embraces the contingency which threatens liberal individualism: People's interactions are actually much more complicated than such notions of individualism allows.

As Brown's approach suggests, questions of normalization and resentment are not limited to the political right, and the implications for identity politics do carry over in varying ways to hooks's and Williams's analysis. Yet I would stress that both authors also set the stage for, if not present, an alternative to the dominant rhetoric of racial injury. For instance, hooks negotiates the legacy of slavery by referencing notions of blackness that are at least implicitly normalizing. While arguing that discovering the true value of the black community entails "breaking through the walls of denial which hide the depth of black self-hatred, inner-anguish, and unreconciled pain" (20), hooks also assumes a certain autonomy for black identity formation, an autonomy that is defined in hooks's analysis by references to black standards. These standards, in turn, mark the road whereby blacks might overcome aspects of denial, acquire mental health, and establish "the right kind of relationship" with their appearance.

Working along similar lines, Patricia Williams's *The Rooster's Egg: On the Persistence of Prejudice* closes with a chapter that discusses the commodificiation and "de-racializing" of black images. In both cases, the authors avoid probing what are otherwise fairly "naturalized" standards for blackness, mental or physical, even though a tendency remains in their critiques to express horror regarding injuries to their conceptions of proper bodies and mental processes. Injuries in both cases can suggest a forced deviation from a natural and/or ideal state that is defined by a race standard. In turn, hooks's version of black self-love is as much a call to a rigorous and explicitly militant political vision as it is an embrace of self-affirmation. hooks argues for a racially defined community that seeks new paradigms and visions, but that is nonetheless primarily focused on reacting first to the veil of denial that allows racial injuries to fester rather than heal (4).

Both authors work in complex and politically strategic fashions that build on certain charged discourses, including black militancy and legal rights activism. But there are also ways in which the authors' own auto-biographically loaded, transferentially oriented explorations of black wounds, including self-hatred, carry with them an aspect of resentment as well as a problematic standardizing of racially oriented critique itself. Here it is particularly important to note the way that race and racism in these examples, as well as in many U.S. race dialogues, become implicitly or explicitly reduced to "black experience." Following Connolly and Brown's analyses, the problem posed by this reduction is not foremost that other groups or histories are excluded (though this is clearly important), but rather that western identity formation generally tends to establish normalizing assumptions—like black equals race—that can be bound to reactionary invocations of unredeemable injuries. As a result, analyses of slavery and its impacts may remain significantly disarticulated from interpretations of colonization, immigration, incarceration, and so on that affect a range of racial groups in the United States. This standardizing dynamic has surely shaped "multicultural" studies in a variety of ways. Far from a blanket condemnation of such studies, I would suggest a deeper engagement, an inquiry guided by a cautious speculation about the rhetoric of injury itself. Because the current sense of impasse appears to be situated in a particular economics of injury and resentment, it will be important to unpack the language of racial injury, with all of its "therapeutic" under- and over-determination. If we are willing to recognize injuries that it would be "inappropriate if not cruel" to ignore, then the project I am suggesting may be thought of as an attempt to conceive an alternative to therapeutic discourse: an alternative critical of normalizing impulses, especially as these have been inflected by liberal individualism and resentment.

INJURY ACROSS DISCIPLINES

Because of the drive to normalization that I have been describing, racial analysis has been left with relatively weak critical and ethical tools for reading conflict. As John Guillory has suggested in his work on the canon debates, fights to gain multicultural inclusion constitute a strategic stage—Brown's period of reprieve—that is now being followed by a global rethinking of what both inclusion and conflict entail.[26] For Guillory, this means a renewed interest in questions of literacy. As producers of particular literacies, disciplines develop specialized approaches to canonical texts as a way of legitimating certain means of reading over and against others. This process perpetuates values that may or may not be acknowledged.[27]

Working in a related vein, Robyn Wiegman addresses the limits of disciplinary discourses by advocating an "alchemy of disloyalty" that grows out of the highly complicated critical terrain wherein race and feminist studies meet. Wiegman argues that a problematic set of anxieties may be driving feminist critique in a manner that leaves it purposefully innocent of contingent, even contradictory, political results. According to this reading, much feminist work has remained insufficiently sensitive to distinctions between race and racism.

This concern with the way that the conceptualization of difference as genderraceandclass occupies a privileged explanatory position in contemporary feminist theory does not discount the importance of studying categorical formations as mechanisms of social control, as this study of race and gender clearly suggests. But it does raise a series of questions that trouble some of feminist theory's most well known critical assumptions. For instance, can we assume that the contents of categories like race and class (and even gender) are already historically and culturally known? that their invocation is a sufficient methodolog-

ical strategy for articulating broad scale social critique? that each category clarifies the structure and functioning of discrete aspects of the
social formation? that a compound ordering of categories necessarily
articulates their imbrications? that the task of political criticism is to
define social organization within the rubric of these categorical relations, that, in fact, only through these categories can we produce the
politics of political criticism? If we cannot assume these things, if categories are not finally transparent epistemologies, what, then, becomes
of the necessary feminist demand for both heterogeneous women and
a discourse committed to social critique? (Wiegman, 186)

Wiegman is quite clear that these difficulties are by no means fatal blows
for feminist or political critique generally. She is, however, equally clear
that many of the guiding assumptions of feminist analysis should be
revisited and interrogated for the baggage that initially conditioned
feminism as a modernist project. Of particular concern, then, is the way
certain procedures and/or systems of knowledge may be assumed to
constitute a form of political guarantee, an assurance of movement toward liberation. Hence, "even an integrationist strategy—adding black
women to feminist histories, for instance—or an inclusivist gesture toward differences—the monosyllabic, infinitely appended *genderraceandclass*—become suspicious elements of a modernist disciplinarity"
(185). In this context, Wiegman counsels a renewed and renewing opportunity for disloyalty, or what might be thought of as a disciplinary
self-consciousness and a transferentially sensitive critique that mines the
historical nuances of politically oriented projects even as it opens questions about the function of historicity itself.

In a similar spirit, I will now turn to debates and experiments regarding injury that have been generated in psychoanalysis, intellectual history, and Critical Race Studies. These particular fields of inquiry have
been highly charged sites for the (re)creation and modification of injury
as a concept. Although these disciplines are not uniquely privileged sites
per se (the analysis here will not maintain an exclusive interest in them),
I would suggest that we are at a juncture in which an interdisciplinary
engagement of injury rhetoric may yield an important window onto the
patterns that have shaped, and will likely continue to shape, definitions

of race and racism in American studies. One goal of such a project would be to reach a more nuanced and subtle contextualization of race dynamics, one that explores the interactive limits of disciplinary practices as well as considers the ways specific fields have both invited and resisted a critical rethinking of race, racism, and injury. Embracing Wiegman's "alchemy of disloyalty," this project brings an awareness of uncritical transferential relations to the practices and concepts normalized by disciplines.

Consider, for instance, that while the Critical Race Studies (CRS) movement has been remarkably powerful in terms of situating the rhetorical battle over definitions of racial injury, and in terms of the ways the law has shaped an often unacknowledged race-consciousness maintaining white privilege, many practitioners have been reluctant to pursue the specific interpenetration of legal issues and larger cultural questions (authors like Patricia Williams and Richard Delgado stand out as exceptions). The link to larger cultural issues—how race in the legal sphere interacts with race in popular culture, the humanities, the social sciences, the "hard" sciences—calls out for further recognition because a number of the best-received CRS authors to date have practiced, if not self-consciously theorized, an exciting rhetorical experiment that often blends literary and legal rhetoric, and is most certainly interdisciplinary in nature. In this vein, texts like Delgado's *The Rodrigo Chronicles,* Williams's *Alchemy of Race and Rights,* and Derrick Bell's *And We Are Not Saved* explore autobiographical and literary dimensions that are clearly poised to invite greater elaboration of psychological dynamics, including aspects of mourning, self-hate, depression, paranoia, nostalgia, and denial as these are worked out in the rules and expectations of legal discourse.

Similarly, significant innovations in historical study, spurred on by the rethinking of the "American" past advocated by the New Western History, are helping resituate American studies. One of the most noted of these efforts, Patricia Limerick's *Legacy of Conquest,* is explicitly framed as an attempt to reconsider the field after the impact of affirmative action histories. Another effort to mine autobiographical and psychological dynamics while registering the play of legal issues, policy battles, and personal reflection (via anecdotes, memoirs, letters), *Legacy of*

Conquest is particularly rich for its framing of the rhetoric of victimization in the United States. As such, Limerick would seem to have much to contribute regarding a history of the way race and injury intersect. However, *Legacy of Conquest* is ultimately seriously limited by Limerick's unwillingness to critically examine the basic psychoanalytic concepts that are very central to the project and to much of the New Western History generally. Ironically, one result of this tendency can be a fairly fundamental displacement of racial dynamics in the New Western historian's explicit drive toward synthetic statements about the region. Ultimately, this problem is tied to the New Western History's avoidance of a methodological issue that necessarily attends the attempt to merge psychoanalysis and history, namely the problem of uncritical transference.

Inasmuch as these issues have guided a small number of interdisciplinary psychological studies of race, a focus on transference is really the exception when psychological analyses take up race and racism.[28] Hence, psychological studies of race and racism have frequently pursued rigid applications of structural paradigms—paradigms which are clearly inflected with the tenets of liberal individualism though they present themselves as universally "human." The playful and speculative discourse of foundational texts like Freud's *Interpretation of Dreams* is eschewed in such writings as authors are drawn to another aspect of Freud's project: the legitimation of psychology as a human science, or as a mode of interpretation and writing somehow protected from the unwieldy aspects of transference by an author's pose of judicious and ultimately ironic neutrality. Assuming universal norms against which pathologies may be defined, these "therapeutic" projects play an important role in race dynamics as they codify particular group behaviors as deviant. As Connolly and Brown argue, the stage is then set for absorbing these groups, or identities, into a blaming structure that extends throughout society, thereby reinforcing an economics of injury.

Rarely touched upon in psychological studies of race is the extended debate surrounding notions of injury that animates a significant aspect of Freud's work. Mitchell Breitwieser's *American Puritanism and the Defense of Mourning* offers an intellectual history of these debates demonstrating how one might follow concepts of injury from antiquity into the present, thereby charting crucial changes in definition and function particularly as these changes reveal the pervasive manner in which injury as such has been politicized. Focusing on Puritan society, Breitwieser explores the way religious rhetoric shaped a response to tremendous losses, especially as a result of the Algonquin war. According to Breitwieser, this "shaping" not only secured the continuing authority of the religious leadership, but also redoubled the community's investment in a particular manner of reading the world around them, a methodology which virtually ensured a melancholic disposition. Although Breitwieser's book is not concerned with racial dynamics per se, despite its focus on the Algonquin war, the text does offer a provocative history of struggles over the meaning (and political import) of mourning as well as psychological health.[29]

Approaching similar problems from a more explicitly theoretical stance, Dominick LaCapra's recent works have reexamined historical practice in psychoanalytic terms by exploring problems of transference and the "working through" of traumatic issues and events. As is the case with Eric Santner's *Stranded Objects: Mourning, Memory and Film in Postwar Germany,* or Shoshana Felman and Dori Laub's *Testimony: Crises of Witnessing in Literature, Psychoanalysis, and History,* LaCapra's latest contributions have considered the representational dynamics engaged by treatments of the Holocaust. However, whereas Santner's approach is oriented toward theories of object relations (especially those developed by D. W. Winnicott), and Felman and Laub's approach is heavily invested in a de Manian practice of deconstruction, LaCapra's works, including *Representing the Holocaust: History, Theory, Trauma,* pursue a more varied mapping of Western engagements with notion of injury. LaCapra's studies are thus open to the play of transitional objects and rigorous linguistic analysis, yet are also concerned with registering the broad range of competing modes in which injury may be critically or uncritically recognized and addressed, modes including working through, acting out, transference, and critique.[30]

Not surprisingly, many of the examples cited in my rough summary of psychological approaches to race issues do not fit neatly into disciplinary definitions, and in fact often explicitly critique the defining projects of disciplines as they have come to organize and legitimate themselves. At the same time, many of these authors are regularly taken to exemplify advanced work in more than one field of inquiry. Not surprisingly, it is in this more interdisciplinary sphere that we find a growing body of exciting literature devoted to recontextualizing assumptions about injury through narrative experimentation. These authors are helping to situate the highly political if not always explicitly politicized discourses of injury, and to set the stage for a more subtle approach to racism. Among other things, their self-conscious, critical approaches to competing disciplinary methods and concepts set the stage for a recognition of the transferential dynamics that may exist between practitioners of particular fields and their "objects of study."

Some of the best work in the interdisciplinary enterprise of American studies is already moving along this path, one that promises to create a critical space for complicating the interpretive and ethical dimensions of how we approach racial injury. Like LaCapra's effort regarding Holocaust representations, this will involve diversifying our attentions and nuancing our understandings of ethics-in-practice, a project that will benefit from a rethinking of the roles assigned to bystanders, collaborators, and resistors. The undertaking will also require us to consider specifically why these kinds of positions have not tended to receive treatment, a problem which returns us with some force to questions of equivalences and their shaping of perpetrator/victim paradigm, as well as to new, more nuanced notions of responsibility. As the discussion of the police trials in my Introduction suggests, addressing the racially defined gap regarding reactions to racial injury must begin with such a rethinking of responsibility.

CHAPTER TWO

COLOR-BLINDNESS, ACTING OUT, AND CULTURE

Adding to the latest chapter in the "culture wars," a number of cultural and literary critics have recently gained national attention by arguing that their academic fields have been significantly harmed by a regime of multiculturalism, a regime they consider fundamentally racist.[1] Walter Benn Michaels provides a prominent example of this trend with his recent rethinking of race and American literary modernism. This work expresses a deep-seated suspicion of historical and cultural inquiry—even as it mobilizes these forms of inquiry to make its point. As is the case with the color-blindness arguments examined in the previous chapter, Michaels animates historical analysis only insofar as it offers exempla of philosophically oriented points. Inasmuch as Michaels believes modern American culture to be defined by a "raced" and therefore racist imperative, his version of modernism constitutes an example of literature gone bad. The readings of particular texts by Michaels, in turn, assert the ways race-consciousness inevitably produces racism. Ultimately, Michaels insists upon a radical break with a whole set of interchangeable, "modern" analytical tools, including the concepts of race, identity, and Holocaust. Michaels's work exhibits a resounding faith in individual agency, and in the individual's ability to disassociate thoroughly from a culture touched by racism: radical, individualized choice is all-important to his analysis. If believing in race is the same as believing in ghosts, which is how Michaels typifies our current predicament, then the invocation of choice in his arguments carries all the freight of an exorcism. Michaels's response to racism is a matter of "just saying no" to all manner of race-consciousness. In this chapter, I will argue that Michaels's approach to racial injury reconstitutes that injury through a form of interpretive violence, a violence that shares important qualities with other products of the "angry white male" backlash which came into its own in the mid-1990s.

Self-consciously provocative, Michaels's arguments tap a variety of political and interpretive trends that might suggest a sea-change of sorts. These writings are, for instance, very much in line with conservative gestures that are now focusing upon Justice Harlan's dissent in *Plessy v. Ferguson,* gestures exemplified in works like Andrew Kull's *The Color-Blind Constitution,* Dinesh D'Souza's *The End of Racism,* and William Henry's *In Defense of Elitism.* Ultimately, the political commitment in Michaels is to a vision of society made up of transparent, individual (trans)actions. At the same time, attempts to posit and interpret group—and especially minority/majority—conflicts are discounted as fundamentally mistaken because the links that supposedly bind such groups are always presumed to be artificial.

However, also working within Michaels's approach is an appeal to a less politically conservative vision which recognizes that aspects of multicultural and minority discourse have in fact stunted critical dialogues about race and culture. In this vein, he builds on a widespread critique of certain crude forms of identity politics. Although he declines to acknowledge this in his works, Michaels's concern is very much in accord with many critics laboring within multicultural and race studies, despite the fact that few of these critics have come to the same conclusions as Michaels regarding the benefits of race-blindness. Michaels thus taps distinct modes of skepticism about the political claims of academic and popular race discourse; ironically, this skepticism also informs in different ways a number of the most significant recent contributions to race theory, including the work of scholars like Robyn Weigman and Wendy Brown.[2] One issue that immediately distinguishes these authors from Michaels, however, is their position on questions of choice and the contingency of individual agency. Where Michaels addresses his concerns about racial discourse by turning to a fundamentally radical act of will and consciousness, critics like Wiegman and Brown extend their skepticism to liberal individualism and its promise of autonomous agency.

Another way to think of the distinctions between these authors would be to consider Michaels's rigid adoption of a Foucauldian, cultural logic paradigm, one eschewed by the other critics who pursue approaches to culture that are more sensitive to the play of hegemony and cultural consumption.[3] To gain a better sense of how this particular commitment to the cultural logic paradigm conditions Michaels's evaluation of race-consciousness, I will turn to his latest book, *Our America: Nativism, Modernism, and Pluralism* as well as to two of his recent projects: one on Holocaust studies and one devoted to white studies.[4] In these projects, Michaels writes himself into a scenario in which his use of cultural logic becomes so rigid that the only recourse left is to make a leap of faith into a transparent political realm evacuated of hegemonic concerns, that is, a realm of liberal individualism.

Walter Benn Michaels's work represents a fully articulated criticism of multiculturalism, a critique that draws upon disaffection with race analysis; because of the nature of this disaffection, my analysis of his work is also concerned with situating the arguments in terms of larger, if nascent, trends toward the censorship of race as a concept. Michaels's work also invites a significant rethinking of tendencies in the theorization of race that have helped set the stage for the attack on race-sensitive analysis. In particular, Michaels's critique compels race studies scholars to reevaluate troubled theoretical relationships posed among social movements, institutional practices, and cultural processes. In this way, his work presents an indirect challenge to scholars who accept academic divisions between disciplinary methodologies, and thereby forego a sufficiently complicated understanding of how race and racial injury operate. In an important way, the ground has been set for such a misreading with texts like Michael Omi and Howard Winant's virtually canonical treatment of racial formation, a treatment that all but writes off cultural issues in favor of studying social movement history.[5] In this context, the experimental narrative interventions that are the subject of the following chapters demonstrate an awareness of the methodological problem and attempt to address it stylistically, as well as theoretically.

In a particularly ironic fashion, Walter Benn Michaels mobilizes philosophical and legalistic analysis in order to narrow the analytical horizon of his engagements with literature. Michaels's goal is to convince a diverse body of literary scholars that their training in matters of cultural critique and historical analysis has been fundamentally in error. Specifically, Michaels "takes on the question of how cultural identity could have been so drastically racialized" in the 1920s, "at a time when in various discourses—literary, sociological, political—race itself was becoming increasingly acknowledged as a limited" and problematic bearer of identity (Gunn, 660). As Giles Gunn points out in his review of *Our America*, "Michaels' answer is brilliantly and disturbingly, if somewhat deceptively, simple." Gunn's description of Michaels's argument is instructive:

> What was effected, most notably in the great texts of American literary modernism, was not so much the rearticulation of race as a marker of cultural identity, but (rather) the reconceptualization of cultural identity (itself) as inherently racial, even racist. (Gunn, 660)

The key for Michaels is that nativism, modernism, and pluralism become manifestations of a single cultural logic: A regime of identity and culture grows out of the white supremacy of the Progressive movement, and this regime takes root in literary America. American modernism's cultural pluralism thus becomes a rearticulation of the "separate but equal" philosophy, but in this instance the notion of racial difference becomes cathected as a new and pervasive object of public discourse. According to Michaels, this process initiates a heretofore unrecognized form of American racism, which lasts right into our present. Among other things, then, Michaels's book offers a genealogy that claims to demonstrate how today's multicultural inquiry came to have essentially racist underpinnings.

At a time when arguments for race censorship are having a notable impact, it is perhaps predictable that a book like Michaels's might appear; *Our America* rides a broad wave of distrust regarding race-oriented analysis, distrust conditioned by various competing claims using the same language and reference points. But where many color-blindness advocates explain the error of our ways with little or no recourse to questions of method, Michaels's approach calls for a significant detour from the methodological trends in his field. In practice, Michaels focuses on a limited range of less problematic literary texts, works that one after another yield the same logic by which cultural identity is collapsed into race-consciousness, and ultimately racism. Tackling the weakness I am describing from another angle, Gunn has argued that "the chief problems with Michaels's thesis stem from the ideologically seamless and ahistorical notion of culture on which [Michaels] depends. . . . Michaels assumes, without ever demonstrating, that cultural concepts possess a logic all their own that inevitably defines and regulates the sorts of instantiation they achieve in discreet historical moments and practices" (660).

Michaels's skepticism regarding historical analysis defines as well his distrust of identity considerations, and so he asks in *Our America*:

> Why does it matter who we are? The answer can't just be the epistemological truism that our account of the past may be partially determined by our own identity, for, of course, this description of the conditions under which we know the past makes no logical difference to the truth or falsity of what we know. It must be instead the ontological claim that we need to know who we are in order to know which past is ours. The real question, however, is not which past should count as ours, but why any past should count as ours. Virtually all the events and actions that we study did not happen to us and were not done by us; it is always the history of people who were in some respects like us and in other respects different. When, however, we claim IT as ours, we commit ourselves to the ontology of "the Negro," to the identity of the we and they and the primacy of race. (Michaels, 128)

History, in the sense of a past not experienced by us, may not be "ours" in the philosophically absolute sense Michaels describes here. But does it necessarily follow that people therefore have no other contingent and still significant relations with the past? The presumed question, announced in this passage and elsewhere in the book, is how people apparently lose and acquire their culture, their past, and their identity. According to Michaels, the American modernists hypostatized difference itself in a race-bound logic of "separate but equal" that completely refigured American nationalism and left U.S. citizens with the fallacious burden of "being ourselves"—in other words, of being true to some preexisting quality out there, a quality presumably not available to the marginalized immigrants flooding America in the early 1900s. In passages like these, the key to the logic being described is the notion of choice—a choice to be, ironically, what we already are. This apparent contradiction becomes a crucial lever for Michaels. Over and against the apparently contradictory bases for choices we might make regarding identity in a world we accept as contingent, Michaels insists upon a universal understanding of truth and falsity that tropes on American pragmatism.

The whole scenario I have been describing is striking for the way historical and cultural factors are assumed *a priori* to matter only insofar as they play a nondeterminant role in one's life choices. Along similar lines, we can also start to see why so many texts treated in *Our America* focus on issues of racial "passing." The "passing" thematic allows Michaels to avoid an analysis of the ways racial identification transcend individual control as well as the ways race issues shape U.S. institutions. As with most of his recent work, Michaels here delegitimates historical and cultural contingency by collapsing it with choice, thereby clearing a path for a whole series of bold substitutions. Any difference between Arthur Schlesinger, Jr., and Toni Morrison on race issues is obliterated because both ultimately submit to the same fantasy deriving from the nativists. At the same time, there is apparently no difference between Faulkner, the character Reverend Shegog in *The Sound and the Fury*, and virtually every other author working in the 1920s. They all presumably exhibit a wish for transubstantiation twisted into an incarnation of race-bound identities that are all about keeping the family pure—Quentin Compson being Michaels's paradigmatic figure of this logic.

Michaels suggests an alternative to this incestuous racism by pointing us toward real standards by which to judge "natives" and "aliens" alike. How such universal standards will be discovered is not an issue Michaels seems eager to take up, but early on in *Our America* he does indicate who, or more properly what, he considers the real victim to be in this racist cultural logic. As Michaels reads his paradigmatic text, *The Sound and the Fury*, what gets truncated by the incestuous and racist drive to protect the family is the legal contract that should be codified by exogamous marriage (Michaels, 6–12).

In Michaels's case, the legally sanctioned heterosexual marriage stands out as a primary institutional alternative to current cultural logic. However, this alternative is all but buried in Michaels's text, and in this he is again quite consistent with regard to larger trends animating conservative approaches to the affirmative action and curriculum revision debates. While conservative strategists are crafting laws and policies that will detrimentally affect women, people of color, gays, and lesbians, these strategists are trying hard to play the race card so as to deflect questions about how the laws and policies actually target more than race-consciousness. One lesson of Proposition 209's success in California is that this sleight of hand works. The opposition's failure to build effective coalition in the Proposition 209 election played a key role in the dismantling of affirmative action in California; the rhetorical agenda I have been describing contributed a great deal to that failed alliance.

With its recourse to state-sanctioned marriage, *Our America* posits legal ritual as a principal means of accessing truth and falsity in an era marked by racial and racist sophistry. Displacing the debate regarding how to read the U.S. Constitution that animated much of legal scholarship during the 1980s, Michaels offers a thoroughly philosophical solution to race issues. According to Michaels, we can either engage in the folly of choosing a race-bound past and identity to fit our current needs, or we can accept universal standards free of history's mock restraints. He thus takes readers through a literary history in order to disparage historical understanding as an untrustworthy enterprise.

In Michaels's subsequent work on Holocaust studies, these arguments are taken a step further as he directly ties together the concept of an American identity, multiculturalism, and the logic of Holocaust itself. Michaels begins the essay by undertaking an analysis of Art Spiegelman's *Maus*. This analysis focuses on categorizing the various characters according to their apparently systematic representation as different species of animals. After probing possible links between species and race, nationality and religion, Michaels decides that, in fact, the only wholly consistent way to make sense of Spiegelman's designations is to assume that such designations are justified "by their proximate relation to the Holocaust" itself. Putting it another way, Michaels argues that *Maus* "invokes the concept of Holocaust as a mechanism of collective identity."

Critiquing various arguments for a distinct and/or "exceptional" American culture and identity, Michaels goes on to claim that all concepts of identity depend exactly on an analogous concept of Holocaust. Unpacking "Holocaust" as a logic, Michaels insists that there is a collapse of physical and cultural concerns in the way critics and historians have mobilized ideas about genocide. This slippage enables a hierarchy in which the loss of a people—of a culture—outweighs murder, which is simply a threat to individual people's lives. As a result, according to Michaels, the Holocaust-oriented regime of cultural identity makes possible the subsequent notion that assimilation is paradigmatically comparable to genocide.

Michaels is particularly concerned with the way in which an almost omnipotent valorization of identity undercuts any pursuit of disagreements. His concern is that a reduction of all values to those affecting survival and extinction will displace healthy criticism and debate. This is clearly an important concern that has resonance. Many scholars working in minority discourse and race studies know how some positions, built around threats to group survival, can be used to deny the diversity of particular communities. It is very unfortunate, then, that Michaels ignores the parallel work that has taken place in multicultural studies, especially because he might better situate his claims and their applicability, particularly their applicability to cruder forms of identity politics and cultural nationalism.

As it stands, however, Michaels offers an unselfconscious and horribly ironic "final solution" for identity that has been replicated by other prominent American studies scholars.[6] As subtle as his work on Holocaust studies is in terms of its philosophical approach, and in terms of its driving desire for a pure form of consistency, its delegitimation of historical concerns comes with a high price. Consider for instance what it means for someone writing about the Holocaust to pose as a solution a value that was a key part of Hitler's mechanism for choosing personnel. Michaels adamantly seeks to dismantle the concept of identity;

Hitler, of course, sought out and made much use precisely of people with shattered identities.[7]

Although Michaels's essay is not explicit in its engagement of legal practice, the extension of his marriage argument in *Our America* is manifested throughout the Holocaust piece by subtle references to the question of what constitutes a true "crime." In Michaels's view, any critique of American cultural identity per se is treated as a crime by the current multicultural regime. This fundamentally unjust situation will only be remedied, according to Michaels, by completely foregoing the logic of identity.

In a similar argument, Michaels maintains that the "white studies" movement submits to exactly the same sort of cultural logic that defines multicultural study. Here again, Michaels's emphasis falls on the fantasies that he believes underlie racial affiliation. Purely a matter of individual desire and choice, such self-imposed racial identification is, according to Michaels, misread by the academy when it posits race as a meaningful category, a mistake made possible by deceptively adopting an ultimately essentialist position. The proof of the fantastic nature of race in Michaels's essay is bound up with the fact that students of race dynamics have confused "actions" and "choices" with "identities."

Fielding questions after a presentation of this argument at Dartmouth in 1997, Michaels offered a "Marxist" interpretation as a contrast: He claimed that if a member of the proletariat buys a factory and thereby becomes a member of the bourgeoisie, it is this action that defines the person in the Marxist analysis, not recourse to a tautologically derived identity.[8] Whereas Marxist interpretation in this instance is seemingly favored by Michaels, his deployment of it here seems almost parodic since he never considers how a member of the proletariat might gain the resources to buy a factory. Marxist distinctions between the proletariat and the bourgeoisie are meaningful to the extent that they engage and articulate a certain relation to historical conditions. Individuals in this sort of interpretation do not simply choose to participate in one category or the other, and for Michaels to offer an example that so easily ignores this historical conditioning, he has to reduce Marxism to a caricature. This turn of events is not accidental. Once the gate to questions of historical conditioning are open, the horses are out, and Michaels becomes responsible for a much more critical appraisal of choice, individualism, and hegemony. In other words, it is no longer viable to maintain a realm of actions and choices freely distinct from interpersonal, socially derived conceptual categories.

Taking *Our America* and the essays together, we may reread Michaels as promoting a certain set of rhetorical gestures. First, collective identity is suspect in virtually any form and in all cases individual actors constitute the preferred reference point. Second, there is a basic transparency in people's actions. This notion allows for the simplistic treatment of motivations and representational issues tied to the authors discussed by Michaels. Third, historical and cultural concerns need to be severely limited in terms of application to decision making. This concept is of course crucial when Michaels disconnects people from any past they have not directly experienced. Fourth, one's relation to culture and history is posed solely as a matter of choice. Everyone becomes a potential perpetrator; by the same token, questions produced in a results-oriented analysis, or victim-oriented analysis, in other words, those results so critical to the development of affirmative action and harassment laws, are radically devalued. And finally, language is taken to be transparent. Issues of representation and linguistic ambiguity that have fueled critical debate about *The Sound and the Fury* and *Maus* and so many other texts are pushed aside as a very mechanical rationalism avoids at all costs issues of translation.

Each of these rhetorical gestures exemplifies a fundamental aspect of legal discourse in this country. Feminist Legal Critics, as well as Critical Legal and Critical Races Studies scholars, have built much of their respective enterprises around challenging precisely these gestures.[9] Even though the tools these scholars have developed have the potential to enrich further analysis of Michaels's arguments, we are ultimately left to consider just why it is that one of the more comprehensive literary histories of twentieth-century America reads better as legal rhetoric than it does as literary history, despite its self-presentation as an example of the latter.

Michaels's version is certainly not the only way to approach the notion of cultural logics and the limits of identity politics, and in a similar vein I would make it clear that I am not interested in replacing

Michaels's demonization of culture/identity/Holocaust/race with my own demonization of legal rhetoric. Instead, I am suggesting that scholars explore the effect of the intellectual amputation that goes along with the practice of color-blindness. Another way to think of the problem is to ask what kind of work is accomplished by embracing the color-blind approach? Michaels has posed the paradigmatic value of multiculturalism as survival, but why, for instance, could not one think of multiculturalism's projects in terms of "working through" intermediate and less absolute injuries and the traumas associated with them, rather than the threat of totalizing extinction?

Since Michaels posits a race "fantasy" of national if not international proportions, might not his recourse to the concepts of psychoanalysis be turned to suggest that the enormous repression required to unthink race-affiliated injuries simply feeds ongoing racially problematic responses? In *Stranded Objects: Mourning, Memory, and Film in Postwar Germany,* Santner contends that particular objects can become cathected points of displaced and problematic focus when more viable mechanisms for working through traumas are resisted or repressed. In this context, Santner reads the reconstruction of Germany as a project that, to an extent, substituted for the work of coming to terms with the trauma of a Nazi past. Inasmuch as this substitution deferred a "working through" of that trauma, the reconstruction itself could become, according to Santner, a kind of stranded object that cannot adequately address the problem which gave rise to its special status as a project in the first place. Herein lies my speculation: Could the myriad substitutions that are being produced by scholars like Michaels—substitutions among such concepts as racism, race, culture, identity, and Holocaust, as well as substitutions among real and imagined actors—be themselves a sign of melancholic exhaustion, an exhaustion demonstrated in a series of "stranded objects," or more properly, "stranded judgments," given the recourse to legal discourse I have been describing? Might Michaels's argument itself indicate just how far we are from adequately addressing racial and other forms of injury?

Specifically, I would suggest that efforts like Michaels's to wrestle with questions of race and racism end up "acting out" rather than working through critical problems associated with understanding either race or racism. At stake in the distinction is the question of whether we can gain a critical distance from, and yet a successful engagement with, highly conflictual issues. If such critical engagement is truncated because the interpretive process is insufficiently self-conscious, thereby conditioning that process to replicate problems inherent in the object of study, then a form of acting out may be at work. In this context, one need not understand working through and acting out as mutually exclusive concepts, and here LaCapra's treatment of the problem is constructive:

> The relation between acting-out and working-through should not be seen in terms of a from/to relationship in which the latter is presented as the dialectical transcendence of the former.... particularly in the cases of trauma, acting out may be necessary and perhaps never fully overcome. Indeed, it may be intimately bound up with working through problems. But it should not be isolated, theoretically fixated on, or one-sidedly valorized as the horizon of thought or life. (LaCapra, 205)

LaCapra's final warning has bearing on the principal limitation in Michaels's approach to race issues: the insistence upon reducing all racially marked interactions to a narrow philosophical interpretation that symptomatically reproduces the injury in an ever-widening circle of error, the legacy of Michaels's rigid notion of cultural logic.

Taking on a parallel problem, Judith Butler has offered a subtle critique of the movement for hate speech legislation, a movement that has attempted to develop policy and laws that would punish injurious references to race.

> That such language carries trauma is not a reason to forbid its use. There is no purifying language of its traumatic residue, and no way to work through trauma except through the arduous effort it takes to direct the course of its repetition. It may be that trauma constitutes a strange kind of resource, and repetition, its vexed but promising instrument. After all, to be named by another is traumatic: it is an act that precedes my will, an act that brings me into a linguistic world in which I might then begin to exercise agency at all. . . . The terms by which we are hailed are rarely the ones we choose . . . ; but these terms we never really choose are the

occasion for something we still might call agency, the repetition of an originary subordination for another purpose, one whose future is partially open. (Butler, 38)

For Butler, there is something like a constitutive trauma that all people experience as linguistic beings, a trauma that is tapped and exacerbated with the use of racist speech. The question of how to reduce injuries, and productively respond to them, in turn, requires a careful consideration of the ways censorship may well act out resentments that are ultimately directed toward the contingency that accompanies our very construction as linguistic beings. Of particular concern for Butler is the sovereign sense of self that would presumably be guaranteed by a person's interpellation into the structure of the state. One result, according to this analysis, is that legal remedies—like statutes challenging race hate speech—may inadvertently end up fixing the language of racism in an even more cathected and powerful position. Butler therefore suggests a more wary and imaginative engagement with (and appropriation of) racist language, an engagement that takes a thoroughly critical stance toward the legal mechanisms of blind neutrality. While Butler may be guilty of fixating on an ultimately abstract and potentially reductive notion of traumatic aporia framing our entrance into language, her intervention focuses badly needed attention on the mediation of race among diverse spheres of professional and cultural activity.

As I will demonstrate in my treatment of Critical Race Studies, these sorts of concerns lead legal scholars like Patricia Williams to assert that "Racism inscribes culture with generalized preferences and routinized notions of propriety. It is an aspiration as much as a condemnation; it is an aesthetic" ("Metro," 198). In this context, it is the judicial desire to simplify and exclude particular interpretations that comes into question. For both Williams and Butler, a skepticism about the law's predilection toward linguistic fixity and reduction translates into a wary assessment of the law's ability to remedy racial injury. But it is Williams's notion of an aesthetic that I would follow up, because it suggests a way of rethinking Michaels's arguments in light of what I would suggest are complementary cultural products. Reading Michaels's texts less as literary history miraculously transcending a pervasive racist cultural logic and more as the product of a particular moment, we can situate a variety of works, including his own, in a particular episode, one that has been typified as the backlash of the "angry white male," an upheaval that was announced in part by the dramatic electoral changes in the U.S. Congress in 1994.

From its inception, the definition of the angry white male has been contested. Largely the product of the mainstream media, the phrase became an explanation for the November 1994 Republican electoral sweep. By December 1994, the *Wall Street Journal* had found a poster boy for this newly legitimated movement: 49-year-old lab technician Sidney Tracy, of Munford, Tennessee. Reporting that the recently unemployed Tracy blamed his plight "in fair measure on affirmative action" because "the President got up there and did everything for blacks and gays," the *Journal* created a reference point that was explicitly cited by publications across the country.[10] As Linda Hirshman discovered, however, there was one problem; Tracy was a devoted Democrat who was misquoted. He had speculated for the *Wall Street Journal* reporter about the forces behind the Republican sweep, but he blamed his own circumstances on corporate downsizing and adamantly protested that his own unemployment had nothing to do with affirmative action (in fact, his entire plant had been closed).

At least in part a product of fantasy from the outset, the angry white male type that Sidney Tracy was forced to model drew on fertile soil in the culture industry. Two of the more notable films in this vein are *Falling Down* (directed by Joel Schumacher, 1993), a film taken by many critics as a bold rejection of multiculturalism, and *Disclosure* (directed by Barry Levinson, 1994), an attack on sexual harassment policies. The former was so definitive as regards the angry white male concept that its lead character, an out-of-work defense industry engineer played by Michael Douglas and known only by his car's license plate, D-FENS, graced the cover of numerous publications, including *Newsweek*, as a representative figure of the backlash.[11] In the film, Douglas plays a deranged motorist who sets off on a pedestrian rampage after finding that he can no longer maintain the illusion of driving to the job he lost weeks prior. Abandoning his car in a Los Angeles traffic jam, D-Fens sets out for his ex-wife's home so that he might celebrate his daughter's birthday, but it is quickly apparent that his ex-wife is terrified of D-Fens, and with good reason.

Although restoring the nuclear family is D-Fens's ostensible goal, the means is the focus of the film, and hence the audience spends much of its time watching D-Fens "cut a swath through the dysfunctional infrastructure, human and architectural, of Los Angeles urban life" (Doherty, 370–371). While D-Fens makes his journey, parallel editing establishes a soon-to-retire police detective, Prendergast, as D-Fens's alter ego. A cop wrestling with problems comparable to those faced by D-Fens—a troubled home life, rotten job, the same traffic jam—this character seems to have at least as many reasons to go off the deep end, but instead, he is posed as a "stable" fellow, especially in comparison to his quarry, D-Fens. While the film builds to a climactic confrontation between the two at its conclusion, much of D-Fens's damage is already done as he moves through various parts of the city to get home. Alternately assuming the mantle of victim and of vigilante, D-Fens amasses a considerable arsenal while crossing the city. Although the scatter-shot that ensues is seemingly dictated by accidental encounters, numerous critics have noted that the casualty rate is hardly distributed evenly. As Tom Doherty notes, the list of the wounded offers "a fair sampling of white collar, white male hate objects" (371). All of this violence is embellished within the movie with nostalgic diatribes that express a wish for a nonexistent earlier period of unchallenged white male privilege, a point that is especially apparent in D-Fens's threats to his wife and in videotaped images of D-Fens's previous married life.

A good part of the appeal of the film is the surrogate experience of vigilantism it offers the audience. This pleasure is based on the audience's ability to imaginatively identify with D-Fens's racially focused acting out, an acting out which repeats with increasing doses of violence. The rampage is sustained in part because D-Fens has lost meaningful contact with the world; his tunnel vision cannot see beyond the supposed choice to return to a (nonexistent) home he has lost. In this way, *Our America* and *Falling Down* present comparable overvaluations of liberal individualism and choice. As sophisticated as his arguments are, Michaels's journey through twentieth-century American literature is as imaginatively violent as D-Fens's march through Los Angeles because of Michaels's reductive reading practices.

J. P. Telotte explores the violent fantasy in *Falling Down* by noting the film's debt to Federico Fellini's *8½*.[12] Telotte argues that contemporary American life is defined by "a complex contest between the real and the fake, between the authentic and the product of our fantasies," a situation which is leading increasingly to the "displacement of the real by its models," and in this way, to a "confusion that threatens to undermine the power lodged in our fantasies . . . for coping and gaining release from the deadening effects of everyday reality" (Telotte, 19). In order to situate *Falling Down* in this American context, Telotte invokes Fellini's *8½* as one of the film's inspirations, and as its alter ego. For Telotte, *8½* is a paradigm of sorts for the filmic treatment of fantasy, and of affirming the "vital, even redemptive powers of the imagination" (20). Its central character, Guido, is a filmmaker, resembling Fellini, who struggles with himself to complete a fantasy film about people escaping Earth in a rocket. In the process, *8½* "repeatedly, and easily, slips into and out of Guido's fantasies, each of which initially seems to accommodate his conflicting desires, but eventually only frustrates them and leaves Guido brought down once more" (21). Guido's "falling down" reinforces his engagement with those around him, and ultimately he is able to negotiate this social existence as well as his traffic between fantasy and reality. The film project does progress, and it does so in large part because Guido is not completely possessed by his fantasies; he succeeds in maintaining a critical distance, in resisting an "acting out" response, in resisting uncritical possession by the wish to escape.

D-Fens presents a different path, a distinction that becomes more clear as we compare the films' openings. Both works invite the audience to identify with the frustrations of being caught in a traffic jam. Guido responds to his sense of being trapped by flying away from his car and finally over a picturesque beach. Tethered to Earth, he remains symbolically attached, and when he tries to break the bond, an assistant calls out instructions which translate as "definitely down," whereupon Guido plunges, only to wake from his dream before crashing.

In a scene that mimics on numerous levels Guido's introduction, D-Fens likewise abandons his vehicle, but here the fantasy is not broken;

D-Fens acts out his escape uninterrupted. While Guido fantasizes about various violent acts in *8½* (hanging an argumentative screenwriter, shooting himself), he always falls back into a social reality. D-Fens, on the other hand, never appears to awaken, and what's worse, he insists in frequently violent ways that others accept his delusions as well: "There is no negotiation, no contestation for this character; his fantasy must be everyone else's—or else" (Telotte, 22). In one politically loaded encounter after another, D-Fens finds himself playing the role of vigilante, striking out at a variety of white male hate objects as he moves through distinct neighborhoods. D-Fens's "progress" is ultimately mapped by Detective Prendergast, a character who bears similarities to Fellini's Guido inasmuch as his fantasies, for instance about his dead daughter, are not only self-controlled, but are actually strategically invoked during the final confrontation in *Falling Down* as in Prendergast's attempts to defuse D-Fens's violence. The attempt fails, and D-Fens commits suicide rather than accept the loss of his manufactured innocence.

Recalling LaCapra's complication of the acting out/working through distinction, I would invite readers to credit *Falling Down* with its own type of inquiry regarding "working through"; in this sense, the film may be more of a compliment to *8½* than the diminution of its project which Telotte suggests. *Falling Down* is interesting for the ways it represents an aspect of acting out that is central to the assertion of white privilege in the 1990s; this assertion finds expression in arguments for race-blindness that isolate, theoretically fixate upon, and one-sidedly valorize acting out. This privilege has never existed unchallenged or untainted, and thus a certain injury has always accompanied what ultimately is a white supremacist project.

There is a significant parallel between the race censorship being advocated by critics like Walter Benn Michaels and the representation of white male anger bound up in D-Fens. While D-Fens journeys through various barrios, Michaels tracks through various fields of multicultural inquiry (identity politics, race studies, Holocaust studies, white studies), repeatedly refusing to acknowledge viable negotiations that he might strike up with the works under examination because everything he encounters is presumably tainted with a cultural logic that collapses race and racism. Like D-Fens, he appears fully committed to protecting the exercise of choice as a redemptive path. It is, of course, no accident that vigilante D-Fens and Michaels are so heavily imbued in legal dynamics. Both have a crucial investment in "turning back" the laws of multicultural America. But in the final assessment, it may well be that the film—despite its mainstream reception—does the most to critically situate the law, its promise, and its limitations. Detective Prendergast saves the day by playing D-Fens's executioner, and in the process is infected to a degree by some of the same impulses that drive D-Fens (in the final scenes, Prendergast "puts his wife in her place" and in an explicitly Dirty Harry moment, tells his captain to "fuck off"). Yet Prendergast also appears capable of communicating with and understanding others in a manner that is not wholly dependent on invoking the law (vigilantes, after all, are defined by taking the law into their own hands). In this way, Prendergast is less the policeman than is either D-Fens or Michaels. Inasmuch as a violent censorship aligns both Michaels's and D-Fens's projects, they offer an account of racial injury that forecloses the possibility of a critical response (Butler, *Excitable Speech,* 19) and guarantee injury's continued effects. Such exorcisms of race and racism cannot succeed, and in fact set the stage for haunting presences that defy the intellectual amputation carried out in the name of the law.

PART TWO

NARRATIVE
INTERVENTIONS

CHAPTER THREE

CRITICAL RACE STORIES
AND THE PROBLEM
OF REMEDY

The original sense of discrimination was one of discernment, of re-
finement, of choice, of value judgment—the courteous deflection
to the noble rather than to the base. It is this complicated social mi-
lieu that must be remembered as the backdrop to what both the
majority and dissenters refer to as "preferences" in [*Metro v. FCC*].
Racism inscribes culture with generalized preferences and routinized notions of propriety. It is aspiration as much as condemnation; it is an aesthetic.

—Patricia Williams, "*Metro Broadcasting, Inc. v. FCC*," 198

Although the Critical Legal Studies (CLS) movement is often credited
with elaborating a detailed "deconstruction" of legal practice, Critical
Race Studies (CRS) has been unique in attempting to reconstruct the
law by virtue of reference to a core race literacy processed "from the bottom up," or by means of a certain proximate relation to racial injury.[1] In
"looking to and from the bottom," and thereby critically connecting
with communities subject to racial victimization, CRS authors have, as
Richard Delgado argues, undertaken a process of understanding the
competition between stories as told by diverse legal actors.[2] Working
from the position that race is a prime factor shaping most facets of society, these authors have defined for themselves a radically interdisciplinary activity, even as it retains a focus on the law per se.

As I have suggested earlier, one may think of the CRS larger project in terms of its focus on transferential aspects of scholarship and

adjudication, aspects that the CRS authors trace to the variety of displacements, paradoxes and inconsistencies that animate legal discourse when it addresses race injuries, and even when legal discourse only seems to retain the faintest connections to such conflicts. Participating scholars attempt to "work through" the implications of these racial dynamics in order to affect the "vexed bond between law and racial power" (Kimberlé Crenshaw et al., *Critical Race Theory*, xiii). Taking up such concerns, Richard Delgado, for instance, frames this CRS intervention in terms of the critical storytelling the authors pursue, storytelling that reveals both "tellers" and "listeners" constructing realities in ways that negotiate complex desires.[3] Wary of the pitfalls associated with race-oriented essentialism, as well as the difficulties that may come when the law is projected as an instrument of an autonomous racism "out there" in society, the CRS authors have engaged and critiqued civil rights discourse in order to rethink the law and race. For many of these CRS scholars, this project is especially urgent given that racial disparities remain a damaging part of U.S. social structure. Arguing for the "absolute centrality of history and context in any analysis" of race and law, prominent members of the CRS movement have ultimately crafted an ambivalent relation to civil rights strategies, for while integration as a goal is assumed to foreclose a crucial avenue of critique, the CRS scholars are not ready to follow arguments offered by some members of the CLS movement, arguments that presume rights-oriented activism is all but hopeless.[4] It is in the context of this debate that many CRS scholars look to alternative paradigms and reconsider the black power movement.[5]

Although CRS projects align in varied ways with the theories of institutional racism developed in the sixties and seventies, one way to think of the overall linkage is in terms of a recombination that draws together the radical critique leveled by black nationalist scholars—especially sociologists—with a continued investment in the rights discourse which was an imaginative center during the civil rights era. Certain topics developed in this dialectical frame have been of particular interest for the CRS movement. These include (1) the critique of merit as a neutral concept; (2) the rethinking of social interaction—especially in institutional venues—along the lines of group dynamics; and (3) the advocacy of significant material redistribution in society (reparations made for injuries suffered by groups over time).[6] The CRS scholars thus rework key aspects of the black nationalist agenda, while simultaneously shifting the focus of the critique away from its racially separatist and essentialist origins. What readers tend to find, then, are "multicultural" projects, projects devoted to analyzing a dialectics of minority and majority interaction. The posture developed by the CRS scholars, therefore, rethinks the nature of "radical" critique, suggesting that effective political change engages the full spectrum of U.S. social and cultural practices.

Building on notions of institutional racism, the CRS scholars attempt to map the specific dynamics of the courts; at the same time, they argue for reforms initiated from within the institution. One irony of this intervention is that the excitement it has generated in many distantly related fields has outweighed actual reforms undertaken in law schools, or legal practice generally. Given the rhetorical goals pursued by CRS scholars, these difficulties are perhaps somewhat predictable; the scope of their critique is ambitious and suggests fundamental changes in legal training and practice. At the same time, the CRS authors "look to the bottom" and try to critically connect with communities subject to racial victimization, thereby undertaking a process of translation that at least opens the question of whether their "products" will be accessible to the various communities they presumably address.[7]

Although CRS authors like Delgado have offered critically important analyses regarding legal storytelling as an intervention, some of the most prominent "maps" of the movement (presented in the "Introductions" to the three collections of CRS writing to date) overlook or quickly gloss this rhetorical complexity.[8] Perhaps most startling, these self-appraisals have largely neglected to analyze an important aspect of the CRS rhetorical strategy, an aspect that in fact has been responsible for much of the excitement generated by the movement. Here I am thinking of the experimental critical prose that has woven together autobiography, anecdote, fantasy, legal decisions, and novelistic discourse: in other words, varied modes of telling stories. Not all CRS authors participate in this experimentation; nonetheless, the tendency toward this kind of rhetorical intervention is marked and is coming to define the movement. Writers, including Patricia Williams, Derrick Bell, Gerald Lopez, and Richard

Delgado, should therefore be credited with generating tremendous interest in the possibilities of such "formal" experiment.[9]

One way to make sense of the apparent disjuncture between the CRS self-appraisals and the excitement regarding storytelling would be to consider the distinct consequences of the different "figures" or models used by the scholars to define racial injury. For instance, it is common to find CRS essays arguing both that racism manifests itself in acts of exclusion, and that racism is perpetuated through entrenched processes of social, political, and cultural value judgments, including, for example, meritocracy. Although these various aspects of racism are linked in the writings to substantial evidence of existing social dynamics, the implications of this bifurcated approach (emphasizing exclusion on the one hand, meritocracy on the other) do not suggest a simple response, or an easily synthesized political project.

As I noted previously with regard to Wendy Brown's work, an emphasis on injury-as-exclusion can place progressive political causes in the questionable position of fighting for a spot in a bureaucratic machine almost wholly unaltered by the remediating "inclusion." Leaving the larger rhetorical and political structuring intact, such multiplication of local claims can foster a backward-looking, resentful *quid pro quo* in which injury is converted into pacifying inclusion (Brown, 156–164). Such a transaction can easily reconfirm the dominant value and decision-making system in place at the time of the injury.

Along these lines, I would suggest that some of the more exciting examples of the CRS project (including Delgado's *Rodrigo Chronicles,* Derrick Bell's *And We Are Not Saved,* Patricia Williams's *Alchemy of Race and Rights*) target forms of cultural literacy. However, the difficulties of a thorough rethinking of cultural literacy are great indeed. Readers may take the argument for reparations as a case in point. Although a number of other CRS scholars have championed reparations, Mari Matsuda was one of the first within the movement to offer the reparations strategy as a response to CLS skepticism regarding rights activism.[10] In the process, Matsuda points to the experience of minority suffering as a way of grounding ethically a privileging of minority scholarship. In other words, Matsuda argues that minority scholars constitute organic intellectuals because of their proximity to racial victimization. In this vein,

Matsuda suggests that reparations for racial injuries deserve a second look because this response to racism is the considered strategy developed by these scholars.[11]

While framing the reparations argument in this moment of suffering, Matsuda also notes the difficulties that attend the implementation of reparations.[12] Besides potentially promoting a commodification of injuries, such policies may be co-opted, either by "buying off" protest; by unfairly limiting the effects of injuries (especially temporally); or by pitting disadvantaged groups against one another in what is posed as a zero-sum game of resource allocation. It is unfortunate that these concerns are developed only briefly at the conclusion of Matsuda's influential essay, because it is here that she most explicitly struggles against the sorts of problematic dynamics that come with emphasizing inclusion and exclusion.

Matsuda claims that "reparations will result in a new form of disadvantage only if they are made outside of a broader consciousness that always looks to the needs of the bottom" (76). This notion of a radical change in consciousness is a lynchpin in Matsuda's thinking, and appears in other CRS treatments of reparations, including Derrick Bell's *And We Are Not Saved*.[13] Exploring the tensions between rights-oriented remedies (emphasizing inclusion) and global critiques of legal and political practice embodied in notions like merit, neutrality, and objectivity, scholars like Delgado, Bell and Williams engage very broad questions of consciousness and cultural literacy in the hopes of enabling a broadly conceived political intervention through the reference to, and practice of, certain kinds of storytelling. While it may be that an inclusive intervention of minority voices has the potential to propel a broader change of consciousness, many CRS works, and certainly the Introductions to the collections noted, do not make clear how these reforms might actually proceed, especially as they depend on an articulation with culture. Given the existence of texts like Delgado's "Storytelling for Oppositionists and Others," and the notable narrative experiments available in numerous CRS texts, the failure in the Introductions to address storytelling dynamics (as thematic and as practice) likely correlates in some meaningful way with the ongoing struggle to articulate more clearly the relationship between inclusion-oriented rights discourse and the "aesthetics" of racism that cuts across different cultural spheres, including the legal.

Although this difficulty of articulating culture and racial injury pervades the genre of race analysis (regardless of its political stripe), opponents of the CRS movement have nonetheless seized upon the limits of inclusion-oriented rhetoric in order to throw the problem back into the movement's face. For Richard Posner, the issue is the questionable "typicality" of racism assumed by CRS authors[14] (in this view, events like the dragging murder of James Byrd, Jr., in Jasper, Texas and the beating of Rodney King by LAPD officers are hyped by a media that distorts reality); for Dinesh D'Souza and a host of others, the issue is whether recognizing race—rather than presuming a universal Western heritage—itself promotes racism.[15] In such reactions, racial injury is presumed to be "exceptional," and the very engagement with the idea constitutes an exclusion in its own right of a more representative reality. Advocates of color-blindness are therefore equally capable of rethinking our larger cultural reality, and at the same time quite adept at using the normalizing impulse of inclusion arguments (we should all be treated the same) in order to posit that in fact the goal (sameness) can best be achieved by simply willing a denial of race (consigning it to the atypical). As proven by Proposition 209 in California, the color-blindness movement has succeeded in convincing many people that censorship is itself liberating. In an ironic turn of events, the political right has therefore reversed its highly successful strategies of the Reagan-era 1980s (when the Left was aligned with nay-saying, politically correct censorship) and sold color-blindness as a new means of self-fulfillment, and as a choice to construct a better, more positive reality. In the meantime, advocates of race-conscious programs and analyses are once again left to figure out how to more effectively engage many voters' desires.

In part, this problem for advocates of race-consciousness stems from the often implicit assumption that "uncovering" the dynamics of racism will result in a correction of these dynamics, an assumption that goes hand in hand with a politics of visibility that has recently come under much fire.[16] Simply making power and injury visible in no way guarantees a more liberated society, although of course recognition of these injuries can be a crucial initial step. The key is appropriately mediating between such recognitions and the literacy that governs the interpretation of social and cultural problems generally. Without this mediation, the making visible of injury can easily be co-opted into a project in which conflicts are subdued, or worse yet, completely robbed of their ability to generate "alternative" political thought. Here, Wiegman's and Brown's critiques of liberal political thinking are quite compatible, inasmuch as both are concerned with the ways in which reform-oriented actions can ultimately be reactive. Consider, for instance, the way courts can turn to anthropology and sociology in order to verify culturally specific definitions—for instance, the meaning of "tribe" in cases involving Native American claims.[17] As scholars like Vine Deloria, Jr., have argued, this situation often leads to a highly problematic reimposition of mainstream academic interests and biases that seriously disadvantage Native American legal actions.[18]

CRS is tremendously exciting and also at times frustrating for the ways it both attends to and displaces this problematic. As Cornell West has noted, the movement aims to remake "the world to reveal the silenced suffering and relieve social misery," but to accomplish such an undertaking the CRS scholars are also required to rethink the tools of their analysis. Along these lines, the CRS critique of meritocracy carries with it one of the single strongest methodological interventions drawing the movement together, because the critique opens global questions of constructing and assigning value, questions that are at the core of battles over competing forms of literacy. This approach speaks directly to the impasse described by Matsuda: Once injuries are legible in their complexity, how do we negotiate a process of healing, or working through, that does not incorporate social and cultural difference into existing bureaucratic norms? Whether the discursive frame of reference is provided by culture, history, or law, there remains a tendency, evidenced in the Introductions to the CRS collections, to visualize racial injury as though it were a transparent object upon which an ethical project might be built. This mode of understanding injury is clearly not the only one at work in CRS writings, but it does play a crucial role in the Introductions when the editors explain the political purchase of their approach to race.

Critics' efforts to contend with racial injuries are, of course, complicated by the fact that such injuries are always approached in a rhetorical field of struggle that is shaded by the designs of the interpreters. At different points in its development, the CRS movement has acknowledged this or similar problematics, and hence when the first CRS conference was convened, it took as a goal the elaboration of "a theoretical vocabulary for progressive racial politics in contemporary America."[19] The results are summarized by Kimberlé Crenshaw, Neil Gotanda, Gary Peller, and Kendall Thomas in their Introduction to *Critical Race Theory*;[20] these theoretical innovations include:

1. "deconstruction," especially as applied to notions of color-blindness.
2. the charting of logical inconsistencies with regard to the legal treatment and recognition of social groups.
3. the analysis of political interest in supposedly neutral legal decision making.
4. an exploration of the denial mobilized by legal authorities who displace racial politics by invoking concepts like legal precedent.

Although the methodological map offered by the editors marks the start of a larger theoretical program, this list does not provide a full sense of how the tools shape the rhetorical and narrative experiments found in some of the most exciting CRS writing. In fact, little in this list distinguishes the Critical Race Theory from the Critical Legal Studies tenets that preceded it, at least in methodological terms. Deconstruction; an emphasis on legal inconsistency and politicization; law-as-denial—all are notions very much at the center of the CLS project.[21] I would suggest, then, that for the CRS to fully develop a notion of racial remedy, it will need to engage more consistently the question of why racial injury in particular holds such a unique claim in terms of the CRS ability to frame an analysis of phenomena like meritocracy. A key part of this development would profitably include an extension of Delgado's rethinking of narrative experiments, experiments that have already made it possible for CRS innovators to transgress disciplinary boundaries as they have approached the tremendous breadth of racialized experience in this country.

∼

> Equal opportunity is not only about assuming circumstances of hypo-
> thetically indistinguishable individuals; it is also about accommodating
> the living, shifting fortunes of those who are very differently situated.
> What happens to one may be the repercussive history that repeats itself in
> the futures of us all.
> —Patricia Williams, "*Metro Broadcasting v. FCC*," 199

Echoing the haunting close of Ralph Ellison's *Invisible Man,* Patricia Williams ends her discussion of the *Metro v. FCC* U.S. Supreme
Court decision with a point that flies directly in the face of established judicial process, inasmuch as that process is committed to reading isolated individuals acting on transparent intentions in a highly
circumscribed temporal frame. The gesture is entirely fitting, given
Williams's desire to reveal the alchemical qualities of race in America.
But the gesture also speaks directly to the *Metro* case itself, in that
Williams believes it may be perceived "as the last hurrah of a dying
liberal order" ("*Metro,*" 191). One goal of Williams's essay, then, is to
convince readers of the *Metro* decision's continuing significance, and
especially of the ways the case reconfirms the appropriateness of racial
group claims.

Of particular concern for Williams are the "costs of pitting individual rights against group interests at a moment in our history when
the groupings race and class intersect in such a way that race increasingly defines class, and such that the property interests of large numbers of white individuals are understood to be in irreconcilable tension with the collective dispossession of large numbers of people of
color" (191). In this context, Williams challenges a certain nostalgia
that might be applied to the *Metro* decision, arguing instead for a rethinking of future-oriented goals based on *Metro* as an active and vital
precedent. In this sense, the first paragraph of Williams's essay elaborates a careful rhetorical negotiation that claims one injury (*Metro*
read as tombstone for an era) while it wrestles with the resentment-
producing paradigms of liberal politics that pit "individual rights
against group interests" (191), thereby imposing a problematic logic of
moral equivalence. Taking issue with this zero-sum game, Williams
argues that

affirmative action and minority set-aside programs are vastly more complicated than this "you're in, I'm out" conception suggests. Nothing in this rigid win/lose dichotomy permits the notion that everyone could end up a beneficiary, that expansion rather than substitution might be possible, and that the favoring of multiple cultures is an enhancement of the total rather than a sweepingly reflexive act of favoritism for anything other than the monolithic purity of an all-white nation. (Williams, "*Metro*," 197)

The argument bears all of the trademarks of previous institutional racism studies, yet there are important differences here as well. For instance, Williams is quite self-conscious regarding the pitfalls of a global notion of racism that appears to transcend recognizable agency. In fact, one of Williams's first criticisms of the majority in the *Metro* case has to do with its subtle tendency to view racism as either individually based or societal, but in either case somehow beyond the scope of the repairs available in the law. Not surprisingly, Williams concludes her essay by reinvoking this problem in an even more critical light, arguing that in certain instances, the enormity of racism can itself become an excuse, even a racist rationale, for inaction (198). One of Williams's particular contributions in this arena is a rethinking of agency: exploring the way choices are usually crosscut by various intersecting interests, including those defined by institutional agendas. To this end, Williams is particularly adept at elaborating the ways in which the culture of contract law shapes our notions of race and of racial injury.

The courts provide a privileged site for this rethinking of agency neither because the law is an autonomous political force, nor because the law is an instrument of external social forces. Rather, the law in Williams's reading offers a crucial site of social and cultural exchange (and contract law particularly so for its "regulating" of exchange). This understanding also leads Williams to argue for a more active engagement of racial issues in the legal setting:

The reflexive referral of all but the most privatized controversies to the legislature obscures the fact that even the narrowest contract or property dispute is never really as private as theory would have it. Courts always have to consider social ramifications that are rarely limited to the named parties, whether that consideration is of "policy" (the contemporaneous society of those similarly situated) or whether the consideration is funneled into issues of "precedent" (the prior or subsequent society of others). (Williams, "*Metro*," 196)

The point with regard to precedent is an important one, inasmuch as it frames the rhetorical goal of the essay as a whole. Directed particularly at those legal actors who will be reproducing and, to an extent, making anew, interpretations of canonical moments in the law, this essay highlights precedent in order to appeal to tradition, while simultaneously transvaluing precedent by drawing it from an ethereal realm of universal norms into the convoluted history of the law's own intersection with race, media, culture, commerce, and society.[22]

At the conclusion of her essay on the *Metro* decision, Williams argues that racism "is an aesthetic" (198). One of the most accomplished CRS writers, Williams develops this intersection of legal and cultural issues by actually examining cultural texts and trends in a way that is organically and dialogically linked to the problems she engages. Whether Williams is focusing on *The Cosby Show*, a manner of dress, or the assumptions of Protestant religion, there is evidence in the writing of a careful scholar who combines the interests of a semiotician, a linguist, a historian, an ethnographer and more, in order to address the results of racism as these have shaped our most naturalized tools of communication and understanding.

This orientation, developed across a range of examples, contributes to Williams's rethinking of legal practice as an adjectival war, or as an ongoing battle over basic definitions.[23] In the *Metro* case, this war saw words "inflated like balloons in order to make the issue of diversity large or trivial, compelling or merely important, natural or momentary, grandly futuristic or of the local past" (191). Williams challenges this linguistic inflation through a careful, rhetorically sensitive and etymologically oriented critique. One of the most striking examples may be found at the close of the essay when she considers how, in the current political moment, "discrimination" is defined against color-blindness. Racial and ethnic identification as that against which one ought not to discriminate has been twisted; now those very same racial and ethnic classifications are what discriminate. The infinite convertibility of the terms is, I suppose, what makes the commerce of American rhetoric so very fascinating, but these linguistic flip-flops disguise an immense stasis of power, and they derail the will to undo it. (Williams, "*Metro*," 197–198)

Placing "discrimination" in a less circumscribed and more historically sensitive framework, Williams goes on to draw a link between the term and intellectual activity as a whole by highlighting the ways Western culture has aligned discrimination with the ability to judge in general. Framed in part by Williams's disgust at the way racial preferences have been equated with racism, this etymological venture has brought Williams, and her readers, to a door, if not through it. That door marks the passage beyond conventional rhetorics of racial injury, at least as maintained by the law. On the other side lies a presumably "multicultural" interpretation of injury which can conceive of racial differentiation and discrimination in a manner that may be distanced from the practice of racism itself—in other words, an approach to racial injury that refuses the intellectual censorship demanded by the doctrine of color-blindness.

This alternative process involves more than a collection of historical data, linguistic or otherwise. Williams's writing is speculative without trading away its claims for an ethical power, and this capacity defines a crucial facet of Williams's, and to an extent, the movements' attainment. Most importantly, Williams's more general queries about discrimination stress the interwoven (intersectional) variety of racially bound activity that cannot be reduced to a rhetoric of inclusion and exclusion. When Williams argues, in "*Metro*," that terms like "poverty" and "low achievement" have been used to recode the consequences of racism and group discrimination as the natural results of isolated contracts (195), she is not simply claiming that language in general may act as an instrument of racism. Instead, her approach to language and racism affords a much riskier ground, one that continually challenges the writer with complex negotiations. As such, Williams's stance with regard to language is anything but the ironic historian viewing the past from on high.

With regard to Williams's approach to language, then, I would highlight two points. First, she assumes that all people are as much worked by language as they themselves work it. Language is a social phenomenon that requires actors to wrestle with each other at every turn, even if certain assumptions about language are rigorously naturalized. Second, given that this process is highly political, it requires a careful probing of local cases as critics build a sense of broader social and cultural patterns. In this sense, Williams is committed to a discursive analysis that is echoed by Michel Foucault's when he argues that, "we must not imagine a world of discourse divided between accepted discourse and excluded discourse, or between a dominant discourse and the dominated discourse; but as a multiplicity of discursive elements that can come into play in various strategies" (*History of Sexuality*, I, 100).

Taken together, these aspects of Williams's approach to language point toward an important complication of contemporary race politics, a complication that emphasizes the transferential qualities of linguistic performance.

The term "transferential" here indicates those ways in which the problems embedded in objects of study may come to replicate themselves in unselfconscious ways during analysis. Although not making use of this particular terminology, the CRS effort to trace displacements, paradoxes, and inconsistencies that animate legal discourse in fact demonstrates a keen sensitivity to this dynamic. While the CRS project is diverse, this interest in transference marks an important point of intersection, and, as I will argue, this interest may help us understand the promise attributed to storytelling which has recently been both celebrated and debated in race studies and legal studies generally.[24]

A transferentially sensitive approach to language suggests the crucial need for linguistic self-consciousness and experimentation. Without such care, the transferential propensities of our communication may themselves perpetuate racial injury. Although scholars might amass a significant set of data giving testimony to the historical impacts of this racism, writings by the more experimental CRS authors indicate that the impact of this archival process is bound not to "factual" accumulation, but rather to the ways current notions of racial literacy are challenged and remade. The CRS self-assessments establish a similar rhetorical sensitivity, when the editors of the major collections argue that "legal scholarship about race in America can never be written from a distance of detachment or with an attitude of objectivity" (Crenshaw et al., *Critical Race Theory,* xiii); the CRS authors aim not simply to explicate, but more importantly to "intervene in the ideological contestation of race in America, in order to create new, oppositionist accounts of race" (xiii). Even though the CRS movement often crafts its claim of analytic privilege for "organic" scholars around the figure of "looking to, and from, the bottom," many of the more experimental writers also suggest that any such privileging is crucially tied to the practice of alternative forms of literacy. How we read and narrativize has everything to do with how we see the "bottom."

I would therefore suggest that some of the most successful CRS writings have avoided transferentially repeating key problems in the law by shifting emphasis away from visibility (one legacy of identity politics), or at least by questioning the opportunities for reform in the politics of recognition: a politics that appears to be but a part of a complicated battle among competing forms of literacy. Williams's notion of multiculturalism—as distinct from identity politics—is thus focused on various forms of discursive mediation as she attempts to work through racial injuries that permeate society as an aesthetic.

Like Cheryl Harris and others who would carry questions of race and culture to the mainstream, Williams probes the way whiteness is naturalized as a nonracial norm, as well as the way this racial denial then gets reproduced in a transferential displacement.[25] Here, separations of white and racially defined social and cultural dynamics, rigorously maintained by the schools, courts, and the media, manifest themselves in all sorts of arguments which presume that what is important about race in America resides exclusively in the barrios, the ghettos, the sweatshops, the plantations, and not in the boardrooms, the editorial offices, the malls.

Williams tackles this problem in the *Metro* essay by arguing against the notion that the mass media is race-neutral. Instead, she argues for "a view of the market in which there are not merely isolated interest groups, of which the 'mass market' may be one, but in which 'mass' accurately reflects the complicated variety of many peoples and connotes 'interactive' and 'accommodative' rather than dominant or even just majoritarian"(192). At the same time, this interactive imperative complicates Williams's own understanding of how her analysis is shaped—by transferential relations she may hold with the history of racism she studies. As is the case with many CRS scholars, Williams explicitly maintains that a certain proximity to racial injury makes for a privileged reader of racism:

> If we cannot conclude absolutely that the victims of racial oppression are always the best architects of its cure, we must nevertheless assume that the best insight and inspiration for its amelioration will come from those most immediately and negatively affected. This allowance is not merely a concession in a random contest of cultures; it is a recognition central to the checking and balancing, the fine line of restraint, that distinguishes a fluidly majoritarian society from a singularly tyrannical one. (Williams, "*Metro,*" 192)

Though this passage argues for a recognition of injury and group identity, the proximity cited offers no guarantee of ethical purity. This passage is most certainly not essentialist, and the only way to frame it as such is to ignore the history and impacts of the injuries Williams references.

In an attempt to address the limitations of her analysis, Williams touches on not only the accidental, idiosyncratic nature of any one critic's perspective, but also on the way injuries may reverberate through communities. Here, Williams asks her readers to:

> Imagine a glass half full (or half empty) of blue marbles. Their very hard-edged, discrete, yet identical nature makes it possible for the community of blue marbles to say to one another with perfect consistency both "we are the same" and, if a few roll away, and are lost in the sidewalk grate, "that's just their experience, fate, choice, bad luck." If, on the other hand, one imagines a glass full of soap bubbles, with shifting permeable boundaries, expanding and contracting in size like a living organism, then it is

not possible for the collective bubbles to describe themselves as "all the same." Furthermore, if one of the bubbles bursts, it cannot be isolated as a singular phenomenon. It will be felt as a tremor, a realignment, a reclustering among all. (Williams, "*Metro*," 199)

This figure may also be used to understand Williams's project as a whole, especially as regards her strategic engagement of extra-legal forms of writing. For instance, in *Alchemy of Race and Rights*, Williams introduces her book by arguing that, "Law too often seeks to avoid [the truth of life's complexity] by making up its own breed of narrower, simpler, but hypnotically powerful rhetorical truths. Acknowledging, challenging, playing with these *as* rhetorical gestures is, it seems to me, necessary for any conception of justice" (10). As Williams goes on to note, one of the crucial benefits of this conceptual shift from "objective truth" to "rhetorical event" will be a "more nuanced sense of legal and social responsibility" (11).

According to Williams's analysis, the law perpetuates a myth of unmediated, objective voice, as part of a process that would "make property of others," even "while denying such connections" (11). Williams in turn offers a partial list of the rhetorical gestures that make this possible. In the first instance, the law draws "bright lines and clear taxonomies that purport to make life simpler in the face of life's complication." In the second, the law insists upon the "existence of transcendent, acontextual, universal legal truths or pure procedures." And finally, legal practice legitimates the notion of "objective, unmediated voices by which those transcendent, universal truths find their expression" (9–10). The remainder of Williams's book is thus posed as an elaboration regarding how these rhetorical gestures play out in specific legal domains, "ranging from contracts to crimes, from property to civil liberties" (9).

Williams's goal is to write in a way that will "reveal the intersubjectivity of legal constructions" and at the same time force "the reader both to participate in the construction of meaning and to be conscious of the process." To this end, Williams "exploits all sorts of literary devices, including parody, parable, poetry" (7–8). Williams is certainly not the first to suggest that literary analysis might open an important window onto the law, nor is she the first to suggest that there is a creative (and constructive) element at work in the law.[26] What is unique about her approach is its commitment to tracing out these interactions in a fashion that respects their inextricable linkages. As Paul Gewirtz points out in *Law's Stories: Narrative and Rhetoric in the Law,* the tendency has been to read legal and literary interplays either in terms of "law in literature" ("work that examines the representations of law and lawyers in fiction") or in terms of "law as literature" (work that "examines law and legal texts the way a literary text might be examined").[27] Although these distinctions seem apposite for the "law and literature" movement as a whole, Williams charts a different course, preferring to consider life's complexities beyond those contours legitimated by the intellectual disciplines that have defined and limited the kinds of questions critics and lawyers can bring to these life experiences.

This commitment to studying complex mediations—an analysis intent upon mining the interconnectedness of different cultural and social spheres—also imposes a certain responsibility for self-criticism, for an awareness of how one's training shapes one's tastes. In this context, Williams's literary experiment pursues a critical autobiography. In turn, these passages yield opportunities to rethink her formation as a student, a teacher, an African American woman, a consumer, a family member, a writer, and so on. Two of these autobiographical passages in particular establish an important tension in *The Alchemy of Race and Rights.*

In one of these moments, Williams describes a visit to a local clothing store. The question held out by Williams as she presents this recollection is why she chose to remain silent when several of the sales clerks included her in a round of anti-Semitic banter. Considering the incident at some length, Williams argues that "such silence is too common, too institutionalized, and too destructive not to examine in the most nuanced way possible" (127). Williams produces a number of reasons why she did not act, many touching upon a basic desire for social inclusion, an inclusion that Williams could not presume for a number of reasons, not the least of which her race. With this and similar stories, Williams subtly unpacks her history as an African American woman who lived in the South immediately after desegregation became law.

Recalling her father's first ventures into formerly "whites only" establishments, Williams acknowledges that

I am always grateful when storekeepers are polite to me; I don't expect courtesy, I value it in a way that resembles love and trust and shelter. I value it in a way that is frequently misleading, for it is neither love nor trust nor shelter. I know that this valuing is a form of fear. I am afraid of being alien and suspect, of being thrown out at any moment; I am relieved when I am not. (Williams, *Alchemy*, 129)

As Williams demonstrates, however, the price for this relief can be participation in a process wherein she makes property of herself. This process moves through different modes according to Williams, modes she describes as she recalls the experience with the anti-Semitic clerks. First, the anti-Semitic store clerks essentially colonize Williams by presuming to make her an approving witness to the scapegoating of the Jewish customers. Second, Williams herself crafts a split consciousness in which her efforts to gain acceptance are contradicted by her awareness that her role as witness is important to the clerks precisely because they identify Williams as vulnerable in a manner similar to the Jewish scapegoats. Her witnessing is thus caught within a subtle contract that would manage her own claims to injury by drawing her into a capitulating silence.

One residue of this exchange is a lingering resentment, a resentment that makes it all the clearer in hindsight how contingent her citizenship in the store really was. Rather than simply dwell in this resentment, Williams probes it, making her critical awareness of this contingency a frame for anti-racist interventions in other contexts. Although she acknowledges that such interventions are risky to say the least, Williams finds a joy, even an exhilaration in them (128–130). In part, this "release" stems from the freedom Williams gains by eschewing the role of mute and complicit witness. This unburdening is about rhetorical empowerment, not the acquisition of the "truth" of racism.[28] In this sense, *Alchemy of Race and Rights* is about Williams's attempt to work through a highly charged investment in the discourse of contracts and property, all elements of a process of exchange that is far more complicated than legal theory allows, particularly as the exchanges intersect racial dynamics.

This type of self-critical effort is crucial if the CRS movement is to engage fully the implications of politically invested analysis, the ethical complexity of racism, and the resentment that may come with trying to accommodate the investigation of racial injuries to legal discourse. One risk of the autobiographical gesture is that the exhilaration Williams describes may fail to resonate in different contexts, among differently positioned readers. Even within the contexts Williams describes, her actions and interpretations—if viewed as those of an isolated individual— may be more easily dismissed for their "subjective" framing. The intellectual enfranchisement that goes along with traditional, impersonal scholarly writing may help explain why some CRS writers have hesitated to follow Williams's experiments with similar attempts. It would seem equally possible that the theoretical self-description of the movement displaces this problematic as part of an effort to meet professional expectations, especially those which police the complexity that comes with autobiography.

Questions of power and rhetorical enfranchisement run through another autobiographical passage in which Williams describes her earliest experiences as a law school teacher.

> I am always aware of the ex-pro-football player/student whom I had told in class to read the cases more carefully; he came to my office to tell me that I had humiliated him in front of everyone and he was going to "get you, lady." At that, I ordered him out of my office, whereupon he walked down to the associate dean's office and burst into tears, great heaving, football-player sobs, the tears dripping off the ends of his nose, as it was described to me later. Now I admit that of all the possible ways in which I thought he might try to get me, this was the one for which I was least prepared; but it could not have been more effective in terms of coalescing both the student body and the administration against me. I became a drill sergeant. A militant black woman who took out her rage on her students. Someone who could make a big man cry, and cry hard. (Williams, *Alchemy,* 96)

For Williams, this episode holds out a particular problem: How did her moderated criticism become so powerful and humiliating to this student? Among other things, this question becomes an occasion to probe

87

the authority Williams wields as a teacher. It is an important moment in part because throughout the book there is a clear sense that Williams closely aligns her efforts as a teacher and her goals as a writer. As such, the passage puts under a microscope the difficult negotiations she must make as someone working within the discursive and political system she is trying to radically critique. The humiliated student of the passage thus poses a problem that is emblematic. The student's reaction, and the reactions of those who gathered to support him, make clear that much is at stake—certainly more than can be deduced from the supposedly transparent intentions of individuals.

Williams facilitates this understanding by using this passage to conclude a chapter that has explored various facets of her teaching. Much of this exploration has fallen on the difficulties Williams has faced while teaching the law through an intersubjective lens that refuses to ignore the limits and failings of legal rhetoric, especially as these displace racial injury. In this way, she uses her teaching experiences to anticipate readers' responses. Documenting these fights over injury and method, the bulk of the chapter contextualizes the final story of the humiliated student, placing in relief his own quite effective strategy of claiming victimization. By virtue of the chapter's structure, readers gain a sense of why the fight has taken the shape it has—vying claims to speak of injury—and why Williams's detractors focused on her as an individual drunk with power and committed to blindly acting out her rage by mistreating innocent white individuals.

Among other things, this struggle demonstrates how apparently unquestioned expectations—a student's accountability for reading assignments—may bring crucial literacy issues to the fore. Williams, the descendent of slaves forbidden to read by law, has questioned reading practices in a law school, and she has done so not only by querying a particular student, but also by manipulating legal rhetoric so as to make recognition of this loaded social context, and others like it, inescapable, undeniable. Worse yet, Williams has refused the separatist moment of identity politics. Like Ellison's protagonist, she has instead suggested that, on some level, she may speak not only for African Americans, and women, but for white males as well.

To the extent that Williams's analysis draws on a great variety of experiences and fields of knowledge, it repositions what might otherwise be undervalued as "special interests." The structure of her intervention contributes significantly to her success in part because her narratives draw together complicated facets of lived experience (made available largely through rich anecdotes) and methodological questions at the core of legal training. Ultimately, such structural experimentation may be traced to the earliest practitioners of Critical Races Studies, including Derrick Bell, and define an important aspect of the movement.[29] Along these lines, I would argue that much may be done to draw connections between the CRS project as I have framed it, and the work of "minority" cultural critics who pursue the narrative format. Elsewhere I have argued that a large portion of Chicana/Chicano literature and film engages legal culture in order to rethink its presuppositions and offer alternative methods of adjudication and interpretation.[30] Such cultural texts are examples of the kinds of resources that the CRS authors might engage more explicitly as they consider dynamics of literacy and the promise of storytelling.

I make this suggestion recognizing that there are dangers in too quickly aligning "law and literature." Law does have a coercive force—backed by the state—that distinguishes it from artistic production. Even so, state interest in cultural production, as well as the complex play of coercion and hegemony, shapes politics in important ways. I would therefore invite comparisons among the CRS and artistic projects: projects that foreground struggles over literacy and its relation to effective racial remedies. In both venues, methods of storytelling are important for how they encourage readers to read.

CHAPTER FOUR

HISTORICAL PROPERTIES, UNCOMMON GROUNDS

As a principal contributor to, and spokesperson for, the New Western History, Patricia Limerick has engaged critical problems that speak not only to the grounding assumptions of U.S. Western history, but also to ideas about what constitutes proper historiography more generally. From the outset, the New Western historians have attempted to negotiate a thick ideological context in which Western history writing has served highly charged political purposes deeply influenced by racial issues.[1] The hallmark synthesizing pluralism that one finds in New Western History texts thus constitutes a strategic response to previous historiographic trends, trends that presumably failed in large measure because of their contribution to imperialistic nostalgia and other uncritical modes of nationalistic celebration.[2] In turn, a logic of inclusiveness is a central component of the New Western History's intervention.[3] However, the racial, feminist, and environmental thematics that have been both praised and criticized by reviewers of the movement are not for the most part understood by these New Western historians to be expressions of special political interests.[4] Unlike the CRS movement described in the previous chapter, race does not form the basis for a radical critique of culture, although a sensitivity to racial dynamics does help initiate the New Western History's program of synthesizing pluralism. Instead, the more obvious engagements of ideological issues and historical injuries are posed as part of a larger program with significant methodological implications.[5] Although these methodological issues lead Limerick into a significant rethinking of historical practice and its psychological dimensions, I will argue that Limerick's exciting experiments with narrative in *Legacy of Conquest* are compromised because of the way she finally valorizes issues of property and economics. Elaborating a study of property issues as an alternative to the awkward dynamics of race politics, Limerick misconstrues the complex mediation between property and race. In order to explore this dynamic, this chapter concludes with a reading of Louise Erdrich's *Tracks*, a historical novel that reveals just how divergent notions of property may be.

AN UNCANNY LEGACY

As the New Western historians themselves frame the issue, the most pressing methodological question they face recalls the difficulties encountered by the Critical Race Studies movement: The New Western historians ask how historiography should change in response to the inclusion of experiences that have heretofore constituted "blind spots," spots created when "elements of our social identity . . . limit our vision as sternly as racial assumptions limited Frederick Jackson Turner's vision" (Limerick, "Turnerians All," 715). Turner's exemplary failure is a central one for Limerick as she evaluates the New Western History (NWH) to date in her essay "Turnerians All: The Dream of a Helpful History in an Intelligible World." In this piece, Limerick defines a responsibility that would require her simultaneously to distance herself from, and to posit a proximity to, Turner's work. Most explicitly, this complicating of Limerick's relation to Turner signals a response to critics, as well as to popularizers of the NWH, who would read the movement as a "trashing" of Turner's frontier thesis—in a very real sense the thesis upon which the study of Western U.S. history was founded.[6] For those who have followed the booming rise of the NWH, the effort is bound to spark curiosity, if only because Turner has been treated with, at the very least, a great deal of ambivalence by the New Western historians. While Limerick herself goes to great lengths in *Legacy of Conquest* to posit historical continuities where Turner would posit a radical break with the closing of the frontier (20–23), a number of Limerick's compatriots virtually refuse to acknowledge Turner's existence at all.[7] Given this situation, one can easily understand why the popular media in particular has read the New Western History's offerings as most importantly a dismissal of Turner.

Intervening in this situation, Limerick uses the "Turnerians All" essay to explore the different and at times contradictory strands of thought about the frontier in Turner's writing. Most importantly, according to Limerick, Turner had sufficient evidence to deeply challenge his frontier thesis and yet he refused the task.[8] Limerick frames this failure in terms of Turner's commitment to a method of "presentism," a notion that the present could be made virtually transparent as the historian charts patterns from the past to the contemporary moment. The writing of history, understood thus, is a relatively clear and linear matter, a tracing of movement from past to present as though one were following a railroad track, to use Limerick's typification (704). That Turner should refuse to adhere to this principle and thereby revise his thesis when the railroad track so clearly curved leaves Limerick deeply impressed, especially because her own formation as a historian was shaped by the adoption of a similar methodology. Holding a strong identification with Turner's notion of the historian as a public servant, Limerick, too, sees herself as a scholar speaking to, and of, the present in politically significant ways.

At the same time that Limerick notes compelling links with Turner, she also documents an "ironic" twist to the enduring error that lies at the heart of Turner's frontier thesis, a thesis she strongly rejects. As it turns out, the more New Western historians have worked to discredit the frontier thesis and the historical break it posits, the more forcefully the thesis appears to have rejuvenated itself via renewed attentions gained in the media ("Turnerians All," 697–699). On another, more subtle level, twists coded as ironic by Limerick echo at key moments throughout the essay, setting a pattern that suggests something more than a conventional understanding of the ironic is at play. This pattern is contextualized when Turner's thesis is said to exist in a "bewitched historiographic space" where critique *consistently* leaves the model unscathed if not renewed (698). Limerick, in turn, accentuates this sense of the ironic while she explores the ways Turner's work actually incorporates its own best critique (699–702). Finally, Limerick's complicated identification with Turner is cast with a humorous, if at the same time biting, acknowledgment of his "haunting presence" for the field of Western U.S. history as a whole; in fact, it is this haunting quality which literally defines Turner in the essay (697).

These instances of "irony" have a special resonance because the ironic's presentation here and elsewhere in Limerick's writings brings to mind something very much like the psychoanalytic concept of the uncanny. Although Freud's development of the topic in "Das Unheimliche" (1919) is complex and notably incomplete, the numerous rethinkings of the concept by other scholars have been united by a principle that is summed up with a phrase Freud borrows from Schelling: "The uncanny is the name for everything that ought to have remained . . . secret and hidden, but has come to light" (Freud, "Uncanny," in *Complete Works*, 225). Building on Schelling's notion, and on the etymological slippages that exist between the terms "canny" and "uncanny," Freud suggests that an uncanny experience "is in reality nothing new or alien, but something which is familiar and old-established in the mind and which has become alienated from it only through the process of repression" (241). Whereas subsequent critics have frequently modified or replaced the motors for such repression that were assumed by Freud, the larger model, describing a specific kind of disquieting "rememory," has continued to draw a good deal of critical interest.[9]

Although a mining of the uncanny is not announced in Limerick's works—which for the most part avoid the explicit elaboration of theoretical concerns—the "Turnerians All" piece may be read as a more theoretically invested extension of Limerick's focus on the play of continuities *and* discontinuities in Western history. Implicitly mapping her present as an uncanny repetition of Turner's efforts, Limerick argues that most of her generation of Western historians have worked themselves into the same corners regarding Turner that she has (714). A primary symptom of this repetition is a presentist-oriented faith in reform, a hopefulness that understands the historian as a guide to "more benevolent action in our own time" (714). Although for both Turner and Limerick, this hope remains purely secular, there exists in both contexts a displaced drive toward redemptive plots, a drive that Limerick blames for leading both writers to overestimate the historian's ability to establish the causal linkage of "progress-oriented" events (711–714). The recognition by Limerick of her own participation in this error subsequently leads her into speculation about the ways in which members of her profession might better understand relationships between past and present. In the process, Limerick charts a disillusionment with her earlier "presentist" self in a highly personalized and virtually confessional passage. At issue is her belief that it would be possible with *Legacy of Conquest* to trace "a direct, clear line between past and present"—an action that she later credits with inadvertently fostering an "unhealthy fatalism" (710). The form of this self-critique is at least as important as the ostensible point inasmuch as one of Limerick's trademarks as a historian is her willingness to assume an autobiographical and quasi-literary stance not always celebrated by others in her profession.[10] Whatever the limits of her experimental approach, it does have the virtue of registering key questions about the potentially uncritical transferential relationship that may exist between the historian and her object of study.[11] In many respects, this is the crucial contribution of the "Turnerians All" essay. Although not moving in a similar psychoanalytic register, the best of the work performed by Limerick's essay points toward self-understanding as precisely this kind of negotiation with one's object of study.

CHARTING HISTORICAL INJURY
AND ITS DENIAL

"Turnerians All" is perhaps best read as a stage in an evolving process wherein the NWH is learning to grapple self-consciously with highly charged issues, including racial issues, that have often been subject to processes of repression. In this sense, one might read the untheorized play with the uncanny in Limerick's essay as the tip of an iceberg, the body of which is constituted by the great diversity of conflicts precariously tapped as the NWH attempts to be strategically inclusive, especially where the stories of history's "marginal" players or losers are involved. Responding to this very significant aspect of the NWH's agenda, reviews have at times been very intolerant of the NWH's supposedly "bleak outlook."[12] Here, the engagement of difficult episodes of trauma take center stage, most notably events that have adversely affected minority populations, women, and in an extension of conventional notions of injury, nature. Central texts of the NWH, including Peggy Pascoe's *Relations of Rescue,* Richard White's *It's Your Misfortune and None of My Own,* Donald Worster's *Rivers of Empire,* and of course Limerick's *Legacy of Conquest,* all pursue a similar tactic.

Certainly the tendency to focus on injurious events or their representations, particularly in myth-making, is not "new" in Western U.S. history writing. Richard Slotkin's *Regeneration through Violence,* Henry Nash Smith's *Virgin Land,* and even Turner's frontier thesis itself build in crucial ways on some notion of injury or loss. However, it does appear that as a movement, the NWH has developed the study of certain kinds of injury in a unique and systematic fashion, although a fashion not explicitly informed by the theoretical treatments of trauma and historiography that have taken off in the last decade, especially around studies of the Holocaust.[13] Injury, as explored by the New Western historians, entails at least a double wounding, involving some form of initial victimization as well as a repression within the historical record of the experience of suffering. When NWH writers like Limerick argue that processes of denial are at the core of Western history (*Legacy,* 96–97), the psychoanalytic force of the claim is grounded in this idea of a double wounding that is fed on a network of disciplinary practices.

As Richard White has described the NWH's response to injury, the goal is to produce a relational history in which Western violence is dislodged from its conventional home as a theme of American mythology.[14] White and his fellows would rethink such violence as a result of social struggles that continue into the present. For the most part, however, the principal works of the NWH do not explore specific history texts in which violent events have been politically and ethically repressed, or, as in the case of much American myth study, displaced to a more aesthetically distanced realm of experience. In this sense, the NWH tends to be much more invested in preaching through practice than in engaging polemical debates with predecessors in the field.

Even though specific reference to Turner may be avoided, the fact remains that the relational history pursued by the NWH cadre takes on a political and cultural work that is strikingly at odds with Turner's 1893 speech because participants like Limerick demonstrate in detail exactly how the legacy of the frontier is very much alive. Given that this relational history embraces an inclusivity that must address not simply repressed historical material, but also the means by which historical representations have carried out the work of repression (the doubled wounding), essays like Limerick's "Turnerians All" mark an important step for the NWH. Some of the best critical reviews of the NWH have also concentrated on the need for further methodological elaboration, leading one to suspect that the lack of polemical engagement manifested in prominent NWH texts comes with an important price.[15] In order to map out and contextualize such problematic avoidances, we will turn to Limerick's *Legacy of Conquest* as a case study. The selection of Limerick's text is motivated by several factors, including: Limerick's relative willingness to engage larger historiographic questions; her explicit treatment of racial victimization; and her tendency to be more explicitly polemical than her peers in the NWH.

Limerick's *Legacy of Conquest* begins with an extended exploration of the forms of denial that have allowed Americans benefiting from aggressive policies of conquest to legitimate their actions. Of these forms, one of the most predominant included settlers imagining themselves as uniquely innocent victims of the hardships almost necessarily befalling them as they tried to live out an individualistically oriented escape from the past with the move West (35–54). As an antidote for this legacy, Limerick offers a method built around an ethic of pluralistic witnessing, a method that draws heavily on anecdotal material provided by memoirs and similar sources. On the most explicit front, such multiplicity provides an inclusion of varied castes and social positions as Limerick rethinks the history of the West.

However, such anecdotal material also documents the complex texture of everyday psychology, complementing and even correcting impressions drawn from official documents and policies. To her credit, Limerick is careful not to be overly critical regarding the study of such policies. Instead, she calls for more caution in how we place this work in relation to evidence we have regarding everyday lives. Here, Limerick echoes White's desire to worry (and not to ignore) Western mythologies as they manifest in policy as well as history writing.[16] Within *Legacy of Conquest*, the frontier thesis is the target of choice, and as such, readers might view Limerick's fascination with repressed historical continuities as a reaction to Turner's—and not the West's—legacy. All the same, what gives this book much of its critical force is its ability to present Turner as one highly visible practitioner of a broad cultural logic that displaced to an important degree ethical problems tied to a legacy of social and political conflict. Limerick accomplishes this by mining various historical contexts in order to rethink the optimism associated with Jeffersonian agrarian ideals and to pose this optimism as a crucial aspect of Western denial (*Legacy*, 130–132).

The stress on historical continuities and denial that ostensibly defines *Legacy of Conquest* leads quite naturally to the methodological implications that inform "Turnerians All." Historical repetitions—not continuities proper—seem to be Limerick's real focus in both works, and these gain an interpretive force to the extent that they demonstrate the denial (and its uncanny by-products) which she associates with the Old Western History throughout her writings. Read in this light, Limerick's "Turnerians All" looks to be a logical extension of *Legacy of Conquest*. In both cases, the repetitions Limerick mines are almost always emotionally, politically, and ethically charged by virtue of their association with injurious losses, losses that have been subject to a crucial underdevelopment in the historical record.

Mapping out the process of denial in *Legacy of Conquest*, Limerick argues that migrants from the East were driven by a desire to break with a troubling past that they nonetheless carried with themselves in myriad ways and despite their best efforts. Notions of independent life in the West were maintained against the realities of the mining industry and other forms of labor relations within the migrant communities. In this context, the legitimation of colonial exploitation within and without migrant communities depended from the outset on the manufacture of an "innocence" that could level the field of social responsibility at the same time that victimhood virtually became a democratic right (35–54).

Limerick also explores the ways such innocence can become embattled when she examines the government's attempt to wrestle with compensation for victims of radiation poisoning, a compensation that would have required the atomic energy commission to acknowledge its own part in the "callous" development of resources replaying the worst of the West's boom mentalities (163–165). Glossing the event, Limerick asserts that the controversy presents a perfect example of how the "Western past [repeatedly] refuses burial" (163). It makes a certain sense that such a critically significant moment of the uncanny should focus on issues of inexhaustible by-products that might be buried but refuse finally to "go away"; Limerick's drive toward inclusivity is, after all, at least partially propelled by an awareness of how Western U.S. life and its histories have been shaped by various repressions which nonetheless make themselves felt in the great variety of unselfconscious, unintended repetitions that she charts.

As with almost every other description of such "returns," Limerick overtly emphasizes an element of surprise that ultimately reframes an apparent lack of self-consciousness and intention. Boom-bust mentalities crop up everywhere, as do natives and insects grown tolerant of pesticides. Even Manifest Destiny breathes new life, although in the less glorious body of the Aryan Nation. In terms of tone, the rhetorical effect of these gestures invites the reader to share the uncanny sense associated with the reapproach to repressed material. However, for all the richness that is implied by this mining of repression and the questions that might accompany it, Limerick distances herself from further methodological inquiry as the book develops and racial issues move to the forefront. In a fairly conventional critique of identity politics, her argument ultimately folds into an attack on stereotypes and racial categorization more generally (290–292).

Limerick's sense, while examining minority historians like Rudolfo Acuña, is that racially focused histories have become too invested in legitimating their own displaced voices by positing a hierarchy of victimization (255–258). As problematic as such identity politics may be, Limerick's answer, a "pluralizing" of history, moves too quickly toward an erasure of crucial social and cultural distinctions. For example, in an effort to create a nonhierarchical playing field of victimization in the West, Limerick posits Mormons, Asian Americans, and Latinos as ethnic groups with comparable traumatic experiences (260–292). The slippage between differences historically coded as racial and differences coded as ethnic is troubling, particularly in the quick shift Limerick makes between the Japanese American internment and the Mormon persecutions. My point lies not with who suffered more, but rather with questions about how particular instances of suffering were brought about and legitimated, in other words, with the mechanics—social, cultural, political—that were at play in these distinct episodes. Any blanket condemnation of categorical difference such as that evoked by Limerick threatens to foreclose study of these distinct processes.

When readers come to *Legacy of Conquest*'s final pages, then, and find themselves asked to shed the racial and ethnic categories that have kept them strangers, more than a little skepticism is likely to take hold. As an alternative, Limerick might have considered more self-consciously the implications of the various historiographic displacements that she documents, displacements that are consistently associated with repression. Although her book announces itself as an argument for continuity in the face of traditionally assumed historical breaks—Turner's most obviously—the study's deeper contribution is actually its testimony to this complex process of displacements that has typified understandings of the American West.

Because the incorporation of multicultural issues has been so important for the New Western historians as they have defined their "newness," Limerick's category-phobic displacement of race itself merits a closer look. Midway through *Legacy of Conquest*, Limerick hits one of her most polemical strides as she undertakes a disavowal of her "ethnocentric predecessors" in the historical profession (219). This distancing takes place as Limerick addresses the nagging "persistence of natives" in the West, a persistence that necessarily betrays the "vanishing Indian" trope she would critique. Expanding on this polemic, Limerick claims that complicit historians have posited this premature burial as a way of securing the record of the West as a "white" property (220). Such a moment could provide an important opportunity for reflection regarding the NWH's own synthesis of material from minority historians, historians who do not necessarily share the critical agendas of the NWH movement. Instead, the move to create a relational history produces a form of corporate relativism that appears to blur ethical distinctions and agendas as the argument moves too quickly toward a universal "speaking out for the human dignity of all parties" (221). Ultimately, Limerick sacrifices a fuller engagement of the minority historical projects which she acknowledges have been subject to complicated processes of denial before.

The cost of Limerick's pluralistic intervention is readily apparent as she takes up Southwestern border dynamics (222–258). Here, Limerick valorizes a critical notion of *mestizaje* in a chapter that consistently resolves the extended struggles over nomenclature in Mexican-descent populations by imposing the term "Hispanic." The choice is a highly problematic one given the term's inherent elision of racial mixing. As much as this and similar chapters acknowledge racially defined injuries which too frequently have been ignored or devalued by previous historical efforts, the ethical problems posed by the engagement of these injuries have not been worked through, and, at its most distressing, *Legacy of Conquest* actually manages to "unthink" racial problems yet again. One measure of such difficulties can be found in the way the concept of *mestizaje* is itself essentialized into a blurring of distinctions—a turn of events that appears to be linked in Limerick's account to a frustration with identity politics and racially oriented studies in comparative sinning (257).

In a subsequent chapter, "Racialism on the Run," readers may begin to wonder if Limerick's target is actually race-conscious analysis itself given the deep suspicions of racial categories that are announced. This distrust, combined with Limerick's earlier gloss of *mestizaje*, accentuates the sense that an evacuation is taking place of critical possibilities and ethical distinctions. The suspicions are compounded when Limerick begins to fashion an alternative form of analysis. According to Limerick:

> Minorities and majority in the American West occupied common ground—literally. A conquest for control of the land, for the labor applied to the land, and for the resulting profit set the terms of their meeting. Sharing turf, contesting turf, surrendering turf, Western groups, for all their difficulties, took part in the same story. Each group may well have had its own, self-defined story, but in the contest for property and profit, those stories meet. (*Legacy,* 291–292)

The turn to the dynamics of property and profit is certainly of interest. Yet readers should wonder why Limerick devalues racial dynamics in order to pose the true meeting ground of the West, "property and profit." Most importantly, it seems that she has weakened her study—including its ability to yield insight regarding the complicated displacements at work in Western history—in order to purify the routes of critical inquiry. Putting the problem in the form of a question, one might ask why such an astute writer about the West would hold at bay all the evidence for the ways racism has moved in a nonutilitarian, fiscally destructive fashion, undeniably violating economic rationales?

Given the tendency of other New Western historians to also focus on property, it will be important to speculate further about the conditions that make this shift to economic analysis appear almost self-evidently appropriate. In this context, consider the way *Legacy of Conquest* presents an evolution in its own defining metaphors, an evolution that both reveals and conceals the implications of the uncanny returns situated throughout the text. In the first instance, Limerick opens her book by comparing the historian's task to the experience of someone walking over Colorado mine fields, a situation that could easily plunge the historian "unexpectedly into the legacy of Western history" (18).

Perhaps somewhat predictably, this ability for the past to return with surprising force is presumably mastered at that juncture in the book when Limerick supplants racial analysis with an economic focus. Here she offers a new notion of how the past might be negotiated by turning to

> a thoroughly un-Western metaphor for a complicated phenomenon—a subway system. Every station in the system is a center of sorts—trains and passengers converge on it; in both departure and arrival, the station is the pivot. But get on a train, and you are soon (with any luck) at another station, equally a center and a pivot. Every station is at the center of a particular world, yet that does not leave the observer of the system conceptually muddled, unable to decide which station represents the true point of view from which the entire system should be viewed. (Limerick, 292)

The surprise of the mineshaft is replaced here with a map and a token, but to hearken back to James Baldwin, we may want to ask "what is the price of the ticket?"[17] If the "underground" in the first metaphor is understood to represent the complex workings of denial, a point Limerick stresses early on in her study, could any ticket be purchased that would simplify the historian's life in the manner suggested by the subway concept? Could any ticket free the historian from self-consciously engaging the baggage entailed when making different narrative and stylistic choices? Herein lies the particularly discursive and professional, as opposed to merely biographical, problem, in large part because Limerick finds herself far more within the expectations of history-as-a-discipline at the end of the book than at the outset. Acknowledging the exceptions posed by scholars who engage in more "experimental" forms of historiography, I am working from the notion that the field is still largely committed to the outlook that historians participate in a craft, and that this craft is best pursued when the writer assumes the stance of a detached, and ultimately "ironic" observer, in other words, a stance more typically represented by the control of a subway passenger than a hiker gambling with each step taken over abandoned mine shafts.

Considered in this context, readers might thus approach *Legacy of Conquest* with an eye for the contradictory pulls it evidences between an implicitly psychoanalytic interpretive framework that would play with the uncanny, and a craftsman's framework that would map the West from a securely distanced vantage point. Perhaps no linguistic aspect of this tension is more readily felt than the consistent manner in which Limerick explicitly redefines surprising returns of displaced injuries as instances of the ironic in her writings. Like the shift to the subway metaphor, this evocation of the ironic tends to flatten out otherwise historically deep scenarios, writing them into an essentially atemporal rhetoric of simple, if shocking, juxtaposition and repetition based in a formal understanding of genre.

If such ironic recoding is itself a sign of displacement—a sign of the NWH's inability to sufficiently work through racial traumas in particular—it may be that there is a certain logic guiding Limerick and her NWH peers to settle upon profit as a "common ground," especially as they negotiate a synthesis of multicultural histories in the potential sunset of affirmative action. Inasmuch as a general appeal to functionality follows with the turn to economic interests, this particular interpretive dimension may actually foreclose self-critical avenues while also adding an apparent manageability to the troubling race issues that have acted as one important motor for the movement. Coming to terms with its own participation in uncanny dynamics, the most pressing questions for the NWH may be bound once again to race, namely: Can the record of racial dynamics in the West ground an analysis that would mediate among different spheres of life in the West rather than presume a choice between economic and race issues? Can a movement that was initiated in good measure by a recognition of racial denial remedy its methodological limitations by devaluing racial analysis? New Western historians will find a precedent for work that mediates between race and property in certain literary examples that, like Limerick's *Legacy of Conquest,* experiment with the means of historical representation in order to better understand the lingering effects of conflict in the Western United States. Pursuing this potential exchange, we will now turn to Louise Erdrich's novel, *Tracks,* a work that problematizes the NWH's notion of property as it explores the uncommon ground at the heart of governmental American Indian policies.

LOUISE ERDRICH'S UNCOMMON GROUND: RETHINKING RACE AND PROPERTY

Novelist Louise Erdrich is a literary pillager. A mixed blood, born to Anishinabe and German-American parents, Erdrich is in fact of the Pillager clan, the members of which gained their name in the late 1700s when they demanded toll from particularly offended traders heading across Anishinabe country to further trade with the interior.[18] Following in the tradition of her forbears, Erdrich co-opts Western tools, setting them to work as she critically engages Anglo- and Native American legal interactions. Erdrich thus participates in a recounting of historical legal conflicts undertaken by a number of Native American novelists, including N. Scott Momaday, James Welch, and Leslie M. Silko. Such recountings work together to critique legal rhetoric and its power to shape thought. Developing their own forms of discourse analysis, these authors "return" to legal interactions not simply to rejudge them, but also to pillage: to revise existing historiography. Put another way, these authors explore the rules that inhere when historical narratives compete for legitimacy, the same kinds of rules that compete in Limerick's text as she moves between "history as an abandoned minefield" and "history as a subway." Such rules are, of course, also the bread and butter of the courtroom, one of the most influential institutions for defining proper historiography in this country. Two particular legal battles act as points of focus for Erdrich's intervention in *Tracks*: government land allotment policies that traded property for an individual's effective renunciation of tribal affiliation, and the repatriation of Native American remains and sacred materials.[19] Among other things, this intervention invites us to rethink the "common ground" of property identified by Limerick.

Native American authors participating in such legal critique pursue diverse literary strategies. Erdrich is certainly one of the more open as regards experimenting with "Western" forms, although for many of these authors choosing to work in the novel genre creates a variety of challenges that necessarily attend the transitions between largely oral and largely written cultures. Of particular interest are the ways Erdrich employs Western literary experiment and Native American culture in order to further a critique of the legal rhetoric that conditions Western historiography. Ultimately, Erdrich's literary strategies posit a collective moment of healing, a moment that comes into focus precisely as she analyzes the telling of the "pasts we tell ourselves."

The third novel published of a series, Erdrich's *Tracks* provides a "prequel" to *Love Medicine* and *Beet Queen*. In terms of the history of the writing, *Tracks* was the starting point for the series, and Erdrich, with collaborator Michael Dorris, worked on the book for better than ten years, a process that was apparently quite difficult given what we learn from Erdrich's comments to interviewers (*Conversations*, 222–223, 238). These comments convey a sense of responsibility to history: a responsibility not simply to get the historical materials "right," but also to engage in the sort of historiography that could "do justice" to her characters' tribal heritage. To an extent, this tension is reflected in reviews of the novel, which at times find its engagement of history either didactic or aesthetically flawed.[20] According to Erdrich, *Tracks* challenged her to convey the inevitably political aspects of Anishinabe history while simultaneously avoiding a reductive polemic. At stake in this history were conflicting ideas of responsibility, a battle that pitted American individualism against more collective (tribal) means of social and cultural organization (*Conversations*, 144–147). Trying to convey how this difference works itself out in modes of thinking, Michael Dorris described tribal languages that have no words to signify individuals, only variations on what in English would be the pronoun "we" (147).

Taken together, these aspects of the writing context pose an interesting question when we turn to one of the most prominent stylistic features of the novel: its bifurcation into two seemingly opposed narrators.[21] These narrators not only hold opposite views about Native American culture, but also convey outright hostility toward each other. However, one of the subtleties of the novel is the way its evolving development of the narrators undercuts what seems initially like a simple opposition. To uncover what actually links these narrators, Erdrich invites readers to take stock of their telling (as speakers, as characters), and what such telling has to say about its own contexts.

The story begins in North Dakota in 1912 as one of the Anishinabe elders, Nanapush, describes an epidemic of tuberculosis that seemed "impossible" given everything else that had befallen the tribe. Death hangs over this chapter in terms of its specific setting as well, as Nanapush goes on to relate a discovery made by himself and a tribal police officer of a remote cabin, a cabin inhabited by members of the Pillager clan, all of whom seem on first appearance to have died from exposure. The one member to survive, a young woman named Fleur Pillager, becomes the imaginative, if somewhat distant, center of the novel, as well as a "relative" to Nanapush who nurses her back to life through his storytelling and traditional mourning practices. As the novel unfolds, Fleur joins Nanapush as an advocate for these older tribal practices, especially in the face of government efforts to acculturate tribal peoples by means of suspect deals that grant property on the condition that recipients sever ties with their tribe, therefore relinquishing the basis for legal group claims.

Nanapush addresses his stories to Fleur's daughter, Lulu, who now looks upon these events many years distant. As such, Nanapush speaks to her as a daughter abandoned at the close of the action recounted in the novel, the point at which Fleur is driven from Pillager land to accommodate Anglo development. Nanapush's stories thus have an overt rhetorical setting; he seeks a reuniting of family, and given this goal, his telling is at once an explanation of Fleur's actions and a call for forgiveness. This rhetorical setting is implicitly modeled on his own various examples of talking cures, including an instance in which he saves Lulu herself from exposure by maintaining a thread of words between them. As we learn from Nanapush, such words take on a specific kind of work. From the initial violation of burial custom at the Pillager cabin, to Fleur's removal in a cart loaded down with her clan's grave markers, to Lulu's subsequent anger, this novel suggests in its various layerings that the history of this people is also the tracking of injury and its legacy.

The narrator who alternates chapters with Nanapush is Pauline Puyat, a mixed blood who from the outset of the novel is highly sensitive to the power dynamics between native and Western peoples and who in turn tries desperately to identify with Anglo culture. This desire for acculturation leads her through a strange series of actions that culminate in her complete denial of her mixed blood background, a denial that is a prerequisite if she is to undertake training as a Catholic nun. Despite her extreme attempts to assimilate, however, Pauline never makes the complete break upon which she obsessively fixes. Instead, she returns physically and in spiritual form again and again, particularly to Fleur, who functions alternately as a surrogate mother to Pauline and as a propagator of a way of life that Pauline supposedly abhors.

Pauline's narrative begins as she describes a period in which both she and Fleur worked in a butcher's shop, located in a small town off the reservation. As if Pauline were not troubled enough by her own cultural struggle, it becomes clear through this retelling that she has been complicit in a rape of Fleur and in subsequent revenge murders of the rapists, acts that she can never quite fully admit to herself although oblique memories haunt her throughout the novel. Here as with other characters in *Tracks,* readers find the struggle with trauma a centerpiece of the work. Carrying the blood of both cultures, but being accepted by neither, Pauline explores mechanisms of complicity, including mechanisms negotiated in both Native American and Anglo institutional spheres.

For instance, feeding off of her turmoil, Pauline becomes an apprentice to the official mourner within the tribe, Bernadette Morrissey. The apprenticeship is not a comfortable one for any of those involved, as it quickly becomes apparent that Pauline likes her job a little too much, experiencing an exhilaration at people's deathbeds that is both ecstatic and vampiristic. As far as Nanapush is concerned, she becomes nothing less than "death's bony whore." The suggestion of a sexual valence is borne out in Pauline's stories as well, as it becomes clear that her subsequent Catholicism embraces the salvific role of suffering precisely because, for her at least, the pain can be converted into masochistic pleasure. Committed to this notion, Pauline exerts much effort in the novel creating new ways to demonstrate her piety through self-torture.

Pauline culminates her narrative by describing what she had hoped would be an epic battle between Native American and Catholic religion. In the episode, she recounts how she had rowed to the middle of a lake said to be inhabited by powerful water spirits closely aligned with Fleur. Once there, she challenges the spirits to wrestle with her as a champion of Catholicism. No reckoning occurs; and when Fleur, standing on the shore, turns away from the event, the moment apparently crushes Pauline. Her leaking boat sinking out from under her feet, Pauline soon finds herself washed up on the shore, all the more ecstatic for having nearly drowned. Accidentally confronted by the father of her own abandoned child, she strangles him, repeating in a sense the revenge murders that have haunted her throughout her narrative.

Much of the criticism would have it that Pauline subsequently descends into madness, and yet more accurately she appears to move deeper and deeper into sublimations of the injuries that shape her stories. To further this sense of sublimation overall, Erdrich leaves Pauline's rhetorical situation undefined; a character seemingly obsessed with belonging, her chapters finally create no apparent connections to others. Yet her stories, and their seemingly endless substitutions for loss, register a desire for connections through storytelling. For all that distinguishes Nanapush and Pauline, they are thus bound by the type of work undertaken as they produce narratives. Despite the bifurcated form of the novel, they form a "we" locked in various negotiations with injury and its aftermath. As Nanapush tells Lulu about "the passing of times she will never know" (2), as Pauline conveys her own cultural estrangement, these narrators suggest that Erdrich's Anishinabe historiography is devoted first and foremost to a fundamentally collective mapping and working through of injury. To the extent that Fleur represents an older way of life, her final departure, wandering with grave markers in hand, reinforces the notion that the novel may be read as a requiem of sorts.

In one of the most aggressive critical attacks on the novel, Gloria Bird in fact takes up this mourning dynamic to accuse Erdrich of participating in cultural colonization. As the argument runs, Erdrich has unwittingly promoted the stereotype of the "vanishing Indian," thereby absolving her mainstream readership of any responsibility, except perhaps to the actions of a distant, virtually forgotten past.[22] Bird is correct as regards the pervasive despair that hangs over *Tracks* (43); Erdrich has taken a significant risk with this novel. Some readers will in fact translate this despair into a kind of hopelessness that will somehow absolve them of responsibilities for current and future Native American claims of injury. But allowing as much does not really acknowledge why Erdrich might be willing to take this risk in the first place. There is, for example, considerable evidence that she has accepted the risk knowingly. Erdrich has noted the "comfortable guilt" created by texts like Dee Brown's *Bury My Heart at Wounded Knee,* and has stated that her aim is "to transfer this guilt into the present reader and say, 'these Americans haven't vanished'" (*Conversations,* 142). In addition, Erdrich has argued for an ongoing Native American investment in legal reform, an investment that is being taken up skeptically, but with the awareness that few if any alternative institutional remedies exist for a people that constitutes less than one half of 1 percent of our nation's population (143).

It is with these statements in mind that I turn to a particularly important legal context for this novel: a context that is alluded to through the novel's study of mourning, and more explicitly through Fleur's final exile from her family home, an exile that finds her laden with grave markers. I refer to the legal battles that have ensued for some time now around the repatriation of Native American remains and burial artifacts, a fight that has resulted in the passage of the Native American Graves Protection and Repatriation Act (1990), as well as numerous state versions. A principal focus of Native American legal rights organizations, these struggles have sought to recover Native American ancestors housed in a variety of institutions, including the Smithsonian, historical societies, museums, and universities. This battle offers a crucial opportunity for rethinking the ways property as a category of analysis is laden with conflict at its conceptual core. In an important sense, the tribal claims fundamentally challenge Western liberal notions of property and hence Limerick's recourse to property as American history's "common ground."

A tremendous body of scholarship has been devoted to the repatriation effort, work I can only sketch here.[23] Perceived as a political, cultural, and economic struggle over religious rights, the repatriation efforts have demanded the enforcement of rights already supposedly guaranteed by the Constitution.[24] Where they exist, reform-oriented repatriation laws install legal means and remedies not afforded American citizens generally because Congress and the courts have recognized a distinct history of discrimination which has disenfranchised Native American tribes. The injury addressed by such laws therefore includes the institutional denial of rights to Native Americans. Legitimating their versions of a historical conflict on the way to passing these repatriation laws, the Native American organizations have thus created in some cases, codified in others, an alternative narrative of U.S. history.

If, as Erdrich has argued, the law is a fundamental battleground in the fight for Native American enfranchisement and national autonomy, then we may well find in the repatriation efforts other indications of broad cultural differences being placed in strategic conflict. And to this end, we may expect to find legal advocates and cultural critics like Erdrich focusing on the law's rhetoric itself. In other words, the repatriation battles may also provide an opportunity for a critique of legal methodology generally. The implications become clearer as we shift to a consideration of what is at stake in the way critics have read the mourning dynamics in *Tracks*.

In *The Sacred Hoop: Recovering the Feminine in American Indian Traditions*, Paula Gunn Allen argues that Native American literature experiments with aspects of tribal ceremony and ritual language practices in large part because these aspects break down false barriers between individuals and an animate world, an "All Spirit" (71). Anishinabe custom dictates a variety of detailed mourning practices for the dead, practices that certainly play a critical part in maintaining "political" structures within the tribal communities; for Anishinabe women survivors in particular, mourning can be an arduous process of subordination to a deceased husband's family.[25] As these customs are played out in novel form, Western adherents of psychoanalysis might well look upon Erdrich's characters as "case studies" interesting for what they teach about how distinct individuals wrestle with mourning, and perhaps succumb to particular "pathologies." However, to the extent they articulate Native American cultural traditions, novels like *Tracks* invite readers to engage a different interpretive register. Pauline and Nanapush's narrations relate in much particularity the processes by which the tribe has been coerced toward a legally defined individualism through government policies, policies which purported to assimilate the Anishinabe into self-sufficiency by tying tribal members to small, taxable farming properties. Focusing on the property-driven assimilation programs undertaken by the U.S. government, and the legacy of such policies, the novel invites its readers to rethink the nature of the collective psychology represented in the novel.

Inasmuch as *Tracks* documents intense ongoing cultural conflict, Erdrich anticipates the difficulty of translating her story for diverse audiences; to this end, she has composed a self-conscious study that is contextualized in the collective repatriation actions. Even as the novel registers the great impact of such individualism, and of the resentment bound to the property-driven acculturation it describes, the collectivity of the repatriation effort provides a crucial context for the "we" that brought this novel together for Erdrich during the writing. It is a "we" that echoes the desire for spiritual community so prevalent in both Nanapush's and Pauline's telling; in this sense these narrators reveal the contours marking tensions between differing communal means of coming to terms with (or failing to come to terms with) injury.

Erdrich's novel suggests that an important part of a culture's binding takes place as specific processes of dealing with loss are propagated over and against alternatives. When Erdrich draws upon the name Nanapush, for instance, she alludes to a complex central figure in Anishinabe storytelling: the trickster figure Nanabush, who created this world precisely by overcoming conflicting mourning processes that were leading to the destruction of the previous world.[26] Erdrich's Nanapush gains a privileged position by virtue of the cultural allusion, and this position in turn contextualizes Nanapush's success with written texts at the close of the novel. Here, he rescues Lulu from a government orphanage by winning a battle fought out in legal documents, a battle that frames Erdrich's own efforts to contribute to Native American culture through novelistic cultural criticism directed at legal issues.

As is the case with Nanapush in the novel, Erdrich validates a critically oriented cultural translation. In the process, she goes to the heart of what is at stake in the repatriation and assimilation policy debates. For all the Western curiosity with Native American remains as academic and historical property, these remains have been used for almost everything but understanding Native American burial and its spiritual implications. Physical anthropology, phrenology, and a host of other "disciplines" have been built on these remains, but almost always in order to justify Anglo superiority and the process of colonization.[27] Erdrich opens the repatriation register foremost to inject a history of property, religion, and their manipulation into these arguments. As such, these "sciences" and histories are inextricably linked to religion, culture, and politics. This effort in turn bears out an interesting parallel to the most successful repatriation cases. Here spiritual evidence presented by contemporary tribes—through accounts of visions and dreams—has been granted equal standing with "scientific" evidence in arguments about the origins of contested remains.[28]

Beyond the inclusion of this evidence, there lies a sense that the language that transports these religious visions effects a crucial intrusion on Western legal discourse. This intrusion calls forth one of the aspects of Erdrich's novel that is the most difficult to convey: the use of narrative voices to evoke language's ability to create, through ritualistic patterns and trickster comedy (and so much more), a complicated response to injury and its culturally specific reception. In this sense, Nanapush constitutes an important reference to Anishinabe and other Native American religions, which, as Walter Echo-Hawk has argued, have been under attack since the colonization of the Americas began (Echo-Hawk, 1). As much as Nanapush might have been drawn as an arch-victim with regard to these injuries, there is very little sense of this as readers move through the novel. Instead, he appears creative and proactive, and hence better able to cope with the lure of resentment, a tendency bound to the forced acculturation that is otherwise "embraced" by characters like Pauline. In particular, Nanapush refuses to think of himself as a sole agent, either as a holder of property or as a spiritual being. In fact he, like Erdrich herself, struggles against the very division of object and spirit (*Conversations*, 69).

Nanapush also refuses to assume that injury is necessarily part of a *quid pro quo* arrangement in which victimization goes hand in hand with guilt: In this way, he refuses the ethic of moral equivalence described by William Connolly. It is for these reasons that he remains a source of promise, even at the most bleak moments in the narrative. For instance, when it becomes apparent that the collective efforts to save Fleur's ancestral home have failed, Nanapush still resists despair, and in this there is of course a lesson for his interlocutor in the novel's frame narrative: Lulu, Fleur's abandoned daughter. Describing what he would have said to Fleur at this moment in his story, if only Fleur could have listened, he argues that

> Power dies, power goes under and gutters out, ungraspable. It is momentary, quick of light and liable to deceive. As soon as you rely on its possession it is gone. Forget that it ever existed and it returns. I never made the mistake of thinking that I owned my own strength, that was my secret. And so I was never alone in my failures. I was never to blame entirely when all was lost, when my desperate cures had no effect on the suffering of those I loved. For who can blame a man waiting, the doors open, the windows open, food offered, arms stretched wide? Who can blame him if the visitor does not arrive? (Erdrich, *Tracks*, 177)

A great example of the kind of "barrier breaking" Allen describes, this passage captures a crucial ethical shift. As someone who functions with a complex form of agency that intersects with those around him, Nanapush dislodges the legal focus on isolated victims and perpetrators. As such, Nanapush can imagine himself, and those around him, as participating in various kinds of collective ethical projects. Unlike Limerick, he refuses to choose between racial and property claims because his agency is spiritually tied to the land and sacred "objects." He speaks to Lulu of this past motivated not by resentment (a result of victimization received) nor by guilt (a result of his contribution to the disaster). Instead, the nonindividualistic ethical imagination his character models offers readers a conceptual horizon in which religious significance and meaning generally are not reduced to the ownership and exchange of property. U.S. law and Indian policy have, of course, played a significant role in institutional efforts to achieve just such a reduction; it would be unfortunate if the New Western History did the same.

CHAPTER FIVE

THE SOCIOLOGY OF RACIALIZED CRIME

No issue so poisons relations between the races as that of black crime.   —Stephen and Abigail Thernstrom, *America in Black and White*, 259

Heralded as one of the most rigorous studies of race relations available, *America in Black and White: One Nation Indivisible* has won praise not only from conservative scholars who share its color-blind ethic, but also from more liberal thinkers, including Henry Louis Gates, Jr., who finds the book "essential reading for anyone wishing to understand the state of race relations."[1] An important part of what makes this book stand out is its method, which blends historical analysis with sociological study. Although *America in Black and White* does not offer new social science evidence—the book depends on previously released studies—the recourse to "facts," as opposed to "feelings," about race issues has been posed as a watershed moment, an aspect of the book that may help explain why this essentially conservative tract has won a crossover audience. This chapter juxtaposes this "factual" reconfiguration of race analysis with the narrative experimentation offered by Jerome Miller in *Search and Destroy: African American Males in the Criminal Justice System*. It also contextualizes ideas about the exercise of choice and racialized crime found in the Thernstroms' and Miller's texts by offering a reading of John Rechy's novel, *The Miraculous Day of Amalia Gómez*, a work that explores the variety of forces acting upon minority decision making, as well as the ideologically loaded rhetoric of choice itself. In the process, this chapter historically contextualizes how crime by minorities

became a justification for the failure of formal equality reforms undertaken in the 1960s. In an important sense, this is the story of how the acquittal of Rodney King's attackers coincides with a generalized logic ex-
plaining the differential treatment of minorities by the criminal justice
system. Like the juror who ascribed total control of the beating to Rodney King himself, this is a tale of how minority actions are divorced from
a field of social interactions, thereby setting the stage for the creation of
racialized monsters who are both fascinating and threatening for the
powers of autonomy attributed to them.

Even though the politics of *America in Black and White* is far from
disinterested (social programs amount to little more than a wrong-
headed vestige of liberal guilt according to the Thernstroms), the larger
message of the history offered is explicitly upbeat: The status of blacks
in America has improved significantly since the 1940s. In this vein, the
authors argue that "racial progress is a train that left the station 50 years
ago and has been chugging along ever since" (12). Directing our attention to the rise of the black middle class, and to a decline in overt racial
discrimination, the authors hope to encourage their readers "to recap-
ture their faith in America" (12). In this way, the authors acknowledge a
desire on their part to build their analysis on an "optimistic premise"
(22). However wishful, this emphasis on improvement, and on the
power of positive thinking, gains legitimacy by its association with a fac-
tually driven analysis. Stephen Thernstrom is a noted scholar who has
made important contributions to the historical discipline, especially
with regard to the question of how best to approach urban problems in
the United States. A blend of qualitative sociologist and social historian,
he is credited with encouraging an interdisciplinary methodology that
grounds historical narratives in hard data.[2]

America in Black and White thus marshals two powerful rhetorical
gestures: It is scientific and at the same time it is almost religiously optimistic. Citing Martin Luther King, Jr., the authors present the audience
with a challenge in their Introduction. Should a reader choose to critique this interpretation of race in America, built as it is on faith and scientific analysis, this person will betray what was presumably most important in Martin Luther King, Jr.'s thought, namely the self-fulfilling
prophecy of hope (12). This book's relationship to its readers is further

complicated by a consistent set of rhetorical gestures that suggest a lay-ered form of audience address. In the Introduction, and again in the chapter devoted to "black crime," the authors describe black interlocu-tors who fail to maintain the faith, at least according to the Thernstroms (*America*, 12, 16). This situation invites the nonblack readership of *America in Black and White* to stand removed from this chastisement. The rhetorical performance is in fact consistent with the Thernstroms' larger argument that it is up to individual blacks to better their social situa-tion. Hence, the initial engagement of the audience only reinforces the broader effort to blame blacks for the poverty they suffer, the crime they experience, and ultimately the social exclusion with which they live. In the book's Preface, the paradigmatic figures of black pessimism are John Hope Franklin, head of President Clinton's Advisory Board on race, Camille Cosby, and Derrick Bell, all critics of the color-blind policy rec-ommendations favored by the authors (12). The book certainly targets white liberal thinkers as well, but it is instructive that *America in Black and White* begins by presenting blacks as their own worst enemy in a world of choices between faith and betrayal, between self-fulfilling opti-mism and self-destructive pessimism.

Within *America in Black and White*'s wide-ranging survey of race re-lations, one issue is afforded unique standing: black crime. In a strategic reversal of traditional liberal rhetoric—in which black crime is often posed as the product of root causes, including poverty and poor educa-tion—the Thernstroms argue that black crime is in itself an autono-mous motor responsible for racism; the authors therefore suggest that racism in general is a by-product of black criminal behavior, an argu-ment not far removed from that offered by D'Souza when he claims that racism grows out of the contact between civilized Europeans and unciv-ilized non-European natives.[3]

If faith in the continued betterment of the black situation should unify America as "one nation indivisible," then, according to the Thern-stroms, fear of crime is the major impediment to this process. The Th-ernstroms reinforce the point in the opening of their chapter on black crime by noting that both blacks and whites desire a social setting in which fear of black crime might be alleviated. Beginning with a variety of anecdotal evidence, the authors describe the popular view that black crime has exploded in recent decades. They also build on such evidence to demonstrate the way fear of this explosion in crime has made "prisoners" of law-abiding citizens who are afraid to venture out of their homes (261). Supporting these impressions about crime, the authors turn to statistics which purport to reveal dramatic increases in violent crime during the previous three decades (262). Based on these materials, the Thernstroms confirm that "crime on a scale unknown to previous generations is a continuing legacy of the 1960s" (263).

Bringing a racial filter to these statistics, the authors then cite work on arrest rates, research which shows that blacks are arrested at a rate of 2.5 to 4.7 times that of whites for selected crimes (264). Acknowledging that blacks are similarly over-represented in terms of convictions and prison population, the Thernstroms argue that these disparities are in fact merited, and that bias in the criminal justice system has not had a hand in producing these results. In the process, they summarize their opponents' positions, noting that

> The racial bias argument actually takes two quite different forms, although often packaged as one. Prosecutors, juries and judges treating blacks and whites differently is the first. The second implies that disparate treatment is actually just. Blacks should be given a break. . . . Young black men have sunk into the criminal justice system . . . [because] the safety nets have disappeared. . . . Take that argument one small step further and it becomes a full-blown conspiracy theory in which black crime is not simply the consequence of white racism but part of a racist plot. . . . Whites, in other words, are deliberately locking black men up; it's a plot easily carried off. (Thernstrom and Thernstrom, 270–271)

The collapse of these different criticisms of the criminal justice system into the extremist plot theory aside, the strongest arguments for bias in the criminal justice system simply are not represented here. Although the debate about crack versus powder cocaine penalties is briefly treated by the authors elsewhere in the chapter, its omission here is glaring since crack cocaine laws are clearly constructed to target inner-city blacks for stiffer punishments. In fact, the author's best defense of the disparate penalties for crack and powder cocaine is that: (1) the Black

Congressional Caucus supported them, and (2) it is better for black communities to lock up the offenders (278).

Given that close to 90 percent of American black males can expect to be arrested during their lives, many on drug charges, and given that these arrests—warranted or not—will have significant impacts on employment possibilities, it is not clear that arrests help the black community.[4] It seems even more curious that authors advocating race-blind policymaking should turn to the Black Caucus to justify a racially disparate criminal punishment—an irony that is heightened by the Thernstroms' skepticism regarding all race-sensitive welfare programs. Perhaps more important, however, is the authors' neglect of studies focusing on the informal stages of criminal justice processing, for instance studies that explore the factors at play when police officers decide whom to stop for initial questioning; certain practices, including the racial profiling of suspects, have drawn considerable attention in this regard.[5] Instead, the Thernstroms build their case against bias in the system by citing studies of the formal stages—those subject to the greatest public scrutiny and therefore those likely to be most cautiously approached by police. Even here, however, the authors ignore highly charged material. Citing a 1993 Justice Department study of 10,000 felony cases that shows blacks and whites prosecuted and convicted at comparable rates, the authors conclude that bias is not at work (273–274). Yet in reading the same study, the authors must also contend with the fact that 51 percent of the convicted blacks were sentenced to prison, while only 38 percent of the convicted whites found themselves similarly treated. Although the authors claim that these differences were "entirely attributable" to the serious nature of the crimes, to the prosecution policies of specific locales, and to the blacks' more problematic criminal records, all of these variables are potential indicators of bias.

There is, for instance, very suggestive evidence that prosecutors will pad their records by more aggressively pursuing poor defendants who are less likely to mount a significant defense, especially in the current "get tough on crime" political environment.[6] In turn, poor inner-city blacks may be prosecuted at a similar rate as whites, but for more serious crimes than whites may expect. Where one lives—the inner city—may certainly be affected by one's race and by bias within real estate practices and government housing policies;[7] in this way, blacks may face distinctly aggressive local prosecution policies by virtue of previous housing discrimination. Finally, prior arrest records may be affected by a propensity for police to stop blacks at disparate rates. A 1993 California State Assembly study, for instance, found that 92 percent of blacks arrested on drug charges were released for insufficient evidence; the record of the arrest, of course, remains with these blacks, making it easier for them to be profiled as recidivists.[8]

In a particularly ironic twist, the Thernstroms read such evidence of overcharging as simply consistent with blacks' heightened criminal behavior (264). For an argument that makes much of the power of self-fulfilling prophecies, readers can wonder why the Thernstroms do not question more critically the 1992 statistical evidence they provide demonstrating that blacks are twice as likely as whites to be wrongly prosecuted for rape, almost 80 percent more likely in drug dealing cases, 30 percent more likely in other drug cases, and 70 percent more likely in the "catch-all" category, "other crimes against persons" (273).

If the effort to assign responsibility for black incarceration to blacks leaves the justice system squeaky clean, the same cannot be said of welfare and other programs. According to the Thernstroms, such programs have been dismal failures in terms of their effects on crime (280). The Thernstroms' analysis is notable for the way in which it obscures a number of variables. Few, if any, sociologists would claim that poverty alone causes crime. Certainly many would argue that welfare and other social programs were never particularly effective because the programs never received adequate resources. But to emphasize either of these points is to miss the Thernstroms' mark, because their goal with these statistical and rhetorical gestures is to shift the blame for racial disparities squarely onto the shoulders of individual blacks who should be held accountable for their injurious choices. When it comes to understanding what keeps America from being "indivisible," the Thernstroms have one prominent answer: "No issue so poisons relations between the races as that of black crime."

Although *America in Black and White* is credited with separating fact from feeling, and adopting this separation as an explicit virtue (16), the conclusion of the Thernstroms' chapter on crime suggests otherwise.

Here the authors look to the larger effect of exploding black criminal behavior. This behavior is associated with, among other things, keeping old stereotypes alive ("blacks are more prone to violence") and keeping residential segregation in place (283–284). Discussing various incidents in which prominent law-abiding blacks have been detained and harassed, the authors predictably conclude that black crime alone is to blame for such racial stigmatization. It is as if the Thernstroms believe that people, including most who never experience black crime, come to know this crime in a purely transparent way, completely free of the potential biases within the media.

To drive home the ways in which blacks perpetuate these fears and stigmas, the authors close their chapter on crime with an anecdote, this time an autobiographical story by Brent Staples, now an editorial writer for the *New York Times*. As a college student, Staples had occasions to walk through predominantly white Chicago neighborhoods at night. In a very disturbing manner, these walks taught Staples, an African American, the way he did violence to the neighborhood whites simply by just "being" (284).

For the first time, it occurred to Staples that he was big—over six feet tall. He tried to be innocuous but didn't know how. He tried to avoid people, letting them clear the lobbies of buildings before he entered, and out of nervousness, began to whistle—popular tunes from the Beatles and Vivaldi's *Four Seasons*. But then . . . he changed, without knowing why. He began to play a game that he called "scatter the pigeons"—terrifying whites by walking aggressively right in their path. It worked every time. Those who encountered Staples on the streets of Chicago's Hyde Park neighborhood had, as he acknowledges, every reason to be scared. "Hyde Park was an island of prosperity in a sea of squalor," he notes. . . . [As] Staples explains, the whites he encountered saw not black, but a friend and neighbor the minute he began to whistle his soothing tunes. "The tension drained from people's bodies when they heard me. A few even smiled as they passed me in the dark," he reports. It took so little, although, understandably he found it too much. But Staples' experience suggests a larger truth: If the African American crime rate suddenly dropped to the current level of the white crime rate, we would eliminate a major force that is driving blacks and whites apart and is destroying the fabric of black urban life. (Thernstrom and Thernstrom, 284–285)

It is hard to imagine an anecdote that could better support the "power of positive thinking" analysis which frames *America in Black and White*. If we are to judge based on this evidence, it would take so little to overcome the stigma rightfully associated with black crime; blacks literally need to whistle a happy tune. The Thernstroms, of course, have something deeper and more meaningful in mind: a token of good will, an indication from law-abiding blacks that they are not one of the "bad" blacks who constitute the explosion of violent crime in the United States.

Perhaps more telling, however, is the way this chapter closes by throwing the responsibility for racism squarely onto the shoulders of blacks. In the performance recounted by the Thernstroms, the whites are justifiably afraid of the black man. He is the one who has the choice to make; will he acknowledge that the whites' fear is justified, or will he choose to feed the racially charged stereotypes by acting aggressively, by "scattering the pigeons"? This passage and others like it in the book (especially in the Introduction) make it clear that black individuals need to choose nonaggressive behaviors and a more optimistic outlook. Social protest itself thus becomes suspect. Government policies are not the answer; after all, according to the Thernstroms, social programs do not affect crime. Hence, readers of *America in Black and White* are left with the black individual and an ethic of personal choices.

～

It may be that the high rate of black offending has caused many researchers to de-emphasize, to the point of ignoring, racial discrimination in the criminal justice system. It is almost as if disproportionate black offending is viewed as a justification for race discrimination. The problem of racism in the justice system is too important to play second fiddle to other criminal justice realities, including disproportionate offending rates. Researchers on either side of the disparity versus discrimination debate have been hesitant to acknowledge that both racial

discrimination and racial disproportion exist, *and* both are problems
that must be addressed.

—Katheryn Russell, *The Color of Crime,* 30

Although a number of reviewers have celebrated the manner in which
the Thernstroms have brought the light of facts to the murky sentimentality of discussions about black crime, the accounting offered in *America in Black and White* is misleading, both in terms of the data presented,
and in terms of the method used to interpret the data.[9] Consider, for instance, the basic premise that crime has exploded in recent decades.
Crime trends are most often measured with reference to the FBI Uniform Crime Report (based on arrest statistics for indexed crimes reported by state and local police), and the National Crime Survey—NCS
(based on a victim survey of 100,000 households). Analyzing the data
from these reports spanning 1979 through 1991, University of Michigan
researchers John Bounds and Scott Boggess concluded that "the UCR reports indeed demonstrated that the index crime had fallen by 2 percent,
while the NCS registered a 27 percent drop in "crime against persons"
and a 31 percent drop in property offenses during those years." Summarizing their findings, Bounds and Boggess note that, "despite the widely
held belief that there was a significant increase in the level of criminal
activity during the 1980s, in general, we find that neither data source de-
picts increasing levels of crime over this period."[10]

As sociologist Jerome Miller has argued, when the raw numbers peri-
odically released to the press by the FBI are "broken down by crimes per
100,000 of population, and are age-adjusted to take into account the
number of those in age categories most at risk, it appears that serious
crime has either been stable or dropping" through the supposed boom
in crime (Miller, 28). Studies focusing on Michigan and Pennsylvania
during roughly the same period confirm these results (14–15). Crime did
not explode, but America's fear of crime did, a phenomenon that has led
a number of sociologists to question the political stakes of manufactur-
ing a crime wave, and the potential self-interest driving the crime industry's presentation of the "crisis."[11]

Likewise, the available data regarding indications of bias within the
criminal justice system do not support the Thernstroms' positive ap-

praisal. Consider, for instance, the Thernstroms' argument that the imprisonment of blacks relative to whites only increased marginally between 1980 and 1993 (279). In fact, the higher rate of incarceration has grown steadily since 1950 when the ratio was approximately 4 to 1. In 1960, it increased to 5 to 1; in 1970, it was 6 to 1, and by 1989 it was 7 to 1.[12] U.S. prisons are in fact growing distinguished by their color, and at an alarming rate. The overall impact has been tremendous, especially on young black males. In this vein, a 1995 study by the Washington-based Sentencing Project revealed that "on an average day in the United States, one in every three African American men ages 20–29 was either in prison, in jail, or on probation/parole" (Mauer, 1).

As Katheryn Russell suggests, such disparities should be examined for the way they may reflect an *interplay* of black criminal behavior and bias (Russell, 30). We have now reached the point where an estimated two-thirds of all federal prisoners have been sentenced for drug-related offenses, and the overwhelming majority of these prisoners are black and Latino (Miller, 83). How does this add up when compared to what we know of criminal behavior?

> While African Americans and Hispanics made up the bulk of those arrested, convicted and sentenced to prison for drug offenses, in 1992, the U.S. Public Health Service's Substance Abuse and Mental Health Services Administration estimated that 76% of the illicit drug users in the United States were white, 14% were black and 8% were Hispanic. (Miller, 81)

Almost 24 million Americans participated in illicit drug trading during 1993, yet only 3 percent of those breaking the drug laws were arrested (Miller, 12). Although 50 percent of crack cocaine users are white, only 4 percent of these whites are convicted; blacks, who account for 38 percent of the use, constitute 85 percent of the convictions (Russell, 31). Readers might wonder as well how the assessment of penalties may reveal disparate treatment. According to Miller,

> In 1991, 90% of the "crack" arrests nationally were of minorities, whereas three-fourths of the arrests for powder cocaine were of whites. However, sentences for possession of crack were usually three to four times harsher

than those for the possession of the same amount of powder cocaine. Blacks were sent to prison in unprecedented numbers and were kept there longer than whites. Ninety-two percent (92%) of all drug possession offenders sentenced to prison in New York were either black or Hispanic, and 71% in California. (Miller, 82)

It is little wonder that the Thernstroms downplay the crack and powder cocaine controversy when mapping the nature of bias in the criminal justice system.

If the war on drugs seems a bit more unsavory on closer examination, the same might be said about the "explosion" of juvenile crime, where "official data on delinquency are tied so loosely to the actual behavior of youth that they are more sensitive to changes in the measurement procedures than they are to the object of measurement" (41). Comparing statistics for the years 1967–72 to actual behavior, criminologists Martin Gold and David Reimer could find no increase in criminal behavior among teenagers despite soaring arrest rates. As they concluded, the data they discovered simply did not give evidence of "rapidly rising rates of juvenile delinquency."[13]

With such data about behavior in hand, it becomes easier to see why some scholars examining black crime find it insufficient to follow the Thernstroms' approach and focus solely on the individual behavior of blacks. Of course the disjunction between behavior and criminal processing raises significant concerns about bias within the criminal justice system. In fact, a recent survey of 169 judges revealed that 98 percent believe racial bias does exist within the system (Miller, 61). Not only are there indications of such bias within the system, there are also indications that the system may impose "a 'treatment' that maims those it touches and exacerbates the very pathologies which lie at the root of crime" (9). Of course, there is far from consensus on this point, and, as Katheryn Russell has noted, "mainstream criminology research leads one to conclude that racial discrimination in the criminal justice system is a historical concept," at most a vestigial and largely insignificant presence (26).

In response, Russell and others argue that existing studies are significantly limited because of (1) tunnel vision that delimits the variable included in the study, (2) the unnecessary assumption that results must either be attributed to disparate behavior *or* discrimination, and (3) neglect of the informal stages of the criminal justice system—stages other than, or between, arrest, conviction, and sentencing (32). Whereas Russell considers these other informal stages, for instance decisions to prosecute for higher drug law penalties (31–32), her primary focus is "how police treat black men *prior* to arrest" (33). Russell argues that "police stops of motorists, which constitute an informal stage, determine in large measure who will be arrested and thus who will enter the criminal justice system" (32). According to the Thernstroms, the criminal justice system is not biased because its sensitivity to blacks is justified by black criminal behavior. However, as Russell notes, "The available research suggests that black men are stopped and questioned at a rate much higher than the level of their involvement in crime. The few studies on this issue indicate that black men are significantly more likely to be stopped than anyone else—at a rate far above their rate of arrest" (39).

It would appear that the racial labeling of prospective criminals affects officers' expectations at this informal level, thereby making it more likely that blacks will enter the criminal justice system. Although this certainly does not account for all of the disparities, it does establish a long-term ripple effect for minority arrestees that calls for interrogation (Russell, 45).

Russell's suggestions for correcting the methodological flaws of current criminology involve two points of focus. She advocates that researchers extend current information-gathering techniques to ignored arenas of social contact. She also invites scholars to complicate their analysis of crime by adopting more interactive models that can better accommodate the variables affecting crime. Although these concerns are also to be found in Miller's *Search and Destroy,* his treatment of the bias question is framed by the broader methodological debates within sociology regarding how one defines social problems in general, as well as by debates among sociologists regarding the relative advantages of assuming "objectivist" or "constructionist" stances when engaging objects of study.

Building on Herbert Blumer's observation that "what we decide to label as social problems are fundamentally products of a process of collective definition," Miller places himself in a "constructionist" camp that views social problems as the result of social manufacture and not "as a set of objective social arrangements with an intrinsic make-up" (Miller, 2–3).

> Blumer's insight is at the center of the contemporary sociological debate over what constitutes a "social problem." "Objectivists" saw our social problems as resulting from an objective set of conditions. "Constructionists" studied the emergence of these crises in terms of "claims-making" and "typification"—that is, how a set of conditions comes to be defined and typified as a "social problem" (e.g. through demonstrations, marketing "think tank" reports, publicizing books, journalistic investigative reports, and political initiative)—and thereby made eligible for anything from public curiosity to public obsession. (Miller, 3)

The approach situates the issue of black crime within a fundamentally rhetorical setting. This method neither dismisses facts nor embraces sentimentality, and in this sense it does not constitute a reversal of the Thernstroms' "factual" intervention in race studies. Instead, Miller advocates a general self-consciousness regarding the social variables that may influence our rhetorical construction of social problems and "data" itself.

> The records by which the justice system memorializes itself—from arrest summaries, to charges brought by prosecutors, to pleading the "facts" of a case by frequently uninterested or incompetent lawyers, to acquittal or conviction, to sentencing based on inadequate and often incorrect information—present truncated and highly distorted versions of reality. Even apparently objective data, such as that generated for statistical reports of criminal justice agencies, cannot be taken at face value. The annual report of the sheriff in pursuit of having a new jail built will present a highly different picture of who will reside therein than that of a sheriff who is satisfied with his jail's present capacity. (Miller, 58)

Unlike the Thernstroms, who adopt an objectivist faith in the facts, including their disinterested production and transparent meaning, Miller suggests that we read "a criminal justice record as a written apologia at each stage of the criminal justice processing for what is about to happen at the next stage" (57).[14]

Miller is not proposing a conspiracy, or a plot against black men. Rather, he suggests that subjective factors filter through the criminal justice system, factors that come into bold relief when we consider that since 1941, 20 black New York City police officers have been shot by their colleagues, while not one white officer has been similarly injured (Glassner, 114). In turn, the drive to positivistic analysis insures that these transferential dynamics will go unaddressed. Exploring these dynamics in a twist on one of the Thernstroms' most valued notions, Miller turns to W. I. Thomas who first defined the concept of the "self-fulfilling prophecy" (Miller, 57). Of particular importance is Thomas's argument that,

> Even the highly subjective record has a value. . . . Very often it is the wide discrepancy between the situation as it seems to others and the situation as it seems to the individual that brings about overt behavior. . . . If men define situations as real, they are real in their consequences. (Thomas, 571–572)

This passage invites us to read for the way facts and fantasies are *mediated*. It also provides a frame for analyzing the methodological catch-22 of *America in Black and White*; because the Thernstroms fail to acknowledge the transferential dynamic, their "factual" correction to the race debates is significantly put into question by the self-fulfilling prophecy they pointedly invoke. As we have seen, this catch-22 is a consistent part of a larger web of color-blind discourse that places great stakes in reducing social dynamics to isolated, individual choices like those attributed to black criminals at the end of the Thernstroms' chapter on crime. In the process, this reduction obliterates any consideration of the crime industry's "interests," or the unintended consequences of the criminal justice system on its subjects and on the public generally. This latter concern was a focal point of a study of U.S. crime released recently by the Eisenhower Foundation.[15] In one of the report's central findings, the authors argued that "Prisons have become our national substitute for effective policies on crime, drugs, mental illness, housing, poverty, and employment of the hardest to employ. . . . In a reasonable culture, we would not say that we had won the war against disease just because we had moved a lot of sick people from their homes to hospital wards. And in a reasonable culture we would not say we have won the war on crime because we have moved a lot of criminals from the community into prison cells."[16] Not surprisingly, spokespeople for the crime industry fell back on public opinion, and opinion about fear in particular, while defending the policies questioned by the report.[17]

Fighting crime is big business in the United States, and it is becoming more lucrative every year. In 1993 alone, more than $31 billion was spent on the drug war nationally. In the mid-1990s, the United States spent approximately $200 billion annually on the crime control industry (Miller, 1–2). According to the *Wall Street Journal,* "The nation's fear of crime had fueled the creation of a new version of the old military industrial complex—an infrastructure born amid political rhetoric and a shower of federal, state and local dollars. . . . These mutually reinforcing interests are forging a formidable new iron triangle similar to the triangle that arms makers, military services and lawmakers formed three decades ago."[18] The rise of this industry has left its mark at the state level as well. As Miller notes:

> A 1994 program audit of the Texas prison system by the state comptroller warned the legislature that a powerful "prison industrial complex" was already in place and could be expected to fight efforts to bring costs down. The auditors noted that this new political entity had "spawned its own self-perpetuating interest groups, complete with consultants, lobbyists, burgeoning state bureaucracies and a rising private corrections industry," and concluded that, like any special-interest group, "the correctional industry is in business to keep its empire growing." (Miller, 231)

At the same time as prison labor, construction, and employment are moving quietly toward privatization, a rapidly growing technical industry is supplying new weapons and means of surveillance, devices that add to the sense that the inner city is now a militarized zone.[19]

The move to think of this industry, and of prisons themselves, as having some sort of agency is relatively new, at least within sociology. As Charles Bright demonstrates in *The Powers That Punish: Prisons and Politics in the Era of the "Big House, 1920–1955,* sociologists have instead tended to treat prisons as (1) distinct morally-deficient cultures, (2) closed systems, and (3) intensifiers of behaviors found both in society, and, in particular, on the streets (6–9). According to Bright, these approaches have led to a conceptual "dead end" that has stunted work in the field, a dead end that inappropriately focuses research on questions of how to understand influences outside the prison *versus* those dynamics inside the prison. Bright builds his intervention on the assumption that such influences are mutual, and that prisons have complex histories that may be profitably traced by examining how prison administrations have mediated their relations both with prison populations (guards and prisoners) and with the "outside" public, including political bodies responsible for allocating resources. As understood by Bright, this process of mediation is thoroughly rhetorical and takes as its principle project the justification of punishment through a careful presentation of prison techniques and rationales, a presentation that may well exist independent of actual practice (14–15).

Bright carries this analysis through detailed readings (focused on Jackson State Prison in Michigan) and through consideration of more global policy trends. Studying these social histories, Bright concludes that punishment, rhetorically speaking, has been less important for controlling crime than it has been for constituting the known criminal as an object of knowledge (19–20). In most eras of punishment, the inmate has been simultaneously excluded from and included in society by virtue of the promise of re-inclusion, a re-inclusion gained through discipline administered in prison. Such a logic for punishment is consistent with Emile Durkheim's argument in *Moral Education.* Here Durkheim claims that punishment is effective to the extent that it both affirms society's rules for the general population as well as makes the criminal feel the weight of society's temporary disapproval and blame (176–180). The deep injury of crime, according to Durkheim, is not only the "natural" consequence of the specific act, but also, and more importantly, the harm inflicted on the entire belief system of the society. It is this injury that justifies punishment according to Durkheim (179). In this context, Bright argues that incarceration constitutes the containment of a revolt: a "necessary" societal vengeance imposed on abnormal behavior.

> The operation of carceral discipline serves to highlight "the form of il-legality that seems to sum up symbolically all the others": the foreign-born bootlegger of the 1920s, the desperado gangster of the 1930s, the dysfunctional psychopath of the 1950s, and the black drug dealer of the 1980s. It is this utility of the prison in the production of "usable illegal-ities" that, in Foucault's view, enabled it to survive and flourish in the face of continual evidence that it failed to correct criminals or control crime. (Bright, 20)

By producing "usable illegalities," the prison industry is able to flourish independent of crime deterrence or evidence of inmate reform. In this context, it would do well to examine how society articulates its venge-ance through the rhetorics of incarceration, rhetorics that justify three strikes legislation, as well as the use of lethal force in prison inmate management.[20]

This project reveals some fairly dramatic changes in the ways U.S. prisons have legitimated themselves. Early industrial models in which prisoners constituted a mass of undifferentiated laborers gave way to a therapeutic paradigm that engaged inmates on a case-by-case basis de-signed for individualized discipline and reform. Most recently, however, U.S. prison policy has shifted course even more notably by largely dis-avowing the rationales of discipline and reform.

> Beginning with the Federal Bureau of Prisons in 1975, one prison sys-tem after another jettisoned rehabilitational programs and abandoned the rhetoric of correction that had underwritten the carceral narrative and the sociologies of the prison for a half-century. The central ques-tion at the core of prison scholarship—what blocks or impedes refor-mation—simply lost its point, and prison managers were fatally com-promised in their efforts to make public concerns about crime and so-cial order fungible with available institutional programs and capacities. (Bright, 312)

If this contemporary period presented a crisis for prison managers, as Bright suggests, the effects have not been particularly deleterious for prison funding efforts. If anything, public support of the crime industry has been exceptional throughout this "crisis." Without an inmate reform agenda, it would seem that the best prison administrators can do at this juncture is tout their managerial efficiency when handling what are essentially lost and disposable souls.

As Bright notes, each era seems to have its archetypal representative of criminal behavior. Might we assume, then, that the black drug dealer's arrival in this role corresponds in some meaningful way with the change in prison rhetoric, and more importantly with society's larger acceptance of this rhetoric? Might the social status of this particular archetypal criminal figure facilitate such a dramatic change in prison rhetoric in the 1980s, a period that also saw the development of the "war on drugs"? A Harvard University study of juvenile delinquency (presumably our next generation of disposable criminals) suggests that we seriously explore such avenues of analysis; it found that two factors were predominant in the decision to incarcerate offending youths: socioeconomic status and space availability.[21]

The crime industry has obvious motives for expanding its services, but these motives do not explain why the public would focus so specifically on racialized criminals at this juncture. For Miller, the answer is primarily a political one. A legacy of racism in this country makes viable various stereotypes that may be directly and indirectly invoked to foster a crucial process of criminal labeling. Fear of crime, in this analysis, is a marketable commodity, one that, as Barry Glassner points out in *The Culture of Fear: Why Americans Are Afraid of the Wrong Things*, may have little basis in reality (xv–xix). It is in this context that Miller challenges the media for its part in constructing a panic about crime; focusing on "dark-skinned predators, crime has become a metaphor for race, hammered home nightly on TV news and exploitative crime shows" (Miller, 149). We might also consider the ways in which newspaper reporters and editors prioritize homicide coverage so as to heighten the awareness of white victims of racialized violence, a practice that has been explicitly acknowledged within the media (Glassner, 111). Miller places the exploitation of such racial capital in a long history of race-baiting that has focused on black crime. Noting the way in which "suspicion" was sufficient cause to lock up blacks at the turn of the century, Miller invites readers to consider the ways in which racially loaded labeling, practiced by the public, conditions interactions between black citizens and police officers. This focus on labeling also invites us to explore the pre-arrest informal suspicion highlighted by Russell and made explicit in various cases in which state troopers have acknowledged the racial targeting of motorists (Russell 40–44).

The prevalence of such racial profiling also instructively frames the ways in which black males are both conditioned for and conditioned by processing in the criminal justice system. In polling, more than 50 percent of blacks have consistently stated that the criminal justice system is biased (Russell, 35). In a number of venues, the NAACP and other organizations are visiting predominantly black high schools to run clinics for black youth on how to arrest well, and most importantly, on how to avoid harm at the hands of police officers (Miller, 100–101). That such concern is founded is confirmed by reports such as the one produced by the Christopher Commission in Los Angeles (1991). This report revealed that more than 25 percent of Los Angeles Police Department officers believe that some officers engage in excessive force against a suspect that is motivated by racial prejudice (Russell, 37–38).

Exploring labeling dynamics in terms of the trauma experienced by blacks incorporated into the justice system (i.e., most black males), Miller asks what the unintended consequences may be for the black community, and also for U.S. society in general. In so doing, Miller challenges the Thernstroms' assumption that the welfare of black communities may be easily separated from the punishment of "black criminals." Miller sets the context for this discussion of trauma by providing considerable data suggesting that black offenders are predominantly acculturated to the criminal justice system not by processing for violent crimes, but rather by attention for lesser, often victimless crimes (12, 35). It is the heightened sensitivity to these lesser offenses that in turn creates a ripple effect which follows black males through the system, and because arrest records persist regardless of whether charges are merited, suspicion is often as damaging as guilt. Fundamentally, we need to ask if criminal justice processing is the best way to address the minor, victimless violations committed by youths, in any circumstances but especially where physical abuse is part of teen detention policy.[22]

For Miller, the effects of labeling heighten the methodological stakes of the crime debates because the processes of informal bias are frequently occluded by the positivistic practices of sociological objectivists and by dominant legal practice. For this reason, Miller strongly advocates a greater role for narrative analysis, which he associates with sociological constructivism. Citing Clifford Shaw, a noted sociologist of the Chicago School and a proponent of narrative research, Miller argues that contemporary crime research must come to terms with "rationalizations, fabrications, prejudices and exaggerations," phenomena that "are quite as valuable as objective description, provided of course that these reactions be properly identified" (Miller, 57).[23]

It is by virtue of such narrative analysis that researchers gain a purchase on the play of formal and informal stages of the justice system. Such analysis also suggests the ways in which the system contributes to the very problem it supposedly addresses: the prevalence of crime in society. A crucial question, then, is how might the criminal justice system act out, rather than work through, the social problem of crime, and of racialized crime specifically? To help frame this question, Miller makes an inviting, if brief, allusion to Holocaust studies.

> Even when memory is grounded in unassailable realities, the ways in which it is carried by each individual may vary greatly—particularly when the memory is of harrowing realities. In looking at Holocaust survivors, for example, Lawrence Langer distinguishes "chronological memory," with its narrative form of a beginning, middle and end (which dims with the passage of time) from "durational memory," which results from having experienced events so horrific and threatening that the memories defy time and suffuse one's total life experience thereafter. Such considerations are impossible for the criminal justice system to absorb. (Miller, 57)

Although it is not clear from Miller's account how such a "durational memory" or acting out may apply to the criminal justice system and the specifics of questioning, arrest, and criminal processing generally, the suggestion here is that the system itself contributes to the repetition of criminal and racial injury in society.

In part, Miller is anticipating inevitable concerns: What is to become of those labeled criminal once society has abandoned the reform and discipline incarceration models? What can society expect of such "disposable" people? But Miller is also asking questions about aspects of sociology's own complicity in the process of discounting harms that register as "indirect" and "informal," or harms that derive from the unanticipated consequences of how we confront crime and the newly minted managerial logic of punishment.

A number of studies have suggested that incarceration does not act as an effective crime deterrent, and may even increase crime (Miller, 93–95, 120). In contrast, rehabilitation does appear to improve significantly a criminal's chances of successfully avoiding further trouble with the law, particularly at the juvenile level (120–22). One crucial difference between the two approaches, especially in the era of mandatory sentencing, is that rehabilitation involves a narrative intervention, both at the time the rehabilitation is awarded and during the process itself. Although rehabilitation is currently out of favor, it offers a context for working through the social problem of crime not otherwise available. In the case of drug rehabilitation, however, even these limited opportunities are shaded by racial bias, as spots in the existing programs are disproportionately given to white offenders (83–84).

Meanwhile, there are a number of indicators that the war on drugs has made the inner cities more, not less, violent (Miller, 91). Social scientists have helped us understand this increase by identifying an "oppositional culture" in the inner city that has been exacerbated by joblessness, racism, and violence—including that violence imported by "get tough on crime" policies. In this setting, young black males are vying for respect in a violent fashion that helps account for recent increases in black-on-black homicide. Given the very high proportion of these youths who are repeatedly processed by the system, we may ask how this violence and craving for respect may be linked to the demoralizing and threatening treatment received from police.[24] In this vein, a Harvard University study of juvenile incarceration in Boston demonstrated that such punishment was not keyed to behavior, and that the experience of incarceration itself made it more likely that youths would participate in criminal activity and be subject to further incarceration.[25]

~

> Despite its pretensions, modern criminal justice is no more about crime control than it is about rehabilitation. Nor is it about deterrence. None of that matters. Rather, it is increasingly about "identifying and managing unruly groups. . . . Having put in place the conditions to ensure a violent self-fulfilling prophecy on crime control, we are poised to move from disciplining an incorrigible population to controlling a disposable one.
>
> —Jerome Miller, *Search and Destroy*, 217, 242

As is evident in Miller's and Bright's arguments, there is a tendency among observers of U.S. prison trends to describe the current trajectory of the institution as thoroughly "managerial," an analysis that was first popularized by Nils Christie in his groundbreaking text *Crime Control as Industry*. Christie argues that the prisons have forsaken a transformative rationale with this transition (164–165) but he does not address why the U.S. public should so heartily endorse this change. Although critics like Charles Bright accurately note the gap, even crisis, in prison rhetoric, the fact remains that the public has largely embraced a thoroughly retributive response to crime. At the same time, this public appears to be less sanguine than ever about the prospects of reintegrating inmates into society.

As Bright suggests, we can learn much about how the conditions were set for this change by looking to the history of prison rhetoric in the United States. Charting the transformation from classical and industrial incarceration to modern "therapeutic" corrections, Bright notes that we moved from "the formal equality of legal subjects to the uneven particularities of therapeutic subjects; the criminal ceased to be like any other save in the commission of a crime and became essentially different—a sick, psychotic, or maladapted personality whose crime was merely the summation of a life that was 'other' than normal" (Bright, 292). This change placed the inmate in a dramatically different position, one characterized most strongly by isolation; "The more crime was naturalized as a deeper asocial deviance that had to be labeled and corrected, the more criminals were made to appear as essentially 'other,' different, set apart, and encountered from a distance" (297).

Such radical "distancing" may itself facilitate the social construction of crime by making the inmate-object all the more available for whatever projections the society may wish to impose. The criminal may be presented as the epitome of evil (Rafael Perez's "monsters"), or the criminal may be studied as a diseased individual, but in either case the policy ramifications are becoming increasingly well-defined, making it easier and easier to write off inmates as lost souls. In response, Bright, who is very careful not to elide the agency of prisons or prisoners, concludes that the project of disciplining social deviants has now moved to the streets. In the contemporary moment, prisons amount to little more than repositories for the by-products of the disciplining project taking place at street level. But, as Bright argues, "this is possible precisely because the 'representative' delinquent in our time is the black male, who is constituted as criminally dangerous prior to imprisonment and is put into prison as a confirmatory act, part of a continuing and generalized process of exclusion" (318–19).

For Miller, the increasingly racial specificity of the inmate is a social problem, one that has nonetheless escaped adequate attention because "the labels we choose to attach to those we define as social deviants are less likely to be born of scientific research than constructed to rationalize prevailing ideologies and consider social class" (Miller, 79). Such calls for greater sensitivity to transferential dynamics can easily be oversimplified into blanket accusations of racism. But taking up Miller's invitation to pursue the "host of reasons" for racially disparate treatment, scholars studying the U.S. crime industry will do well to probe more deeply the retribution dynamic that so clearly facilitates the collapse of race and crime, establishing its own self-fulfilling prophecy.

Public opinion research on the death penalty and the drug war demonstrates that deterrence rationales frequently mask deeper retributive motives (Miller, 95). Faced with the paradoxes of various social policies and their outcomes, as well as with a history of racial inequality, many people have charted the same cognitive path as the Thernstroms: Crime appears to be a black propensity, solidified by individual choices. "They" get what they deserve. Ethical paradoxes that infuse social problems are thereby supplanted by simple equivalences: isolated injuries are tied inextricably to isolated punishments. This dynamic helps explain why certain highly strained hoaxes are made credible by the media and police (for example, the Susan Smith infanticide case in which she accused fictitious black perpetrators) and why rap music artists can be credited with events like the Jonesboro School shooting. In such cases, blacks are granted powers they simply do not have, but powers that are crucial for making sense of the retributive drive to assign blame to people outside society's "norms."

This dependence on ethical equivalences was fostered by a key player in the development of current "get tough on crime" policies, the neoconservative James Q. Wilson, whose advice was actively sought by President Ronald Reagan, New York Mayor Ed Koch, and Senator Edward Kennedy.[26] Wilson offered a risk/benefit paradigm for crime fighting that focused solely on increasing the risks for criminal behavior by increasing penalties. As with the Thernstroms' analysis, the point of this program, realized as the Federal Omnibus Crime Bill, was to affect the isolated and remarkably simple choices supposedly made by potential offenders (Miller, 140–141).

Despite the broad political appeal of formulations like that offered by Wilson, paradox and complexity make themselves apparent at every turn. Greater penalties do not constitute effective deterrence, a failure reinforced by a University of California study of the state's "Three Strikes Law"; hence, advocates of such policies, like the Thernstroms, must ultimately ask their readers to take their conclusions "on faith."[27] In a gesture typical of color-blindness arguments, the Thernstroms celebrate the decline in overt expressions of racism, while forgetting that poll taxes and literacy tests were not race-specific practices, although these two key color-blind tools were remarkably effective at promoting racial inequality. Likewise, the Thernstroms ignore evidence that "white attitudes regarding a variety of racial policies are best predicted by their responses to various measures of racial 'resentment,' and that these measures of racial resentment correlate strongly with traditional stereotypes that blacks are lazy, unintelligent and violent" (Klinkner, 37). Such studies suggest that "the conservative views of whites on matters of racial policy stem more from their anti-black views than from any principled commitment to individualism, meritocracy or limited government" (37).

Although these views may well be "anti-black," the resentment revealed by this research deserves greater attention, especially in light of Durkheim's argument that punishment is important because it confirms society's ideas and values generally. Here I would make recourse to William Connolly's notion that, in addition to confirming general rules and values, punishment may constitute a fundamentally vengeful expression, a by-product of the liberal state's normalizing rule and value system itself (Connolly, 34–35). In this context, the Thernstroms' focus on individual black choice and self-fulfilling prophecy acts as a blaming mechanism that enhances "anti-black" views by funneling them together with more diffuse resentments. Although I would not claim that racism is the product of general liberal resentments, an analysis of the ways racial bias and liberal resentment interact seems merited. If, as I have argued, works like *America in Black and White* "succeed" to the extent that they strategically displace methodological questions about transferential dynamics, such texts may also have much to teach readers about the conditions for perpetuating racial injury, and for maintaining the "durational memory" Miller draws from Holocaust studies. Rather than taking steps to work through racial injury, *America in Black and White* ensures that blame will continue to circulate in a finger-pointing exercise that perpetuates racial division. More crucially, such finger-pointing perpetuates the circulation of resentments in a system of moral equivalences, for example, mechanical sentencing policies like the "three strikes" laws.

As Miller argues in response to sociology's debates over method, narrative analysis offers a fundamentally important supplement to the discipline's grounding in data. Sociological knowledge and the interpretation of race dynamics have never been transparently grounded in raw data. This fact poses a problem that transcends the process of data selection, the relatively simple question of which facts are included and which facts excluded. Sociological data must be woven into propositions that construct meaning; this process is thoroughly rhetorical, as well as open to the rationalizations, fabrications, prejudices, and exaggerations identified by Clifford Shaw.[28] Missing this point, as the Thernstroms do, facilitates the continued "acting out" of injuries and resentments. By contrast, narrative analysis may supplement established sociological method, opening windows onto formerly "minor" arenas of social activity and the complicated play of variables, as well as yielding an opportunity for the analyst to self-critically examine the nature of the stories she and other sociologists inevitably tell.

The modern novel is in an important sense built around a similar exploration of how knowledge is produced. Even though some examples are far more explicit in their engagements of sociological and historical material than others, most novels thrive on exploring exactly those sorts of psychological dynamics elaborated by Shaw. Recent work in intellectual history has also focused on the way certain narratives engage traumatic "limit events" or injuries in order to facilitate their working through. With these developments in mind, we will now turn to a novel that explores resentment and choice for the way these correspond to the racialization of crime in the Southwest at a time when demographic changes promise to thoroughly redraw the racial and political map. In the process, I hope to add an important supplement to the previous discussion of race and crime by considering an alternative historical trajectory, one focusing on the experiences of a Chicana/Chicano population that is frequently lost with the normative assumption in many sociological texts that race in America is solely a matter of black and white. The racialization of crime in the United States simply cannot be fully understood without the study of nonblack racial interactions, including those with people of Mexican heritage. In addition, John Rechy's novel, *The Miraculous Day of Amalia Gómez,* contextualizes the ways in which faith in self-fulfilling prophecy has served exploitative ends pursued by the church, the state, and varied institutions responsible for constructing good consumers. In the process, Rechy offers a powerful critique of the kind of faith so central to the success of *America in Black and White,* as well as a guide to the type of narrative intervention proposed by Miller.

A contemporary novel in large part about contemporary Los Angeles, *The Miraculous Day of Amalia Gómez* opens with its principal character desperately seeking a religious sign that might justify the sorrow and resentment she feels: for the death of her oldest son in jail; for her inability to come to terms with the sexuality (particularly gay sexuality) of her children; for her loss of anything resembling the dream of love that has been subverted by every man she has had contact with; and finally for the loss of her best friend and intellectual guide, Rosario, a fellow sweatshop worker who has "disappeared" after joining others in the revenge murder of an immigration official. The complex interpretations undertaken by Amalia Gómez as she pursues her "signs" foreground particular concerns on Rechy's part which include: (1) the search for an expression of sexuality not bound by violence, exploitation, or humiliation; and (2) the development of a critical stance toward consensual ideologies that keep people like Amalia fixated upon the supposedly empowering exercise of severely limited, even degrading, choices.

As the novel unfolds, Amalia moves through a "typical" Saturday, stripping away layer upon layer of her own denial and disgust in order to piece together various recollected narratives, including a narrative of the previous night when she "betrayed" her "husband" by pursuing an encounter with a "romantic" stranger. That so much of this description should end up in quotes says something about how seeming choices, even to commit adultery, are never quite what they might seem for Rechy's principal character; Amalia's "husband" is in fact a live-in lover still married to an estranged wife but called Amalia's husband for the sake of Amalia's children; Amalia's "betrayal" is precipitated when her "husband" walks out on her; and Amalia's "romantic" suitor is in fact a *coyote* who only plays into her romantic dream so he can recreate a rape fantasy of his own that just happens to reproduce Amalia's initiation into sex. While there is much that might be explored regarding the unfolding of this particular narrative, Rechy's decision to present Amalia's seducer as a *coyote* deserves particular attention. *Coyotes* of course act as "guides" for fellow Latinos, extracting often exorbitant fees as they attempt to bring immigrants secretly into the United States. In this novel in particular, *coyotes* do little more than prey upon their own, cheating the desperate, often subjecting them to sexual assault, and sometimes murdering them. Rechy works carefully to create strong analogies among these *coyotes,* the police, and *la migra* (U.S. immigration officials); hence we find that the INS (Immigration and Naturalization Service) officers in the novel abuse their positions to carry out humiliations, sexual assaults, and murders almost identical to those perpetuated by the *coyotes*.[29] In this way, Rechy demonstrates the complex rhetorical context in which ideas about racial criminality are manufactured. Finally, the justice system and the *coyote* become a unified masculine manifestation of what Latinos, and particularly Latinas, must contend with, "illegal" or not. The vision offered by Rechy startlingly anticipates what we have learned about the LAPD in the Rampart scandal; than again, as polls have suggested, the corruption hardly came as news to many Los Angeles minorities.[30]

Initially, the *coyote*'s manipulation of Amalia's desires would appear to reinforce the notion that Amalia is one more Latina frustrated by an appealing yet unattainable *fabula*: in this case, an ideal of what mutually consenting love should be. Yet Rechy challenges this reading by turning to a critical genealogy of desire and its manipulation. In doing so, he reminds readers that migrants move back and forth across the border while pursuing complex, even conflicting goals. Exploring the complex description of the lives represented in Rechy's novel, readers learn that liberal "choices" to follow specific fantasies are conditioned by complex historical pressures, and that for both Amalia and the migrants, a systematic culture of fear is perpetuated from which little if any respite may be found, even within the Church. Exploring this situation, Rechy presents his principal character as continually agitated about the rise of gang activity in her neighborhood, activity which inspires terror as much for the subsequent increase of police action as anything else (Rechy, 71). Much of what keeps Amalia going under such circumstances is the will to keep her family housed, fed, and secure—desires not easily separated from her wish for mutual sexual fulfillment without fear. Part of Rechy's accomplishment is thus revealing the pervasive practices that would sustain a crucial disciplining and ultimately foster relations of dependency as well as resentment regarding these relations.

Engaging the border culture dynamics that affect the working poor like Amalia, Rechy studies the ideology embraced when people come to believe their own political "disappearance" is the best route to achieving their desires and avoiding police labeling. At the same time, Rechy builds into the novel a counterexample: a model of revolt in the form of a co-worker, Rosario. This co-worker is also explicitly presented as Amalia's model of intellectual strength. Throughout, Rosario questions the political treatment of her fellows in an attempt to make them more critically aware, or as she states, to get them to "think" (77). A stalwart defender of unionization and coalition politics, Rosario finally fails to inspire collective action among her co-workers, and instead pursues guerrilla tactics that force her even farther underground than her peers. A critic of the notion that a person can be defined solely by their criminality—she abhors the idea that a group of people should be called "illegals" (76)— Rosario is finally cut off from her peers when she seeks retribution against *la migra*. Although Rosario's actions significantly challenge Amalia and her co-workers to reconsider the nature of the agency they exercise, these effects are limited because ultimately Rosario cannot dialogue with her peers' steadfast faith in consensual paradigms and in Church doctrine. In other words, Rosario does not effectively speak to how the manufacture of cultural dependency manipulates desire itself, or to the process by which choices are "shaped," and resentment secured. Rosario can decry the politically suspect telenovelas that captivate her peers, but she does not weave alternative stories to engage their imaginations and critical facilities.

Rechy thus offers a lesson in Rosario's failure, a failure that leads readers into questions about the role of Church doctrine and religious martyrdom in particular: the source for many of the narratives that capture the workers' attentions. This doctrine is interestingly reprocessed in the novel, becoming the model for a TV game show—"Queen for a Day"— that rewards contestants who can prove that they have suffered the most (7). The key to this show, and others like it in the novel, is the way it reproduces a particular consensual paradigm. Viewers obsessively participate in the shows, retelling them to fill almost every moment of their leisure time. In turn, the content of the shows reinforces the obsession, particularly by conveying the notion that salvation—a term which slides between material and spiritual manifestations—may be gained by enduring, actually embracing, the apparent absence of any choice, any alternative in one's life. What is modeled, then, is a choice for no choice which will be rewarded in some indefinite future. One's identity as martyr is secured by performing the experience of an enduring and unhealable injury locked in the past; injury in this sense falls very much within that paradigm described by Wendy Brown as she demarcates the resentment that shapes contemporary identity formation. Rechy explores this problematic by offering his own specific history of political identity formation, and the possibility of substituting a logic of moral equivalences with a gift economy reimagined through the language of divine miracles.

Rechy's novel rethinks racial injury by exploring the ideology of consent and the manipulation of definitions of criminality, factors central to the manufacture of minority social dependency and to the institutional reproduction of social relations at the border.[31] In this and numerous other Chicana/Chicano border narratives, such critique situates the social marginalization that maintains the working poor teetering on the edge of disaster even while they place a premium on choosing the American dream, which is, again, choosing to believe that, as a member of the working poor, one has something to celebrate as choice.[32] The Thernstroms' incorporation of Brent Staples's story performs a similar homage to choice. By singling out this dynamic in the novel, Rechy contextualizes: (1) why Chicanas like Amalia might seek sporadic housecleaning jobs over more regular work (thereby establishing a mobile and malleable workforce)—she feels enfranchised by selecting "her" homes; (2) why Amalia is obsessed with the *semanal* "*Camino al Sueño*" ("Road to the Dream"), the soap opera that titillates its viewers with exactly the romantic notion of consent where none exists; and (3) why Amalia should eagerly embrace, at the end of the novel, her 15 minutes of fame under blinding, possibly miracle-inspiring TV lights. Her fame has been won by virtue of being a gunman's victim in an exclusive mall, a mall that would have done anything possible a few moments earlier to make the out-of-place cleaning woman "disappear" (201–203).

Although this final miracle echoes the "Queen for a Day" show Amalia worships, it also synthesizes Rechy's statements about consensual paradigms and resentment. Throughout the novel, but especially in its sexual dynamics and careful study of consensual ideologies, a sometimes subtle, sometimes crude battleground is being reworked. Taking advantage of a novelist's ability to weave certain patterns out of the representation of lived experience, Rechy demonstrates how cultural discourses and liberal ideology validate certain relations to the concept of choice, albeit relations maintained under strict scrutiny. Always waiting for those who overreact to this scrutiny, enforcement, often "legal," mobilizes quickly to contain and to legitimate the self-same actions in the eyes of the mainstream society: The assumption of Rodney King's "control" over his own beating is a reminder of this containment. This is precisely why it has been so important for authors like the Thernstroms to reproduce images and narratives about racial propensities toward criminality and why it has been so important to "forget" the role of the "migratory machine" that has been built precisely to manipulate the desires of "disposable" Latino labor in the borderlands.[33] Asserting criminal stereotypes is part of a larger process by which a culture of fear and the ideology of "choice" work together to maintain a fundamental cultural and social dependency for targeted communities. The resentment that goes along with this internalization of liberal ideology reinforces tendencies toward political disenfranchisement, and likewise accounts for much of the cloud that hangs over the end of the novel. As much as Amalia seems to take control of her life in her final gestures, her commitment to a liberal form of agency is only slightly affected by her revised relationship to her family, and by her partial awareness of the ongoing "gun to her head" posed by the police, the gangs, and the *coyotes* around her (147).

Part of Rechy's accomplishment is having foregrounded an epistemological conflict by building his examination of border culture around his central character's desire to discover and then to appropriately read signs: a process that is conveyed as highly performative. Readers will recall that throughout the novel Amalia tries to make sense of what she would like to consider miraculous visitations—at the novel's opening, a cross that may be a beneficent sign, or a filmy cloud, or smoke, or even an airplane's sky writing (3); at its close, a burst of light which may be the "miraculous mother," or yet another television camera capturing Amalia's victimization (206). What Rechy crafts with this ongoing conflict is a bitingly ironic suggestion that the doctrine of liberal choice necessarily subverts agency. In turn, Amalia endlessly flips between imagining herself as a thoroughly passive benefactor of an omnipotent will, and imagining herself as the autonomous author of her own redemption as she properly reacts to given signs. In this context, the Thernstroms' marketing of self-fulfilling prophecy is anything but an innocent, hopeful project.

In contrast to *America in Black and White*, *The Miraculous Day of Amalia Gómez* makes its readers keenly aware of the racial injury perpetuated by the criminal justice system itself. Jerome Miller underscores this point as he examines the unintended consequences of the "war on drugs", consequences that have effectively militarized barrios like those described in the novel. But perhaps most telling is Rechy's exploration of social responsibility. Ultimately, Rechy's novel demonstrates that such responsibility may be severely limited by a world view premised on liberal choice and on fundamentally individual exchanges that are "morally correct" to the extent that they adhere to a logic of equivalence. As Amalia initially tries to convince herself, her responsibilities (as well as her sympathies and regrets) should, in this world view, only extend as far as her range of essentially reactive choices (13). Hence, she repeatedly tells herself that she cannot be blamed for opportunities she has not had. The "miracle" at the novel's close may in fact reside in the suggestion that Amalia has found a way to imagine divine and human interaction that is open to paradox. The new connections that Amalia imagines to those around her, especially to her family, seem in the final pages of the novel to side-step the damaging effects of liberal choice, effects that severely limited the her notions of social responsibility. Spending most of the novel in anticipation of a divine gift, Amalia finally becomes something of an altruistic agent in her own right, a transition that signals an all-important moderation of fear and a willingness to accept risk. By contrast, this generosity of spirit is markedly absent from a criminal justice system that rejects rehabilitation, thereby consigning more and more people to "illegal persons" status in prisons justified by their managerial efficiency. As I will explore in the next chapter, this struggle over risk and altruism has also greatly affected arguments about race and genetics, and speaks directly to the disposability of racialized prisoners.

CHAPTER SIX

GENETIC LIABILITIES
AND THE PARADOX
OF ALTRUISM

The rhetorical view of science does not deny "the brute facts of nature"; it merely affirms that these "facts," whatever they are, are not
science itself, knowledge itself. Scientific knowledge consists of the
current answers to three questions, answers that are the product of
professional conversation: What range of "brute facts" is worth investigating? How is this range to be investigated? What do the results of these investigations mean? Whatever they are, the "brute
facts" themselves mean nothing; only statements have meaning,
and of the truth of statements we must be persuaded. These
processes, by which problems are chosen and results interpreted,
are essentially rhetorical: only through persuasion are importance
and meaning established.

—Alan Gross, *The Rhetoric of Science*, 4

Since 1969 and the publication of Arthur Jensen's "How Much Can We
Boost IQ and Scholastic Achievement," no argument for a causal link between genes and racially defined IQ disparities has received more attention than Richard Herrnstein and Charles Murray's *The Bell Curve: Intelligence and Class Structure in American Life*. Given that Herrnstein and
Murray's book draws heavily on long-standing psychometric work now
significantly challenged by developments in cognitive science and neuroscience, the remarkable success of *The Bell Curve*, as judged by its best-
seller status, may well say a great deal about the value of savvy marketing and about the book's particular social and historical context.[1] How-

ever, *The Bell Curve* is also notable for the accessible way its authors marshal and present their scientific evidence. It is this well-crafted, scientific framework (if not actual scientific authorization through peer review) that allows the authors to pursue a neoconservative agenda—an agenda to which they have been long committed—and still claim a pose of objectivity and neutrality, thereby increasing their rhetorical credit with a broad audience.[2]

In an era marked by substantial cutbacks to social programs, *The Bell Curve* literally rewrites the nature of social responsibility by tying poverty and crime to immutable, racially distinct genetic codes. Claiming to solve what Stephen Jay Gould has termed the "egalitarian paradox" (Gould, 368), *The Bell Curve*'s authors claim that an affluent society with equal opportunity will *naturally* develop a caste or class system because some members, and notably African Americans as a group, will simply never be fit to function at an elite, or even average level of conduct, no matter how much training or assistance they receive (Herrnstein and Murray, 527–552).

Certainly some of the American public's fascination with *The Bell Curve* stems from its controversial, if implicit, recasting of eugenics. Although Herrnstein and Murray do not entertain questions of state-mandated limits to reproduction—the kind that led to the 1927 *Buck v. Bell* Supreme Court sanctioned sterilization of "feeble" people during the heyday of eugenics—their understanding of society's genetic liabilities leads them to describe two potential outcomes for our current situation: The first is the development of a "custodial state" which would essentially formalize a state of affairs already in existence:

> By custodial state we have in mind a high-tech and more lavish version of the Indian reservation for some substantial minority of the nation's population, while the rest of America tries to go about its business. . . . Extrapolating from current trends, we project that the policies of custodialism will not only be tolerated but actively supported by a consensus of the cognitive elite. . . . The main difference between the position of the cognitive elite that we portray here and the one that exists today is to some extent nothing more than a distinction between tacit and explicit. (Herrnstein and Murray, 526)

The second, more "humane" option would entail "finding a place" for all genetically deficient members of society. Such "place finding" would acknowledge the genetically deficient person's limitations and ameliorate resentments and frustrations for all parties by setting expectations according to the biological facts. In this latter scenario, which I would dub a "kinder, gentler eugenics," Herrnstein and Murray's goal would be to weave our least talented into a supportive network by bonding them to local, "neighborhood" social settings.[3]

In essence, this is advice, directed at poor, low-scoring African Americans, to embrace a genetic life sentence of remedial functionality. Above all else, Herrnstein and Murray are adamant that such a social transition should take place divorced from government programs and spending (540).[4] Judging by the interpretations offered in *The Bell Curve*, which devotes a significant portion of its argument and policy recommendations to racial matters, African Americans as a group would seem to have a choice between newly fashioned internment camps or genetic house arrest in the form of unquestioned social immobility. According to Herrnstein and Murray, the 15-point differential between white and black IQ scores makes these options inevitable (276–280). Even here, there has been controversy regarding the authors' assessment of the differential, which appears in various studies to be shrinking.[5] In an era when prison rehabilitation programs have been jettisoned, what could be more consistent than genetic explanations for criminal behavior that, like *The Bell Curve*'s conclusions generally, make African Americans as a group "disposable"?[6] Yet how telling for this genetically based argument as a whole that the possible policy outcomes posed by the authors parallel the language of incarceration. As sociologist Troy Duster has suggested, genetic explanations can work in concert with understandings of social problems like criminality, thereby dehistoricizing these problems and "absolving" policy- and lawmakers of responsibility for the disparate, politically loaded impacts their work produces.[7]

Of course, *The Bell Curve* is just one moment in an historically rich discourse on race and genetics in the United States.[8] As noted, Harvard psychologist Arthur Jensen also captured the limelight by arguing that educational efforts to boost low black achievement scores constituted wasted energy and that schools across the country needed to learn to "accommodate larger numbers of children who have limited aptitudes for traditional academic achievement."[9] Jensen not only gained attention from the national press, including *Newsweek* and *U.S. News and World Report*; these media vehicles also warned readers to take Jensen's findings seriously as evidence of genetic differences.[10]

The tendency to approach black crime in particular from a biological basis accelerated during the 1990s, leading to controversies over a National Institute of Health conference devoted to "genetic factors in crime," and over the Department of Health and Human Services' Youth Violence Initiative, "an unprecedented nationwide effort to identify youths at risk of committing violence and finding ways to prevent it."[11] The latter $400 million program fell under pointed scrutiny when a high-ranking federal health official associated with the initiative made a speech likening "violence by inner-city youth to the behavior of male monkeys in the jungle."[12] Such embarrassments aside, "responsibility for crime control remains located in agencies dealing with matters of public health: the Department of Health and Human Services and the Centers for Disease Control."[13] We therefore find ourselves at an important juncture in which sociological approaches to crime are being displaced so that government institutions may act increasingly on "genetic predispositions" as they address the presumed crisis, both in crime and poverty. This situation has significant consequences for the engagement of these social problems; as Dorothy Nelkin and M. Susan Lindee note,

> Applied to crime control, the public health model suggests that, as in the case of epidemics, individual rights must be suspended to preserve public order. Reinforced by popular belief in the deterministic powers of the gene, genetic information could open opportunities for social control of unprecedented power as predispositions are employed to predict and avoid potential risk. (Nelkin and Lindee, 159)

One problem with acting on such predispositions is that they are often malleable and subject to complex interactions that may facilitate or stunt their expression as a trait or a disease, especially when we are considering complex behavioral patterns. Even in more apparently simple scenarios, genetic risk alone rarely determines outcomes. For example, a person might be predisposed to heart disease, yet significantly affect the likelihood of experiencing serious illness by controlling environmental factors such as diet, stress, and exercise.

> Terms such as "predisposed" or "at risk" are understood by scientists to mean that the individual is vulnerable to a disease that may or *may not* be expressed in the future. In the quest to identify genetic predispositions, however, the statistically-driven concept of correlation is often reduced to "cause." (Nelkin and Lindee, 165–166)

The confusion of cause and statistical correlation has been enhanced by media reporting and popular science.[14] In the case of reading criminal predispositions, this confusion plays into a long history wherein racial profiling policies have disproportionately drawn more African Americans into the criminal justice system; genetic testing runs the risk of becoming a new technological extension of these profiling practices.

As Nelkin and Lindee demonstrate in *The DNA Mystique,* some scientists have also contributed significantly to the confusion I have described, a complicity tied to the scientists' efforts to gain support for their projects. As Alan G. Gross argues in my epigraph, science has its own rhetoric and, inasmuch as the scientific endeavor depends on state support, this rhetoric is intrinsically bound to accommodating expectations that may greatly influence the practice of scientific objectivity. In the current moment, much evidence suggests that genetic predispositions sell well when they appear to define causes, and in this manner, some scientists themselves have been guilty of dramatically enhancing the "DNA mystique."

Consider, for instance, the selling of the Human Genome Project, a $3 billion, 15-year undertaking funded by the National Institutes of Health and the U.S. Department of Energy. This project, which is being duplicated in Great Britain, Japan, Russia, and Europe, hopes to "locate and determine the exact order of the base pairs in the estimated 100,000 human genes, as well as in many of the sections of DNA with no known function."[15] This mapping has already led to breakthroughs in terms of the identification of disorders caused by single genes (a fairly rare etiology), and is also defining new ways of studying predispositions as scientists are tracing particular groups of genes to the potential development of cystic fibrosis, one form of Alzheimer's disease, and Huntington's disease, among others.[16] The research is also deepening our understanding of predispositions for the development of various forms of cancer, juvenile diabetes, and emphysema.[17] But again, this list reflects the definition of predispositions based on statistical correlations, not on assigned causes. At issue is the element of risk in a complex field of interaction, at a molecular level within a person, as well as between a person and his or her environment; all of these factors should mitigate the sense that genes define fate.

Yet when some scientists characterize the Human Genome Project, they elide or confound this distinction; such scientists have used metaphors that create and/or foster a public misreading of the Human Genome Project, calling the genome "a Delphic oracle," "a time machine," "a trip into the future," and "a medical crystal ball."[18] The explicit message being conveyed by some of the project's champions is that people constitute readouts of their genes, an erroneous interpretation promoted when scientists like Nobel laureate James Watson announced that "our fate is in our genes."[19] In these ways, scientists have contributed to a mystification of genes that transform them into texts, which magically reveal one's true identity and promise to unlock the secrets of life itself.

Grounding this mysticism, one finds an enormous, highly technical map of deoxyribonucleic acid (DNA). The predictive quality erroneously assigned to the genome project is therefore legitimated by the "objective" processes that allow scientists and the public alike to think of these rules as "apolitical." Yet like the metaphors used to describe the genome, maps in any form convey implicit values. The Human Genome Project, posed as a revolutionary mapping, suggests a kind of access to information that is itself misleading. This fact has led more cautious molecular biologists to emphasize that, to the extent they are like words, genes must be contextualized to be understood.[20] As products of evolutionary history, genes are highly complex, frequently ambiguous, and open to varieties of analysis and interpretation.[21]

Scientists, including Watson, have been quick to underscore the great promise of bioengineering advances like the Human Genome Project, but highly reticent to discuss in any detailed way the institutional impacts of the research.[22] Such questions include: What will the burgeoning gene therapy industry look like? What mix of public and private interests will govern the industry's growth? And who will have access? Genetic testing is becoming increasingly available to employers, insurance companies and the criminal justice system, all of whom can justify mandatory testing in ways not regulated by the 1992 Americans with Disabilities Act. What will protect recipients of questionable test results from a life sentence of legal discrimination based upon assigned predispositions? Who will define acceptable and unacceptable levels of risk based on genetic propensities?

In a larger, political frame of reference, we might well ask how the overestimation of the genome's predictive abilities may feed into neoconservative trends that would isolate the responsibility for social problems in the communities which bear their brunt. We have already seen, for instance, how this approach has been used by Stephen and Abigail Thernstrom to reread black crime as solely the product of black choices. In the context of the new eugenics, will those experiencing "social problems" find even their contingent measure of individual choice compromised as these "problem" people become singularly bound to a natural, immutable order permeating every cell in their body?

The experience of poverty and crime may seem distinct from genetically linked illnesses like Huntington's disease and cystic fibrosis. But champions of the Human Genome Project have set their sights beyond such illnesses and are now turning to the genetic codes for "higher human functions" including intelligence.[23] The transition is crucial because such higher function research can appear to explain away the sociological factors in phenomena like crime and poverty as well as simultaneously to absolve the government of responsibility for pursuing programs fostering equal opportunity.

What has been fundamentally unclear in many presentations of this higher function research is that the movement to these functions as an object of study is remarkably plagued by statistical problems of correlation, problems that make the findings significantly more ambiguous, if not irretrievably so. One way to think of the problem is to imagine a bell curve that statistically maps the incidence of particular traits in a cross-section of the population. A trait existing as an easily discernable bump on the periphery of the bell curve appears to constitute a distinct phenomenon, for instance the tendency within a family to give birth to twins. If we find a similarly unique aspect in the genetic code of women whose families tend to bear twins, we may use this overlap to describe a correlation, a statistical probability that may or may not be caused by the gene(s) in question. If the correlation is perfect (and such cases are rare), we might define the gene as a causal agent. Yet even in cases in which correlation is exact, caution and supplemental knowledge remain critically important. My increasing age may appear to correlate perfectly with the growing pace of student enrollment at my university, but the two are clearly not linked in a causal way.

Returning to the bell curve model, one can appreciate how the problems attending correlation increase as we try to decipher genetic links to phenomena—especially to complex behaviors—that tend not to fall on the periphery of the bell curve in a distinct lump, but rather as a minor deviation in its fuller, middle portion. With the loss of truly distinct, anomalous sets of identifiable overlapping traits and genes, scientists move into an ambiguous territory that demands supplemental evidence because the statistics in themselves are simply too cloudy. It is in this terrain that the most controversial battles over race and genetic have taken place. Consider, for instance, Herrnstein and Murray's use of psychometric data: How does one argue that IQ results indicate a relatively stable set of genetic differences when IQ scores have increased by 15 points fairly consistently around the globe in just the last 100 years? But perhaps the most hard-hitting criticism has come from prominent psychology and education scholars who marvel at the way in which *The Bell Curve*'s authors essentially ignore dramatic developments in cognitive science and neuroscience, developments that demonstrate the efficacy of cognitive function interventions from pregnancy through adulthood.[24] In addition, cognitive science has raised important questions about the adequacy of reducing intelligence to a single measure, suggesting instead that it is more appropriate to recognize multiple forms of intelligence, including workplace and social abilities that do not correlate with IQ test results.[25]

The strength of these criticisms overall suggests that we may now shift the nature of our engagement with *The Bell Curve* in order to focus less on how the text fails and more on how its failure presents opportunities for rethinking genetics, biological research, and scientific method as these engage issues of racial injury. With this sort of intervention in mind, I turn now to Stephen Jay Gould's *The Mismeasure of Man*, a work notable for the way it situates the *Bell Curve* debate in the context of evolutionary biology, and in a particularly rich vision of science as a social enterprise.

~

The Bell Curve by Richard J. Herrnstein and Charles Murray provides a superb and unusual opportunity for insight into the meaning of experiment as a method in science. Reduction of confusing variables is the primary desideratum in all experiments. We bring all the buzzing and blooming confusion of the external world into our laboratories and, holding all else constant in our artificial simplicity, try to vary one potential factor at a time. Often, however, we cannot use such an experimental method, particularly for most social phenomena when importation into the laboratory destroys the subject of our investigation.
—Stephen Jay Gould, *The Mismeasure of Man*, 367

As Gould suggests, *The Bell Curve* offers an important example of how the methods of science may project the scientist's desires onto the object of study, thereby transforming that object. Although the particular concern with the role of transformative reduction (especially correlation rewritten as cause) is a consistent theme in *The Mismeasure of Man*, Gould is also fascinated with the interplay of self-fulfilling prophecy and biological determinism. This interest is apparent as Gould considers the appeal of over-reading correlation in scientific work. Here, he argues that,

The spirit of Plato dies hard. We have been unable to escape the philosophical tradition that what we can see and measure in the world is merely the superficial and imperfect representation of an underlying reality. Much of the fascination of statistics lies embedded in our gut feeling—and never trust a gut feeling—that abstract measures summarizing large tables of data must express something more real and fundamental than the data themselves. (Gould, 269)

The focus on this "Platonic" mistake, in fact, frames Gould's study, which begins by linking "the justification for ranking groups by inborn worth" with two centuries of scientific claims (52). These claims have become the new means for arguing that "social and economic roles accurately reflect the innate construction of people" (52). For Plato, this worth was a matter of each individual's construction in terms of metals (hence the expression, a person's "mettle"); now, according to proponents of biodeterminism, it is a matter of genomes. Although Gould suggests that The Bell Curve's reception has been conditioned in fundamental ways by neoconservative politics, he is ultimately more interested in exploring how the methods of science lend themselves to the biodeterminist project that stretches back to Plato.

The revised version of The Mismeasure of Man offers a historically deep, detailed refutation of The Bell Curve's argument that racial differences on IQ tests are the results of immutable genetic factors (367–390). To accept Herrnstein and Murray's argument, readers must agree that: (1) intelligence is depictable as a single number capable of ranking people in linear order; (2) these numbers are genetically based; and (3) these numbers are essentially immutable (368). Presenting a detailed study of Spearman's "g" (the formulation that Herrnstein and Murray draw upon to justify assigning a numerical value to intelligence) and the factor analysis used to achieve it, Gould demonstrates that the value identified by Herrnstein and Murray is at best a reductive abstraction among several equally viable options. Gould also reveals that this option is tied to genetics by weak correlations that are misrepresented in the body of The Bell Curve (375–376). Adding to these problems of misrepresentation, Gould charges Herrnstein and Murray with the omission of such crucial counterevidence as

impressive IQ gains for poor black children adopted into affluent and intellectual homes; average IQ increases in some nations since WWII equal to the entire 15-point difference now separating blacks and whites in America; failure to find any cognitive differences between two cohorts of children born out of wedlock to German women and raised in Germany as Germans, but fathered by black and white American soldiers. (Gould, 370)

As powerful as this critique is, it does not constitute a reversal of *The Bell Curve*'s argument despite the advertisement of Gould's book as a "refutation." Gould carefully avoids reinforcing the traditional dichotomy between nature and nurture being worked by Herrnstein and Murray as they attack the sociological bases for government aid programs. Instead, Gould attempts to transform the terms of the race and genes debate by rethinking this dichotomy and approaching the interplay of genes and environment as a problem of complex, nonadditive mediation. Behaviors and intelligence in this framework simply cannot be reduced to popular formulations that assess traits as 80 percent genetics, 20 percent nurture, or 70 percent genetics, 30 percent nurture.

Gould's insistence on the need to acknowledge a more complicated mediation may be most directly addressed to *The Bell Curve*, but is wholly consistent with Gould's larger critique of scientific method, and what I would designate his "transferential" intervention. In a chapter devoted to "three centuries' perspectives on racism," he carries this critique to science's rhetorical legitimation of its findings in the acquisition of empirical data. Here Gould notes that:

> An old tradition in science proclaims that changes in theory must be driven by observation. Since most scientists believe this simplistic formula, they assume that their own shifts in interpretation only record their better understanding of newly discovered facts. Scientists therefore tend to be unaware of their own mental impositions upon the world's messy and ambiguous factuality. . . . When scientists adopt the myth that theories arise solely from observation, and do not scrutinize the personal and social influences emerging from their own psyches, they not only miss the causes of their changed opinions, but may also fail to comprehend the deep and pervasive mental shift encoded by their own new theory. (Gould, 406)

This passage certainly does not constitute a condemnation of the scientific project, but rather presents a call for the methodological self-critique, a process that would recognize and engage the role of desire.[26]

Inasmuch as Gould's focus is on biodeterminism specifically, and social Darwinism generally, he explains how scientific reduction has justified social inequalities while seriously misreading biology and the meaning of evolutionary diversity:

> Biology is not the enemy of human flexibility, but the source and potentiator (while genetic determinism represents a false theory of biology). Darwinism is not a statement about fixed differences, but the central theory for a discipline—evolutionary biology—that has discovered the sources for human unity in minimal genetic distances among our races and in the geological yesterday of our common origin. (Gould, 390)

One of the great ironies of efforts like *The Bell Curve* is that recent genetic study has demonstrated that our genetic makeup is remarkably consistent across races, with variation within groups far outstripping variations among groups (Gould, 353). At the same time, Gould does not dismiss the limits placed by genetic codes on people's traits and behaviors. What distinguishes Gould's approach from that of many sociobiologists and authors like Herrnstein and Murray is his recognition of a complex level of mediation between genetically inscribed codes and the expression of behaviors.[27] The deep structure rules provided by genes constitute only part of a never-ending puzzle that must accommodate environmental factors as well. In this vein, and consistent with his interpretation of Darwin, Gould emphasizes the critical role of potential and adjustability in evolutionary theory.

> Flexibility is the hallmark of human evolution. If humans evolved, as I believe, by neoteny . . . then we are, in a more than metaphorical sense, permanent children. (In neoteny, rates of development slow down and juvenile stages of ancestors become the adult features of descendants.) Many central features of our anatomy link us with the fetal and juvenile stages of primates: small face, vaulted cranium and large brain in relation to body size, unrotated big toe, foramen magnum under the

skull for correct orientation of the head in upright posture, primary distribution of hair on head, armpits and pubic areas. . . . We retain not only the anatomical stamp of childhood, but its mental flexibility as well. The idea that natural selection would have worked for flexibility in human evolution is not an ad hoc notion born in hope, but an implication of neoteny as a fundamental process in our evolution. Humans are learning animals. (Gould, 363)

Expanding on an evolutionary theory of behavior, this passage focuses on deep biological structures not to pose a narrow utilitarian role for a particular trait, but rather to support the notion that biology has worked to encourage mediating processes between nature and nurture, processes that are simply unaccounted for in works like *The Bell Curve*.

Gould's focus on the distinctiveness of human learning processes also helps contextualize another important tendency in his work: the proclivity to rethink the history of science not as a determined linear progress toward Truth, but rather as a narrative that is subject to repetitions as well as changes and advances. On one level, the structure of *The Mismeasure of Man* itself reveals this sensitivity to science's repetitions. Although the chapters focus on a range of different eras and scientists, the readings offered underscore the periodic repetition of certain basic ideas about genetics, intelligence, and race—ideas that "confirm" the immutable biological inferiority of lower classes and minority "out groups." Gould intervenes not only to challenge biodeterminism, but also to rethink the production of scientific knowledge: to see the production of such knowledge as a process with certain consistent problems rather than as a linear progress transcending them. Of these problems, one seems particularly fundamental: the potential for scientists to legitimate, through their labors, *a priori* ideas and desires. Even the basic drive to reduction associated by Gould with experimentation itself constitutes an *a priori* assumption on the scientist's part regarding the viability of excluding "confusing" factors and still producing results that will accurately reflect how entities, and especially people, interact outside the lab.

Gould does not present himself as a social scientist, but he does suggest some intriguing ideas about those social contexts that appear to foster biodeterminist research. In particular, two aspects of these contexts tend to resurface in Gould's analysis. In the first, Gould correlates the popularity of the biodeterminist research with the "destruction of social generosity" (28). In the second, Gould associates the basic category mistake of treating African Americans as a distinctive genealogical unit with a social tendency to blame victims for the injuries they have suffered (397–398). Although Gould does not analyze these tendencies, or their possible interaction, at significant length, it may be that their role in redefining racial injury is intrinsically related to the biodeterminist project.

Sociologists have explored blaming responses by conducting a variety of studies that confront bystanders with apparently innocent victims.[28] These studies have demonstrated that bystanders lacking information about an injury will tend to blame the victim because of an assumption that such victims are likely to be responsible for whatever has befallen them.[29] Along similar lines, sociologists have crafted a "just world theory," a hypothesis that is consistent with William Connolly's arguments regarding the tendency for people to construct and/or reproduce equivalences when tackling moral problems like those faced by a bystander who must decide how to react to an apparently innocent victim.[30] Confronted by an apparent moral paradox, an injury without assignable fault, bystanders in these studies tend to rely on assumed equivalent relationships: That person got hurt because he or she did something wrong—people simply do not get hurt for no reason.[31] On one level, such responses reassure the bystander by imaginatively reducing the risk of an accident to the predictable outcome of a morally calculated choice.

Social theorists have also used this moral equivalences theory as a way of understanding the expression of altruism.[32] Although Altruism as a term was first used by the French scholar Comte, who also coined the term "sociology," the concept has at best constituted a relatively minor concern in the development of the human sciences.[33] In one of the few interdisciplinary collections devoted fully to exploring altruistic behavior, Lauren Wispé argues that this relative inattention is due in good measure to the basic rules governing social interaction, at least as these ideas are maintained in the human sciences. Here the crucial point is the presumed linkage of self-interest and the equivalent exchange economics, a linkage frequently, if problematically, associated with Adam Smith's theories.[34] Altruism in this context simply does not fit. Certainly efforts have been made to read altruism as displaced, exchange-oriented self-interest (acts undertaken for the good of *one's* family, clan or even species), but these attempts have not been especially satisfying, in large part because they appear highly reductive in their utilitarianism.[35] The act of generosity—untied from a return benefit—presents a paradox to economically oriented theories within the social sciences, a paradox that, like the innocent victim scenario, threatens the presumption of a world governed by moral equivalences.

Extending Gould's argument for human flexibility, one may thus read *The Mismeasure of Man* as an appeal to a new valuation of self-critical adaptability, and as a check on unfortunate projects that erroneously use science to confirm the moral logic of self-interested equivalences. At the core of this intervention lies a challenge to notions regarding what IQ tests and similar measurements reflect.

> What is intelligence, if not the ability to face problems in an unprogrammed (or, as we often say, creative) manner? If intelligence sets us apart among organisms, then I think it probable that natural selection acted to maximize the flexibility of our behavior. What would be more adaptive for a learning and thinking animal: genes selected for aggression, spite and xenophobia; or a selection for learning rules that can generate aggression in appropriate circumstances and peacefulness in others? (Gould, 361)

Rethinking Darwin's work in response to the "social Darwinist" neoconservative attack on governmental social programs, Gould finds in evolutionary biology evidence lending support to the notion that people are *innately* structured to accommodate such paradoxes as altruism and victimization. If this is the case, then people are innately capable of transcending a model of strict moral equivalences; no biological foundation exists for the *quid pro quo* logic and therefore moral paradox is not a "natural" enemy. Of course, the logic of moral equivalences thrives by appearing to avoid paradox as well as reduce risk, and to the extent that scientists contribute to the collapse of statistical correlation and causality, they too foster a discourse of moral equivalences. In the same vein, *The Bell Curve*'s genetically justified caste system tells us precisely that everyone in an unequal society gets exactly what they deserve.

Whereas the authors of *The Bell Curve* are less persuasive because their claimed "objectivity" is compromised by a fairly clear political agenda, the champions of the Human Genome Project may be far more effective in the long run in terms of reinforcing the public's ideas about the causal power of genes. Although these scientists' promises and predictions are even more bold than those that grace the pages of *The Bell Curve*, their scope—all of human behavior—is so varied that it seemingly transcends specific political interests. However, in judging the great shift toward genetic overvaluation, I argue that we would do well to recall Gould's point regarding the correlation of political conservatism and biodeterminism. Certainly this is a concern shared by Henry Louis Gates, Jr., as he examines *The Bell Curve* debate and asks why the text should appear at this particular historical moment when we are wrestling with growing indications of racial segregation and with attacks on social programs.[36]

Theorists studying altruism have been especially concerned with the role of resentment because it is held that altruistic acts may be received as socially exclusive/excluding interactions by those who witness but do not receive benefits from the acts. In this context, altruism is posed as a potentially dangerous activity because of the way it may be perceived to stigmatize excluded third parties;[37] this, presumably, would be the same sort of resentment felt by lower-class white males as they react to affirmative action policies and the like. Although studies of altruism have not critiqued the network of moral equivalences underlying the just world logic (if anything, they tend to reinforce the paradigm by finding ways to justify social aid programs within the logic), they have offered an important appraisal of social mechanisms that manage and effectively contain the resentments that may arise from acts of social exclusion, for instance the creation of "private" families.[38]

Focusing on a variety of rituals and institutional practices, such theorists demonstrate how seemingly exclusive relationships are mediated to defuse potentially resentful responses.[39] For example, they examine ways in which rituals like dating, courtship, and marriage ceremonies reincorporate witnesses and bystanders. In turn, they present proposals for better mediating the resentments attending current governmental social programs.[40] Whereas most of these mediating options are presented as "prophylactic measures" that do not challenge "just world" assumptions,[41] others suggest a more visionary rethinking of social responsibility. Of these, one of the more theoretically promising takes up "bacchanalia, festivals and games"; as Wispé argues, "The function of these carnivals lies in the fact that they tend to democratize and deemphasize the exclusiveness otherwise maintained by certain individuals. In certain instances they provide open access to otherwise privatized interaction, thus, in effect, trivializing them" (323).

Whether such excluding relations are trivialized in carnival processes is a point of some debate; such processes may play with private relations to significantly revise and even strengthen them.[42] However, the democratizing impulse located here certainly reaches beyond the "prophylactic." Carnival, as conveyed in this passage, has at least the potential for transforming the rules of social responsibility, and this is the case to the extent that carnival practices promulgate social adaptability and an embrace of risk.

A literary historian working under highly restrictive political circumstances (early twentieth-century Russia), M. M. Bakhtin developed a highly influential theory regarding the democratizing possibilities of carnival and argued that, to the degree they remain viable in the modern context, these possibilities may live on in narrative experimentation, and in certain forms of novelistic discourse in particular.[43] With Bakhtin's argument in mind, it is tempting to reconsider Gould's book as a scientific history informed in muted but nonetheless important ways by narrative play, play that asks us to read the book's author as autobiographer, scientist, historian, psychologist, political scientist, and storyteller. According to Bakhtin, novelistic discourse may provide a cannibalistic medium in which authors combine various discourses (for instance, legal, medical, scientific, religious) in order to develop a critical sense of how we produce knowledge. This production is, for Bakhtin, a complicated, conflictual, flexible dialogue that is often taken for granted by language users who fall under the illusion that linguistic meaning is somehow transparent, a matter of "common sense."[44] In something akin to the novelistic discourse described by Bakhtin, Gould presents a variety of interacting discourses in his prose (biology, history, sociology, philosophy) in order to reassert the risk of language, whether this language takes the form of words, statistics, or genes.

In the realm of science fiction, numerous examples of carnivalesque play correlate in interesting ways with Gould's rethinking of racial injury as it is conditioned by biodeterminism. For instance, the 1992 film *Alien 3* presents its viewers with a biodeterminist dilemma in which a racialized community of criminals find their punishment enhanced—they are condemned to a hellish prison planet—because of violent predispositions locked in their XYY genetic codes. The "alien," both woman and monster, arrives in this all-male setting to disrupt in a grotesque carnival the discipline of the prison community as well as this community's embrace of its own genetic sentence. (The inmates have chosen to stay on the planet despite the official closing of the prison, in part because they view themselves as biologically fated to this existence.) Ultimately the central figures in this prison drama die while taking altruistic risks, made in defiance of the prison system and for the good of a larger population that would be subject to that system's terrorist use of the monster. For the prisoners in particular, such risk-taking entails an overcoming of significant resentments that have been buried within the religiously structured discipline they have adopted. Ultimately, the prisoners shift from a biologically and religiously mandated fate to a struggle for survival that acknowledges and contests power dynamics in an environment defined by risk.

The 1982 cult classic *Blade Runner* works a similar ground by retelling the Frankenstein story in a futuristic bioengineering setting. Here a band of conspicuously white escaped slaves return to a racially diverse Los Angeles in order to challenge their maker and their deliberately limited, bioengineered life-spans. In a visual framework akin to a photographic negative, these white escaped slaves follow a variety of conventions borrowed from classic slave narratives, including a final escape to northern freedom. This escape is made possible when one of the last fugitives, Roy Batty, altruistically spares the life of his bounty hunter, Rick Deckard, during a carnivalesque scene that visually confuses the identities of humans and their bioengineered offspring. Again, one of the most crucial moments in the film demonstrates an overcoming of resentment as Roy Batty's vengeful pursuit of his hunter yields to a gift of life without recompense. In this sense, Roy Batty's humanity is defined by his embrace of altruistic paradox.

The 1997 film *Gattaca* explores in depth the allure of genetic risk management as well as the ensuing social "price." Like the other films described here, *Gattaca* responds to the scientific effort to enhance the DNA mystique, including the collapse of correlation with cause, predisposition with prediction. Of these stories, *Gattaca* is the least explicit about racial dynamics, although the central character, Vincent Freeman, invites speculation as he describes in voice-over a world that has discovered new ways of perpetuating discrimination. What makes the film so interesting for the rethinking of racial injury is the focused way it examines biologically justified discrimination, risk, and altruism. Although in our current moment, race is not a biological category as far as scientists are concerned, *Gattaca* asks what racism might look like in a world where people could be classed by their genetic (re)construction.

Gattaca presents a ("not too distant") future in which ubiquitous bioengineering makes it obligatory for parents to select for their children advantageous traits like high intelligence and near-perfect physical stature. People born without this genetic assistance are deemed "in-valids," or "de-gene-rates," and are otherwise stigmatized in a remarkable vision of what it would mean to "find one's place" as counseled by the authors of *The Bell Curve*. Viewers, in turn, follow Vincent's progress as he attempts to overcome his status as an "in-valid" who is both myopic and saddled with a predisposition for heart failure by the age of 30.2 years. Alienated from his own family, Vincent makes his way in a marginalized community of fellow in-valids, eventually gaining menial employment at a space flight center, Gattaca. In order to follow his lifelong dream of exploring the stars, Vincent assumes the false identity of a genetically very well endowed, yet suicidal, figure, Jerome Eugene, who has failed to live up to his prescribed expectations. Vincent ascends through Gattaca's ranks by employing a host of ingenious deceptions, and is chosen for a mission to Titan, one of Jupiter's moons. Along the way, he becomes romantically involved with a fellow astronaut-in-training, Irene, who appears to gain insight into Vincent because she is also subject to genetic discrimination.

Vincent's plans become compromised when his mission director is killed and a DNA clue at Gattaca sends detectives searching for Vincent's in-valid alter-identity. Vincent's "valid" brother, one of the investigating detectives, discovers his deception but finally does not expose him, in part because Vincent is exonerated in the murder case and in part because Vincent saves his brother's life (for the second time) during a swimming contest. In this contest, Vincent challenges his brother's faith in biodeterminism by performing beyond the limits prescribed by either one's genes. For all of its boyish macho, the scene encapsulates a statement regarding the way the scientific institutional management of risk may itself become a prison house. Ultimately Vincent does defy the odds and make the flight.

Two aspects of this film stand out as we consider its rethinking of injury. From its opening credits on, *Gattaca* eschews any mystery regarding Vincent's identity; viewers are immediately made a part of the deception, lured into the intricate mechanics that maintain Vincent's assumed self—including the careful dissemination of false hair, fingerprints, blood, and urine. These mechanics hold a special function in the film, emphasizing as they do Vincent's alternative, non-bioengineered intelligence. At the same time, viewers learn that Vincent's success has only been possible because a significant network of collaborators have altruistically risked their careers, sometimes their lives. Irene plays a central role in this regard, as does a genetic technician at Gattaca, but the ultimate sacrifice is offered by Jerome Eugene, who makes good on his earlier suicidal intent by self-immolating during Vincent's flight. In this way, he cedes his genetic identity to Jerome, an identity guaranteed by a lifetime supply of human by-products stored for Vincent's return. A demonstration of this society's failure to accommodate those who do not live up to their genetically coded expectations, this suicide is both a condemnation of the risk-averse culture and a gift to Vincent who has found, with the help of others, the means to resist.

Like most science fiction, *Gattaca* presents an allegory, a vision of contemporary tendencies played to emphatic fruition. (The name *Gattaca* itself is drawn from the components of DNA, abbreviated as G, A,

T, and C and thus highlights the film's responsiveness to current genetic debates.) In the film, the DNA mystique becomes a primary logic of social organization, one into which people have slowly evolved. As viewers might expect, *Gattaca* announces that "there is no gene for the human spirit" and "no gene for fate." What is more telling than such odes to resistance is the exploration of altruism as a counter to scientific risk management. Vincent's ingenuity, as impressive as it is, cannot succeed without the altruistic supplement, which is truly paradoxical in this future society, built as it is on biologically based merit and on rewards rigidly indexed to this merit. Ultimately, *Gattaca* focuses not on the hero, but rather on the altruism that stands in distinct opposition to the socially dominant biodeterminism.

Interpersonal connection outside of this merit network is so strained in *Gattaca* that it seems almost impossible. Even casual dating is governed by genetic predispositions as potential suitors surreptitiously steal genetic samples in order to confirm their prospective partner's biological prospects. This tension is conveyed during Vincent and Irene's love scene when the director, Brian Robbins, inverts the entire scene and overlays it with reflections of crashing waves and filtered light coming from outside the room. Such playful manipulations of image parallel the disorientation conveyed in the shooting of the climactic swim contest between the brothers in which fog and darkness mask both the shore and the horizon. Both visually carnivalesque moments rely on thematic and stylistic elements to suggest a disruption of the reigning social logic, the genetic meritocracy and reward system. These scenes, as example of carnivalesque bacchanalia and games, also suggest a movement beyond the resentment both Irene and Vincent's brother have been taught to hold against Vincent as an in-valid stepping beyond his DNA ladder.

Ultimately these recent films contribute to a reservoir of critical thought regarding the DNA mystique. As a supplement to arguments like those offered by Nelkin, Lindee, and Gould, such fictions are invaluable, particularly because they experiment with the carnivalesque in ways that may guide a creative rethinking of racial injury as it is being conditioned by scientific discourse. In the process, these narratives also yield valuable speculation about the shape of racism to come. As if to prove Gould's point that the history of science evidences repetition as well as change, films like *Gattaca* stand out both as indicators of the vitality that may still be attached to old ideas like eugenics, and as cautionary tales regarding the dangers of tying policymaking to an overvaluation of genetic determination.

CONCLUSION

Inasmuch as claiming and representing injury is a thoroughly rhetorical endeavor, it follows that witnessing as an activity is intimately related to the problematics explored over the course of this book. Consider, for instance, the debate that was generated in response to the events dubbed "the casino child murder" by the national media.[1] On May 25, 1997, Jeremy Strohmeyer, a white teenager, sexually molested and murdered a seven-year-old African American girl, Sherrice Iverson, in the restroom of a casino located near Las Vegas.[2] The crime drew attention for a variety of reasons, including the killer's extreme disassociation from human suffering (as conveyed in statements after his arrest), and the fact that the victim's father had left her unattended in the casino at four in the morning while he played slot machines.[3] These aspects alone would have likely drawn interest, but this case involved yet another element that became a lightning rod for debate regarding the nature of social responsibility. Jeremy Strohmeyer had been accompanied to the casino by a close friend, David Cash, Jr., who entered the restroom during Strohmeyer's assault of Iverson and heard Strohmeyer threaten to kill the girl. According to Cash, he tried but failed to interrupt Strohmeyer, then left the restroom without reporting what he had seen and without taking any steps to assist Iverson.[4] When Strohmeyer was arrested some days later, and the story of the crime was pieced together by investigators, Cash found himself completely free of any legal charges because the state of Nevada had no so-called "good Samaritan" law that would require either assistance to a victim or the reporting of an emergency.[5]

As one might expect, editorials across the country expressed horror at Cash's inaction, particularly when he let it be known in interviews that he remained quiet, not out of fear, but rather because he believed he had no obligation whatsoever to another person, no matter what that person's situation might be.[6] The response worsened when he later announced that the notoriety of the case was making it easier for him to get dates.[7] The callousness of Cash's remarks fostered an unsuccessful campaign to have him expelled from the University of California at Berkeley, where he was an undergraduate student.[8] This upheaval, which culminated on August 26, 1998 with a rally on the Berkeley campus, prompted Chancellor Robert Berdahl to disseminate the following statement:

> As a public institution the university has due process procedures it must follow in cases of dismissal. This student has not been charged with any violation of criminal law or the campus student code that would provide a basis for any such review. We cannot set aside due process based upon our outrage over a particular instance.
>
> The demonstration that was held today on this campus is an appropriate means of launching a discussion of the adequacy of existing legislation. We need to build a safer society by ensuring that each of us takes the safety and well-being of our fellow citizens as our own personal responsibility. As a public university we strive to educate students to assume that responsibility.[9]

David Cash remained at Berkeley, exempt from any formal responsibility for the role he played in Sherrice Iverson's murder; however, his conduct did inspire the introduction of legislative bills in both the Nevada State Assembly and the U.S. Congress, bills that would make it a crime to disassociate in the manner Cash had celebrated.[10]

The justice system's reaction to a person like David Cash, and the debates over good Samaritan laws (like the ones standing in Vermont and Minnesota)[11] bring to the fore the complicated ethical stakes that pertain to acting as a witness. In the process of unpacking these stakes, it is crucial to remember that, like the term "injury," "witness" has an etymological history that emphasizes the way witnesses sustain the field of rhetorical assumptions within which they speak.[12] As with Durkheim's argument regarding the most basic purposes of punishment, witnessing most often sustains fundamental values and shared ideals within a society.[13] With this point in mind, we may therefore reframe the outrage provoked by David Cash as an engagement with a basic paradox that lies at the heart of witnessing, especially as it is understood in the courtroom.

On the one hand, witnesses are instructed by courts to disassociate from feelings, opinions, and biases; their credibility with jurors is supposed to be based on such "objective" disassociation.[14] At the same time, we tend to expect witnesses to evidence compassion when recounting injuries; to do anything less appears cold, potentially pathological, and even calculated. In this vein, we might recall the Australian case of Lindy Chamberlain, a Seventh-Day Adventist whose baby was killed by dingos during a family outing in 1980.[15] Originally cleared of any wrongdoing, Chamberlain was later accused of infanticide, a charge that was bolstered by a media frenzy that grew as Chamberlain became increasingly stoical about the death, a stoicism directly related to her religious beliefs. Subsequently convicted of the crime, Chamberlain spent five years in prison before new evidence was found that proved dingos had in fact killed the child. Chamberlain's experience is an extreme but nonetheless telling example of what can happen if witnesses appear too disassociated, and, ironically, too adept at following the letter of the law.

Studies of good Samaritan laws also reveal a paradox at work as mandates to assist victims may in fact discourage those who could offer assistance but instead avoid any contact with potential victims for fear of subsequent liability issues.[16] Such laws have also been criticized for overlooking the potential endangerment of witnesses, thereby opening a calculus of competing injuries.[17] These difficulties have helped ensure that the few good Samaritan laws in existence carry the weakest of penalties; typically their violation constitutes a misdemeanor offense.[18]

Despite the difficult terrain opened by such good Samaritan propositions, public discussions about them remain animated.[19] Like efforts at reparation and group apology (for slavery, for actions in war), the good Samaritan debate evidences an engagement with paradoxical formulations of social responsibility.[20] The results, in turn, frequently demonstrate the weaknesses of various institutions and discourses in terms of registering nuanced, complicated ideas of responsibility. The impulse to respond to ethical paradoxes by adopting a model of moral equivalences—where every injury has an assigned agent, every loss an assigned blame—leaves these institutions and discourses largely incapable of registering the larger spectrum of interaction that exists beyond the roles of perpetrator and victim, including the positions of witnesses, bystanders, collaborators, and resistors. These positions are appropriate for describing many people's experiences of racism in the United States, yet our discussions to date of these positions and their relationships to ameliorative programs have been severely truncated by the intellectually limited, ethically reductive perpetrator/victim paradigm promoted by legal practice as well as by academic discourse. This reductive quality is in evidence during the trials and in the racial profiling that I described at the outset of this study. In the Diallo acquittal, the officers were read as victims of their own terror, and Amadou Diallo was recast as an unfathomable perpetrator, because the jury was instructed to wholly identify with the officers and thereby forget the responsibilities that were specific to their roles as witnesses. Rodney King was similarly transformed into a perpetrator, even when he was apparently unconscious. Racial profiling, for example the NYPD's Stop and Frisk policy, also severely limits the dynamics of witnessing by encouraging officers to misconstrue what they encounter on the street; in the process, these officers may turn almost any minority into a presumed criminal.

The preceding chapters provide examples of authors struggling to work out these difficulties as they engage both racism specifically and the construction of social problems more generally. In each case, distinct methods and objects of study help determine how race and racism are understood. These chapters have also explored how certain ideas about narrative appeal to scholars in different disciplines as they rethink issues of responsibility. Patricia Williams asks readers to rethink what might constitute effective remedy by exploring, among other things, the way the media functions as both witness to, and at times collaborator in, racial injury. Analyzing the implications of her own scholarship and teaching, she offers narrative, and especially autobiography, as a powerful means of unpacking the transferential aspects of witnessing. The chapters on the New Western History and the sociology of crime demonstrate the ways in which an overvaluation of individual choice may obscure important social and cultural variables. This overvaluation underlies Limerick's suggestion that historians chose property and economics rather than racial struggle as the common ground in the West. Although Limerick concludes *Legacy of Conquest* with this problematic gesture, the early portions of her study contain very promising ideas regarding the complicated, transferential role of the historian-as-witness, and the existence of uncanny, historical returns. Because Stephen and Abigail Thernstrom are so committed to crafting a history of progressive racial improvement, their analysis does not allow a similar acknowledgment of the uncanny, returns that are identified by Jerome Miller when he examines the criminal justice system. The Thernstroms' tunnel vision, focusing only on the individual's decontextualized choices, frees them from thinking about responsibilities attending witnessing, and instead unleashes their own self-fulfilling fantasies.

Both the history and the sociology chapters provide literary examples in order to situate notions regarding liberal choice found in Limerick's and the Thernstroms' works. In Erdrich's novel, the narrators Nanapush and Pauline weave together evidence of exactly how contingent their lives are upon the land and the people around them. With these characters, Erdrich asks readers to look beyond the illusory, if sometimes satisfying, fantasy of the autonomous "I," and to dwell within the world of a communal "we." In Rechy's novel, Amalia Gómez explores forms of collective agency as she forges new ties with family and community, a process that requires a greater critical sense of the institutions (particularly the Church and the media) which would make her a grateful spiritual and material consumer. In both novels, characters wrestle with issues of responsibility and witnessing by exercising critical postures toward the discourses—legal, religious, political, economic—that constitute them as linguistic subjects. Although these characters suffer racial injuries, the authors do not present them as victims foremost; instead, the characters are conveyed as subtle interpreters of the mediation between their actions and their contexts. This mediation is a fundamental part of the critical narratives that these characters construct.

Anticipating aspects of Limerick's work, Stephen Jay Gould recasts the history of science as a process of repetition and change, a process open to uncanny retrievals of racist thinking that are intimately tied to social and political contexts. Analyzing *The Bell Curve* in this light, Gould asks readers to consider what it might mean to approach genetics from an altruistic stance. His invitation suggests that we read the unfolding complexity of genetics not as a story whereby our racially defined fates are set, but rather as an opportunity to embrace our potential as creatures unique for their adaptive qualities. As I suggest in readings of science fiction, various artists join Gould in conjecturing about the tensions that exist between genetic fatalism and altruism. Asking us to view genetic discrimination through the eyes of those who witness, collaborate with, and resist such injury, works like *Gattaca* suggest that altruistic witnesses gain crucial insight regarding social responsibility and its nuances.

Overall, such experimentation with narrative evidences the vitality of race studies as an integral part of how disciplines might wrestle with the ethical paradoxes that inevitably attend the formulation of social problems. At the same time, the previous chapters also reveal an important rethinking of injury. As a final gesture, I would suggest that this rethinking is tied in a fundamental way to altering conceptions of witnessing. Here witnessing is understood both as an object of study (what do witnesses do? what counts as witnessing?) and as a set of implications for writers who treat race (implications touching the psychologically complex relationships interpreters maintain with their contexts and objects of study).

Patricia Williams offers a rich venue for discussing this dynamic when she analyzes her interactions with anti-Semitic shopkeepers; readers will recall that Williams posits a kind of joy at escaping the role of mute and complicit witness. Such mute roles are reinforced as expressions of shared responsibility and sympathy are culled out of actors who embrace the notion that they must choose among being a victim or a perpetrator or someone otherwise entirely removed from the situation (the position unapologetically adopted by David Cash). As Williams subtly demonstrates, such disassociation (as mute yet complicit witness) rarely leads to the kind of vilification David Cash received, but may in fact even translate into a type of currency in social exchanges tied to the granting of power and community. In turn, this field of exchange helps explain the significant privileges bestowed on people of color who advance color-blind positions.[21] The success of such racially defined advocates goes beyond their ironic racial capital as speakers for, and against, "their people"; such advocates tap basic resentments that obtain to liberal social interactions generally, and gain a specific power through the reference to race-sensitive, remedial policies specifically.[22] By, among other things, disassociating the individual from the social, these figures feed a growing resentment of social programs as a whole, while simultaneously limiting notions of social responsibility.

Supporters of affirmative action and similar programs may contribute to the promulgation of resentments by justifying these policies via claims of racial injuries that reinforce the logic of moral equivalence.[23] Hence the preceding chapters suggest a need to rethink the basis for coalition building among communities historically subject to discrimination. Representing racial losses and injuries in a rhetorically narrow fashion, advocates of race-sensitive analysis and decision making may lose chances to persuade diverse segments of the U.S. public that race-conscious, "affirmative" policies touch their lives in other than (1) punitive ways that are only justified if one accepts the highly circumscribed role of perpetrator, or (2) beneficent ways that require coding injuries within a calculus of competing claims, a calculus not unlike Amalia Gómez's "Queen for a Day" performance. Assessing alternative visions, my arguments have focused on numerous "disciplinary" struggles over race in which authors develop new articulations of responsibility: articulations that do not subsume race in denial, and that do recognize witnesses as complex and ethically bound. As long as witnesses are paradoxically and selectively discouraged from embracing effective relationships with racial others, there is little hope that ameliorative programs will gain broad-based support.

Trying to move beyond the resentful reactions to affirmative action, Harvard University's Civil Rights Project recently conducted a study of prestigious public and private law schools and found that an overwhelming majority of students considered race-sensitive admissions and related policies to be a highly valuable resource for their education and professional lives.[24] Key findings of the study include the following:

- 89 percent of Harvard Law School students and 91 percent of Michigan Law School students reported a "positive" impact—the large majority reporting a "strongly positive" impact—of diversity on their total educational experience.
- Nearly two-thirds of students surveyed reported that diversity improved class discussions.
- 62 percent of respondents reported that diversity clearly or moderately enhanced their ability to work more effectively and/or get along better with others.
- By a ratio of more than 10 to 1, students who were enrolled in both racially homogeneous and racially diverse classes viewed racially mixed classes as superior. "I can't imagine how serious discussions of law, which affects all Americans, can take place without the points of view of all different races," commented one respondent.
- Seven out of eight students reported that contact with students of diverse backgrounds led them to change their views on civil rights.
- An overwhelming majority of students at both schools (78 percent at Harvard and 85 percent at Michigan) reported that discussions with students from different racial and ethnic backgrounds changed their views of "conditions in various social and economic institutions."
- A large majority of students at both schools (78 percent at Harvard and 84 percent at Michigan) indicated that discussions with students from various racial and ethnic backgrounds resulted in a "significant" impact on their views on the criminal justice system.
- 80 percent of students at both Harvard and Michigan favored strengthening or maintaining the existing admissions policy aimed at increasing enrollment of students of color. (Orfield and Whitla, 1–2)

The study is notable in part because advocates of race-sensitive policies have almost wholly neglected to prove the assumption that diversity is a benefit to education (a key tenet of the 1978 U.S. Supreme Court Bakke ruling that permits race as a factor in decision making and a tenet recently rejected in two federal court rulings).[25] But beyond the very strong show of support for these policies, the study also suggests that the majority of these students have adopted an alternative understanding of both racial injury and witnessing, an understanding premised on the notion that racial interaction is, in their experience, personally transformative. These transferential dynamics were registered when the students emphasized shifts in how they thought about a variety of legal and social issues.[26] Ultimately, their responses detail a case of witnesses significantly and beneficially affected by race-conscious contacts.

The long-term impact of the Harvard study is hard to predict; it focuses on an elite group, but one to which Supreme Court justices can easily relate. The overall influence may depend most on how the study as an undertaking is translated into projects with broader public reach. However, as I have demonstrated, the Harvard study does not stand alone. In many instances, across a variety of disciplines, scholars and artists are rethinking the race debates as a struggle among competing notions of literacy (of how to read, of how to interpret). Taken together, their body of work yields powerful evidence of the valuable ways in which students of race in America are negotiating the complex dynamics of working through racial injury.

NOTES

Notes to the Introduction

1. David Lauter, "Jurors' Race Not Key to Simpson Verdicts, Most Say," *Los Angeles Times*, February 8, 1997, A1 (quoting Derrick Bell); see also Katheryn Russell, *The Color of Crime*, 47–68.

2. Lauter, "Jurors' Race Not Key," A1.

3. Ibid.

4. With regard to the King beating, Lou Cannon describes the reactions of senior African American officers in the LAPD and contrasts it with the reactions of the department in general (*Official Negligence*, 84–85); for a description of reactions to the Diallo killing, see Timothy Williams, "Giuliani's Popularity Has Fallen Since Diallo Shooting, Poll Finds," *Record* (Bergen County, New Jersey), April 9, 1999, A1.

5. Jim Newton, "Rampart Revelations Upset City Residents, Undercut Confidence," *Los Angeles Times*, April 9, 2000, A1; Josh Getlin, "Despite Pressure, NYPD Resists Call for Reforms," *Los Angeles Times*, March 20, 2000, A1; Josh Getlin, "NY Case Triggers Police Racial Profiling Debate," *Los Angeles Times*, October 25, 1999, A1. These results are consistent with general assessments of racial bias offered by blacks and whites; see Russell, *The Color of Crime*, 35.

6. Josh Getlin, "Cop Trials Move," *Los Angeles Times*, December 27, 1999, A1.

7. Kimberlé Crenshaw and Gary Peller, "Reel Time/Real Justice," 56–57, 67–69.

8. See Richard A. Serrano and Tracy Wilkinson, "All 4 in King Beating Acquitted," *Los Angeles Times*, April 30, 1992, A1.

9. The juror's statement is cited in Thomas Dumm's essay, "New Enclosures," 184.

10. See for instance Giuliani's claim that the NYPD was simply reacting to reports of crime that identified suspects by race; Giuliani is cited in Getlin, "Despite Pressure," A1. Virginia Fields, Manhattan Borough President and the New York's highest ranking African American elected official, criticized Giuliani's stance, arguing that the city's leadership is in denial about the extensive minority estrangement from the NYPD that is the product of aggressive policing (cited in Getlin, "Despite Pressure," A1).

11. Getlin, "NY Case Triggers Police Racial Profiling Debate," A1; Michele McPhee, "Governor Rips Rudy on Diallo," *New York Daily News*, March 22, 1999, A16.

12. Josh Getlin, "NY Case Triggers Police Racial Profiling Debate," A1.

13. Jerome Miller explores this problem in *Search and Destroy,* 48–88.

14. My summary of Diallo's killing is drawn from John Goldman, "4 White Officers Are Acquitted in Death of Diallo," *Los Angeles Times,* February 26, 2000, A1.

15. "Officers Acquitted on All Charges in Diallo Shooting Trial," *CNN.COM,* February 25, 2000, <http://www.cnn.com/2000/US/02/25/diallo.verdict.01/index.html>.

16. Getlin, "Cop Trials Move," A1.

17. "Officers Acquitted on All Charges," *CNN.COM,* February 25, 2000.

18. Goldman, "4 White Officers Are Acquitted," A20.

19. Ibid.

20. Ibid.

21. Judith Butler, "Endangered/Endangering," 20–22.

22. Ibid., 15–22.

23. Ibid.

24. Goldman, "4 White Officers Are Acquitted," A20.

25. "Officers Acquitted on All Charges," *CNN.COM,* February 25, 2000.

26. Goldman, "4 White Officers Are Acquitted," A20.

27. Ibid.

28. Scott Glover and Matt Lait, "A Tearful Perez Gets 5 Years," *Los Angeles Times,* February 26, 2000, A1.

29. Rafael Perez, "I Succumbed to the Seductress of Power," *Los Angeles Times,* February 26, 2000, A25.

30. Ibid.; Scott Glover and Matt Lait, "4th Officer Is Charged in Corruption Scandal," *Los Angeles Times,* July 11, 2000, A1.

31. Scott Glover and Matt Lait, "71 More Cases May Be Voided Due to Rampart," *Los Angeles Times,* April 18, 2000, A20.

32. Ibid.; Twila Decker, "Judge Ponders Arguments on Request for Rampart Retrial," *Los Angeles Times,* December 22, 2000, B3.

33. Joe Domanick, "Sheriff Baca's Bold Move to Keep Deputies Accountable," *Los Angeles Times,* July 9, 2000, A1.

34. Scott Glover and Matt Lait, "Parks Says Agencies Share Rampart Blame," *Los Angeles Times,* March 2, 2000, A1; Jim Newton and Tina Daunt, "Feuds Over Rampart Report to Test Divided Police Panel," *Los Angeles Times,* March 2, 2000, A1.

35. "LAPD Probe Grows Beyond Rampart," *Orange County Register,* April 1, 2000; Tina Daunt, "Reform May Cost Hundreds of Millions of Dollars, Official Says," *Los Angeles Times,* November 17, 2000, A34.

36. Perez, "I Succumbed to the Seductress of Power," A25.

37. Ibid.

38. Glover and Lait, "A Tearful Perez," A25.

39. For a description of such victims, see Scott Glover and Matt Lait, "2 Women Say Rampart Squad Framed Them," *Los Angeles Times,* April 27, 2000, A1.

40. Ibid.; Getlin, "NY Case Triggers Police Racial Profiling Debate," A1.

41. For a summary of the assault on Louima, see Getlin, "Cop Trials Move," A1.

42. Scott Glover and Matt Lait, "Chief Parks Orders Current Anti-Gang Units Disbanded," *Los Angeles Times*, March 4, 2000, A1.

43. Ibid.

44. Ibid.

45. Newton and Daunt, "Feuds over Rampart," A1.

46. Glover and Lait, "Chief Parks Orders Current Anti-Gang Units Disbanded," A1.

47. Ibid.

48. Newton and Daunt, "Feuds over Rampart," A1.

49. Glover and Lait, "A Tearful Perez," A25.

50. Jim Newton, "Rampart Revelations Upset City Residents," A1.

51. Ibid.

52. Ibid.; the approval rating for the LAPD reached a low of 36 percent in the wake of Rampart, a figure not matched since the rating of 34 percent received the month after the assault on King.

53. Ibid.

54. Ibid.

55. Ibid.

56. Ibid.

57. Jim Newton, "Riordan Analyzes Roots of Police Scandal," *Los Angeles Times*, April 27, 2000, B1.

58. Jim Newton, "City Near Critical Choice as 4th Officer Faces Charges," *Los Angeles Times*, July 9, 2000, A1.

59. A five-member civilian police commission was in place before and during the scandal; however, observers have questioned the effectiveness of the panel, particularly because it is appointed by the mayor and may unduly feel his influences. See Domanick, "Sheriff Baca's Bold Move," M1.

60. Crenshaw and Peller, "Reel Time," 67–69.

61. Jerome Miller offers such an analysis in *Search and Destroy,* a text discussed in Chapter 5.

62. See Alfredo Mirandé, *Gringo Justice,* 1–26, and Carl Gutiérrez-Jones, *Rethinking the Borderlands,* 1–8.

63. Miller, *Search and Destroy,* 89–136.

64. Ibid., 81–86.

65. Richard Delgado, *The Rodrigo Chronicles,* 1377.

66. Ibid.

67. Crenshaw and Peller, "Reel Time/Real Justice," 56–72.

68. Josh Getlin, "Despite Pressure, NYPD Resists Call for Reforms," *Los Angeles Times,* March 20, 2000, A1; Jim Newton and Tina Daunt, "City Reaches Deal with U.S. on Police Reform Package," *Los Angeles Times,* November 1, 2000, B1.

69. See Richard Delgado, "Storytelling for Oppositionists and Others," 2411–2441; Derrick Bell, *And We Are Not Saved*.

70. For example, see Butler, *Excitable Speech*, 127–163.

71. See Richard Delgado and Jean Stefancic, *Must We Defend Nazis?*

72. Like the verb form "to injure," "injury" marks an act against "jur," against the law, rights, and accepted privilege. For a discussion of the term's etymology, see Chapter 1.

73. Although "working through" is a psychoanalytic term that has been defined in a largely clinical context (see, for example, J. Laplanche's and J.-B. Pontalis' description in *The Language of Psycho-Analysis*), the concept has been particularly useful for intellectual historians and race theorists who would grapple with the problem of how best to address the continued effects of sociopsychic injuries. Although the two concepts are intimately related, "working through" may be understood as an alternative to "acting out," "an action in which the subject, in the grip of his unconscious wishes and phantasies, relives these in the present with a sensation of immediacy which is heightened by his refusal to recognize their source and their repetitive nature" (Laplanche and Pontalis, *The Language of Psycho-Analysis*, 4). In this context, "working through" is understood to be "a sort of psychical work which allows the subject to accept certain repressed elements and to free himself from the grip of mechanisms of repetition"; this process is expedited "by interpretations from the analyst which consist chiefly in showing how the meanings in question may be recognised in different contexts" (488). As Dominick LaCapra notes, Laplanche and Pontalis are careful not to pose "working through" as a "simple ideology of liberation from the constraints of the past" (*Representing the Holocaust*, 209); instead, Laplanche and Pontalis argue that "working through is undoubtedly a repetition, albeit one modified by interpretation and—for this reason—liable to facilitate the subject's freeing himself from repetition mechanisms" (488–489). Carrying these concepts to considerations of ethics, as well as to an analysis of historical methodology, LaCapra argues that "working through" involves a mode of repetition that offers "a measure of critical purchase on problems and responsible control in action which would permit desirable change" (*Representing the Holocaust*, 209). In demonstrating the ways that "working through" might be pursued as an alternative to possession by the repressed past, to repetition compulsions, to unworked-through transference, and to inconsolable melancholy (209), LaCapra suggests important avenues for race studies scholars who would address the perpetuation of racial injuries.

74. John Guillory was one of the first scholars to develop this analysis; see his 1987 essay, "Canonical and Non-Canonical: A Critique of the Current Debate." As discussed in the following chapter, recent work by Wendy Brown and Robyn Wiegman also explores the inclusion/exclusion paradigm of racial injury and extends the interrogation of race literacies announced by Guillory.

75. Dorothy Nelkin and M. Susan Lindee, *The DNA Mystique*, 5–9, 57.

76. See, for example, Miller, *Search and Destroy,* 89–136.

77. Ibid.

78. Mikhail Bakhtin, *The Dialogic Imagination* (see especially "Discourse in the Novel," 259–422).

79. See Abdul R. JanMohamed and David Lloyd's "Introduction" to the special issue of *Cultural Critique* entitled "The Nature and Context of Minority Discourse."

80. See Guillory's "Canonical and Non-Canonical"; Henry Louis Gates, Jr.'s *"Race," Writing, and Difference* (especially the "Editor's Introduction"); Vine Deloria, Jr.'s *Custer Died for Your Sins*; and Miller's *Search and Destroy.*

Notes to Chapter 1

1. See, for example, John Guillory's essay, "Canonical and Non-Canonical," as well as Wendy Brown's essay "Injury, Identity, Politics."

2. The presidential initiative regarding race, as well as apology for the Tuskegee experiment, helped focus attention on efforts by some members of Congress to produce a national apology for slavery, efforts which have been ongoing since 1989. Questions about the efficacy of such gestures have been a growing concern internationally, with considerable attention being given to apologies mounted in Argentina and Germany. For a summary of these "efficacy" debates in a global context, see Michael Ignatieff's article, "Healing Nations."

3. The debate regarding the measure is recounted by Teresa Watanabe, "Measure Urges Japan to Apologize for Atrocities," *Los Angeles Times,* August 24, 1999, A1.

4. See, for instance, Ann Scales's front-page article, "US Dialogue on Race May Lack Shared Language," published in the *Boston Globe* shortly after President Clinton's announcement; as I am arguing, the problem is not so much a lack of shared language as an overabundance of interpretive flux. Participants in the debates tend to use the same language, but with significantly different ideas about what the terms signify.

5. *Compact Edition of the Oxford English Dictionary,* "Injury," 1439.

6. See Cathy Caruth's collection, *Trauma: Explorations in Memory,* as well as Shoshana Felman and Dori Laub's *Testimony: Crises of Witnessing in Literature, Psychoanalysis, and History.*

7. The authors of the Introduction to *Critical Race Theory: The Key Writings That Formed the Movement* note the shifting dynamics whereby political left and right were aligned with the simultaneous collapsing of race and racism; see especially page xiv.

8. Examples in this vein include Andrew Kull's *The Color-Blind Constitution,* and William Henry, III's *In Defense of Elitism.* As I will argue below, important works on this topic that have made an effort to set out definitions often nonetheless collapse distinctions between race and racism.

9. Building on James Baldwin's assertion that "there has been almost no

language" to describe "the horrors" of black life, hooks argues that "a fundamental task of black critical thinkers has been the struggle to break with the hegemonic modes of seeing, thinking and being that block our capacity to see ourselves oppositionally, to imagine, describe, and invent ourselves in ways that are liberatory" (*Black Looks*, 2). In turn, the institutionalization of specific representations of race by the mass media becomes hooks's focus as she levels a critique of white supremacist patriarchy in general.

10. With regard to the highly problematic representation of black injuries, see Barry Glassner's *The Culture of Fear* (112–114); here Glassner explores the racially disparate treatment openly acknowledged by reporters and editors.

11. Omi and Winant note that although Carmichael and Hamilton were highly successful at popularizing the concept of institutional racism, the basic concept was circulating widely at the time, and was an important part of President Lyndon B. Johnson's noted address at Howard University in 1965, "To Fulfill These Rights" (*Racial Formation*, 186, n. 50).

12. For discussion of these methodological stakes, see the final chapter of Mark Kelman's *A Guide to Critical Legal Studies* (269–295), and the first chapter of Patricia Williams's *The Alchemy of Race and Rights* (3–14).

13. Kelman elaborates on the efficacy of these rigorous rhetorical limitations at the close of *A Guide to Critical Legal Studies* (269–295).

14. The notion of transference is considered a cornerstone of psychoanalysis by Freud, and has played a crucial role in the subsequent explorations of how psychoanalysis might be critically merged with the study of history and historiography. For an overview of the possibilities, see Dominick LaCapra's essay, "History and Psychoanalysis."

15. In *History and Memory after Auschwitz*, LaCapra argues that insufficient attention has been given to the role of Holocaust bystanders, collaborators, and resistors, a fact that suggests an important skewing of analyses to date. Carrying over this concern to debates about Paul de Man's actions during and after the Holocaust, LaCapra raises crucial questions regarding modes of working through, acting out, and critique.

16. My own experiences speaking in public forums prior to the passage of prop. 209—the anti-affirmative action initiative in California—confirm this sense inasmuch as many participants expressed bewilderment at the apparent slippage in language which allowed both sides to use the same language but mean entirely different things. Claims of injury, in terms of violations of fairness and equality, were regularly made by both sides, while each also intimated or announced explicitly that the opponent was racist.

17. For examples, see Stanley Fish's essay "Reverse Racism, or How the Pot Got to Call the Kettle Black," and William Connolly's *Identity/Difference* discussed below.

18. See the discussion of Mitchell Breitwieser's *American Puritanism and the Defense of Mourning* below.

19. Summarizing Nietzsche, Connolly writes that the creation of a Christian God was an act of "imaginary revenge," one that would grant a responsible agent who would dole out reward and punishment according to a new set of Christian, victim-oriented equivalences. Eventually, this revenge is transformed into a command to assume the posture of honesty, meekness, and industriousness and in this way weakness becomes merit. In turn, "what the slaves must be becomes the standard against which every difference is defined as a deviation to be punished, re-formed or converted" (*Identical Difference*, 79). Arguing that masters themselves become attracted to this revolt in morality because it speaks to "a more pervasive human dream of a world without injustice" Nietzsche contends that all people resent the transiency, suffering and uncertainty of redemption that mark the human condition" (79). Carrying this reading to our modern (liberal) setting where religious institutions and values have been significantly displaced, Nietzsche suggests that people have tended to substitute themselves for the lost responsible agent (god or nature). Existential suffering regains meaning by virtue of this assumption of agency, an assumption which also ensures the vitality and the constitutive ressentiment of the liberal individual.

20. For a summary of the enforcement difficulties related to "hate crime" laws, see Mark Gladstone, "Hate Crimes Spur Lawmakers to Seek $5 Million Fund for Prosecutions," *Los Angeles Times*, August 24, 1999, A3.

21. For the most part, Freud's writings avoid explicit definitions of healthy or normal behavior. However, in his later work, particularly *Civilization and Its Discontents*, he speculated about larger social pathologies, a speculation that led him to acknowledge the power dynamic which is essential for maintaining and acting upon such norms. To the extent that authors like Omi and Winant have demonstrated the pervasive hold of assimilationist paradigms in contemporary U.S. racial politics, it is easy to imagine how a "therapeutic" moment enters these political debates, where the therapeutic is aligned with normalizing tendencies (Omi and Winant, *Racial Formation*, 15).

22. See Butler, *Excitable Speech*, 127–164.

23. The Weber decision is a centerpiece of Cohen's arguments about reverse discrimination in employment; see in particular chapters 4 and 5.

24. Here, an absolute focus on individuals is the price of justice (Cohen, *Naked Racial Preference*, 220). In this interpretation, liberal individualism completely displaces group dynamics, and, as a result, people embracing this ideology subject themselves to an economy in which all merits, and all suffering, are theirs alone. Initial resentment for a suffering outside their control is in turn converted into a resentment for deviations from a system of norms that determines how equivalences between responsibility, reward, and punishment will be worked out.

25. In probably one of the most famous cases, Tom Wood, co-author of California's anti-affirmative action measure (Proposition 209) was featured on *Frontline* (aired January 18, 1996). Wood's claims that he had been the victim of reverse

discrimination were seriously undermined by the investigative reporting produced by the *Frontline* staff.

26. In this vein, see Gerald Graff's *Professing Literature,* Guillory's "Canonical and Non-Canonical"; and Robyn Wiegman's *American Anatomies.*

27. Guillory's essay, "Canonical and Non-Canonical," develops an extended analysis of how values are maintained by institutionalized reading practices. Anthropology might be taken as an example of how some fields are undergoing significant self-criticism in this regard; see Renato Rosaldo's *Culture and Truth* for an assessment of this process.

28. Robert Guthrie's *Even the Rat was White* remains one of the most far-reaching critiques of psychology as regards the field's complicity in racist ideologies. Although similar calls to rethink methodological practice are still being made, the profession as a whole does not appear to be granting the problem priority. For an example of a recent attempt to focus the profession on these questions, see the *American Psychological Association's Psychological Perspectives on Human Diversity in America* (1991), and especially Jacqueline Goodchilds' "Preface" as well as the lead essay by James M. Jones, "Psychological Models of Race: What Have They Been and What Should They Be?" See also Daryl Scott's *Contempt and Pity* for an excellent history of the ways pathological images ascribed to blacks have been mobilized for political gain. Although Scott's study is not organized to pose the broader methodological questions raised by Jones and Guthrie, it successfully contextualizes the political stakes at play in current psychological debates, including those centered on black intelligence in the wake of *The Bell Curve* (note in particular in Scott's final chapter).

29. Breitwieser's analysis focuses on a captivity narrative written by Mary Rowlandson. With careful attention to the ways Rowlandson resisted the interpretive restrictions placed upon her by the colony's puritan leadership, Breitwieser argues that she managed to gain a critical purchase on the colony's essentially melancholic modes of interaction. Although there may be some ways in which the analysis suggests Rowlandson herself as a model of relative health, the greater sense is that her text acts as a site of intense negotiation wherein the practices of her captors infect the ideological mandates of the Puritan leadership, creating a subtle field for registering ethical and moral concerns, as well as for working through the losses sustained by the colony and by Rowlandson herself.

30. For an overview of how these modes address injury, or what LaCapra refers to as "trauma," see especially the conclusion to *Representing the Holocaust.*

Notes to Chapter 2

1. This philosophy is the foundation of the newly formed Association of Literary Scholars and Critics which claims to offer its members an avenue for the serious study of literature, as opposed to the current trend, "the conversion of literature into

a mere vehicle for the investigation of race, class and gender" (Robert Alter, recruitment letter, August 18, 1997).

2. See the discussion of Wiegman's *American Anatomies*, and Brown's "Injury, Identity, Politics" in the Introduction.

3. For example, see Michel de Certeau, *The Practice of Everyday Life*.

4. The Holocaust treatment was delivered at Dartmouth College, June 22, 1996; a version of this argument has been published under the title "You Who Never Was There: Slavery and the New Historicism, Deconstruction, and the Holocaust." The essay treating white studies has been published as "Autobiographies of the Ex-White Men: Why Race Is Not a Social Construction."

5. See Omi and Winant's treatment of race and culture in *Racial Formation*, 65.

6. Jonathan Arac, for instance, argued that American studies would be best served if participating scholars completely banished the concept of identity immediately, in part because identity study is a symptom of a collective fantasy. His talk, entitled "American Pedagogies," was presented at Dartmouth College, August 14, 1997.

7. Dominick LaCapra noted this irony during an exchange with Michaels at Dartmouth College, June 24, 1996.

8. This talk, titled "Autobiographies of the Ex-White Men: Why Race Is Not a Social Construction," was delivered at Dartmouth College, August 15, 1997.

9. See Mark Kelman's *A Guide to Critical Legal Studies* (269–295) for an example of this rhetorical overlap; see also the discussion of Critical Race Studies in Chapter 3.

10. Linda Hirshman, "Angry Rewrite Man," 11.

11. David Gates, "White Male Paranoia," *Newsweek* 121:13 (March 29, 1993): 48–54.

12. J. P. Telotte, "Definitely *Falling Down*," 19–25.

Notes to Chapter 3

1. One of the definitive Critical Race Studies essays in this regard is Mari Matsuda's "Looking to the Bottom."

2. See Richard Delgado, "Storytelling for Oppositionists and Others: A Plea for Narrative."

3. Ibid., 2416.

4. For a review of the CLS critique of rights activism, see Matsuda's "Looking to the Bottom," 64–65.

5. Gary Peller, "Race-Consciousness," 127–158.

6. Kimberlé Crenshaw, et al., Introduction to *Critical Race Theory*, xiii–xxxii.

7. Gerald Torres and Kathryn Milun outline these translation problematics in their essay "Translating 'Yonnondio' by Precedent and Evidence: The Mashpee Indian Case," 178.

8. Two of these collections of CRS writings include summaries of the movement that make little mention of this rhetorical experimentation; see the Introductions to

Critical Race Theory (edited by Kimberlé Crenshaw, et al.) and *Critical Race Theory* (edited by Richard Delgado). The third recent collection, *Critical Race Feminism*, edited by Adrien Katherine Wing, may be taken as an exception, but even here the Introduction never fully explores the promise of storytelling. Storytelling is acknowledged as an exciting aspect of what the Critical Race Feminists are doing, but the potential efficacy of storytelling as a tool of resistance and liberation is not developed (6).

9. See Patricia Williams's *Alchemy of Race and Rights*; Derrick Bell's *And We Are Not Saved*; Gerald Lopez's *Rebellious Lawyering*; and Richard Delgado's *Rodrigo Chronicles*.

10. See Matsuda's "Looking to the Bottom."

11. Ibid., 63.

12. Ibid., 75–76.

13. Bell, *And We Are Not Saved*, 239–258.

14. Richard Posner, "Legal Narratology," 742–747.

15. See the discussion of D'Souza in Chapter 1, and the discussion of Michaels in Chapter 2.

16. Robyn Wiegman's *American Anatomies* develops this critique at length (115–148); see also Renato Rosaldo's essay "Imperialist Nostalgia," (110, 121).

17. See Torres and Milun, "Translating 'Yonnondio'" by Precedent and Evidence," 184–188.

18. Vine Deloria, Jr., pursues a broad critique of these "interests and biases" in *Custer Died for Your Sins*.

19. Crenshaw, et al., *Critical Race Theory*, xxvii.

20. Ibid., xxviii–xxxii.

21. Mark Kelman, *A Guide to Critical Legal Studies*, 269–295.

22. This rhetorical aim may help explain why this essay is less experimental than others published by Williams. At the same time, few of Williams's offerings wrestle quite as explicitly with questions of culture, and for this reason the *Metro* essay offers an important opportunity for rethinking Williams's methodological innovations.

23. For a fuller description of this "war," see Williams, *The Alchemy of Race and Rights*, 98–132.

24. Peter Brooks and Paul Gewirtz trace these dynamics in *Law's Stories* (see especially 1–22).

25. See Cheryl Harris, "Whiteness as Property."

26. Two early contributions to this burgeoning field were *Interpreting Law and Literature*, edited by Sanford Levinson and Steven Mailloux; and *Doing What Comes Naturally*, by Stanley Fish.

27. See Gewirtz's summary of the "Law and Literature movement" in his chapter "Narrative and Rhetoric in the Law," 3–4.

28. In this sense, Williams's project has much in common with Marta Minow's

efforts in *Making All the Difference* (173–224); both authors counsel a displacement of philosophical truths by politically sensitive rhetorical analysis.

29. See Bell, *And We Are Not Saved.*

30. See my Introduction to *Rethinking the Borderlands,* 1–8.

Notes to Chapter 4

1. Donald Worster, *Under Western Skies,* 12–16.

2. Ibid.

3. Jerome Frisk, "The Theoretical (Re)Positions," 18–19.

4. Jerome Frisk and Forrest G. Robinson, "Introduction," 6–7.

5. For a discussion of these implications, especially as concerns the use of narrative, see Frisk, "Theoretical (Re)Positions," 44–46; see also Patricia Limerick, "Turnerians All" (discussed below).

6. Frederick Jackson Turner, *The Frontier in American History,* 1–38; see also Larry McMurtry, "How the West Was Won or Lost" and Alan Brinkley, "The Western Historians: Don't Fence Them In."

7. See, for example, Richard White, *It's Your Misfortune and None of My Own.* One of the principal contributions of the New Western History movement, White's 630-page account of the West offers almost no recognition of Turner whatsoever.

8. Despite changing ideas about agrarianism, and the rise of the factory, Turner apparently chose not to revise his thesis, a decision Limerick ties to his fear of jeopardizing his professional standing, built as it was around what must have seemed an increasingly compromised notion. See Limerick, "Turnerians All," 699–708.

9. In an essay entitled "The Sideshow," Samuel Weber has produced a Derridean reading that links Freud's theories about castration to post-structuralist explorations of difference per se; in "Fiction and Its Phantoms," Hélène Cixous has considered Freud's "uncanny" in terms of the ambivalences it expresses regarding women, especially as played out in textual and literary fashion; and Allan Lloyd-Smith, author of *Uncanny American Fiction,* attempts to build on the feminist analysis by further historicizing Freud's thinking about women.

10. Limerick meditates on these stylistic points and the response they have drawn in a recent essay entitled, "What Raymond Chandler Knew and Western Historians Forgot."

11. As I have noted earlier, the notion of a transferential relationship would designate a potentially unselfconscious, insufficiently critical, replication by the historian of problematics imbedded in the object of study.

12. See, for example, McMurtry, "How the West Was Won or Lost."

13. Some central texts in this growing field include Caruth's *Trauma;* Felman and Laub's *Testimony;* and LaCapra's *Representing the Holocaust.*

14. White, *It's Your Misfortune,* 3–4.

15. In "The 'New Western History' Comes of Age," Donald Pisani argues that

New Western "historians have not been notably successful in finding 'a new narrative form more appropriate to a pluralistic concept of history'"(170); in "The Politics and Anti-Politics of Western History," Johnson and Ostler offer an in-depth critique that is very suspicious of the NWH's incorporation of minority and women's issues, arguing that these end up being pushed aside for economic issues.

16. White, *It's Your Misfortune*, 613–632.

17. James Baldwin, "The Price of the Ticket."

18. Harold Hickerson describes the origins of the Pillager clan and their response to colonial trade in *Chippewa Indians*, 62–64.

19. For a summary of the repatriation movement and the 1990 Native American Graves Protection and Repatriation Act, see Walter Echo-Hawk, Preface, 1–8.

20. Jean Strouse emphasized this didactic quality in her review of *Tracks* for the *New York Times Book Review*.

21. For a discussion of this stylistic feature, see R. Z. Sheppard, "Review of *Tracks*."

22. Bird's argument in "Searching for Evidence" resonates with that offered by Renato Rosaldo in "Imperialistic Nostalgia." In Bird's case, however, the attempt to read the novel as a set of relatively static stereotypes loses what is dynamic in a character like Nanapush. The effort also leads Bird to undervalue Erdrich's study of the history that led up to tribal factionalization, especially those forces that are at work after the treaty-era proper yet constitute an important moment in the process of coerced acculturation.

23. Perhaps one of the best collections on the topic is a special issue of the *American Indian Culture and Research Journal* 16:2 (1992), with a preface by Walter Echo-Hawk that offers an excellent summary of the repatriation movement. The collection also contains an essay by Vine Deloria, Jr., which contextualizes these battles in terms of larger conflicts between U.S. religions and civil society. See also U.S. Congress, *Native American Grave Protection and Repatriation Act* (*NAGPRA*), for a wealth of testimony and documentation. Readers will also find a summary of the legal arguments that have determined repatriation decisions to date in Edward Halealoha Ayau's article, "Restoring the Ancestral Foundation."

24. Echo-Hawk, Preface, 5.

25. For an extended discussion of Anishinabe mourning customs, see Frances Densmore, *Chippewa Customs*, 73–78.

26. See Sam Snake, et al., *The Adventures of Nanabush*.

27. For a summary of this argument, see U.S. Congress, *NAGPRA*, 63.

28. With regard to a dispute between the Hui Malama tribe of Hawaii and the Phoebe Apperson Museum at the University of California, Berkeley, a NAGPRA review committee accepted spiritual testimony from the tribe, and granted it equal standing with existing scientific evidence. Because the latter was inconclusive, the committee recommended, on the basis of the spiritual evidence, that the remains in question be repatriated to the tribe (*NAGPRA*, 111–112).

Notes to Chapter 5

1. See Henry Louis Gates, Jr.'s assessment of *America in Black and White* on the back cover of the paperback edition.

2. Alan Wolfe, "*America in Black and White*," 27–33.

3. Dinesh D'Souza, *The End of Racism*, 527.

4. Jerome Miller, *Search and Destroy*, 6–7.

5. In one of the most high-profile cases, the U.S. Department of Justice forced New Jersey State Troopers to end their practice of racial profiling after years of debate by threatening protracted litigation. Numerous individual cases of racial profiling have made their way into the national media, including the recent complaint filed by a black woman judge from Virginia who was stopped by the LAPD after they misidentified her car's license. After the jurist was removed from her car, she was handcuffed and forced to lie face down on hot asphalt for half an hour. To make matters worse, no one at the LAPD would take a formal complaint from the victim. The jurist subsequently filed a federal lawsuit. See David Rosenzweig, "Judge's Suit Accuses Police of Racial Profiling," *Los Angeles Times*, December 7, 1999, A1. Such cases have also prompted the ACLU to offer a website titled "On Racial Profiling and Driving while Black" (http://www.aclu.org/profiling/).

6. Miller, *Search and Destroy*, 35, 65.

7. For an analysis of FHA housing policies and their racially disparate impacts, see George Lipsitz, *The Possessive Investment in Whiteness*, 6–27.

8. Miller, *Search and Destroy*, 8.

9. For example, see Wolfe, "America in Black and White," 27.

10. See Boggess and Bounds, *Comparison Study of UCR, NCS and Imprisonment Rates*, 24; cited in Miller, *Search and Destroy*, 29.

11. The business side of the crisis in crime is explored by Nils Christie in *Crime Control as Industry* (see especially 21–22) and by Miller in *Search and Destroy* (228–233).

12. Miller, *Search and Destroy*, 88.

13. Martin Gold and David J. Reimer, "Changing Patterns of Delinquent Behavior among Americans 13 through 16 Years Old: 1967–1972," *Crime and Delinquency* 7:4 (December 1975): 483–517.

14. Miller gives a sense of the growing concern regarding the bias such apologias may mask by citing a presidential address delivered by John Hagan to a 1987 meeting of the American Criminological Society. In this address, Hagan warned that "one of the clearest things these [studies on racial bias in the criminal justice system] tell us is that criminal justice records are potentially problematic not only for the etiological study of criminal behavior, but also for the study of reactions to this behavior in the form of processing decisions" (Miller, 57).

15. *To Establish Justice, to Insure Domestic Tranquility*, Washington, DC: Milton S. Eisenhower Foundation, December 1999.

16. Ibid., 1–2.

17. For a summary of the Eisenhower Report and the reactions it drew, see Eric Lichtblau, "U.S. Crime Study Sees a Society in Trouble," *Los Angeles Times,* December 6, 1999, A1.

18. "Making Crime Pay: Triangle of Interests Creates Infrastructure to Fight Lawlessness," *Wall Street Journal,* May 12, 1994, A1.

19. For an analysis of this urban militarization, see Mike Davis, *City of Quartz,* 221–264.

20. In an article exploring a shooting incident at California's Lancaster Prison, Mark Arax notes that "During the last decade, California's practice of mixing rival gang members into the same small exercise yards and then shooting them if they did not stop fighting resulted in 39 inmate deaths and more than 200 woundings." See the article, "Guard's Shooting of Prisoner at Lancaster Probed," *Los Angeles Times,* June 30, 1999, A3. California's use of lethal force to break up fistfights is unique among state prison systems; California prisons also house a disproportionate number of the nation's convicts.

21. See Robert Coates, Alden Miller, and Lloyd Ohlin's "Juvenile Detention and Its Consequences"; cited in Miller, 124–125.

22. At issue are harsh, military-style camps intended for rehabilitating troubled teens. For a summary of the debate, see the Reuters article, "Teen's Death at Camp Fuels Debate, Inquiry," *Los Angeles Times,* December 5, 1999, A13.

23. Clifford Shaw, *The Jack Roller,* 1–2.

24. As Miller notes, "The stigma of being labeled an offender further alienates the individual from society and promotes the building of closer relationships with others who have been similarly ostracized, contributing to further acting out and creating a self-fulfilling prophecy" (112).

25. See Coates, et al., "Juvenile Detention and Its Consequences"; cited by Miller, *Search and Destroy,* 124–125.

26. For an example of Wilson's work, see *Crime and Human Nature.*

27. For a summary of the University of California report and the reactions it garnered, see Dan Morain, "3-Strikes Law Called No Deterrent," *Los Angeles Times,* November 9, 1999, A3.

28. Shaw, *The Jack Roller,* 1–2.

29. Sebastian Rotella documents the remarkable turnover of INS officers in the San Diego corrido as well the poor training and notorious abuses that appear to stem from the situation; he notes, for instance, that 1,000 officers were replaced in 1989 alone, and this in a sector that has roughly 1,000 positions total; see Rotella's "Light Brigade."

30. See the discussion in the Introduction.

31. Carl Gutiérrez-Jones, *Rethinking the Borderlands,* 1–8.

32. Ibid.

33. Carl Gutiérrez-Jones, "Resisting Cultural Dependency."

Notes to Chapter 6

1. Richard Nisbett, "Race, IQ, and Scientism," 45–48.

2. Gould makes a similar point when he takes issue with reviewers of *The Bell Curve* for their tendency to defer too quickly to Herrnstein and Murray's scientific evidence because of its complexity. As Gould notes, *The Bell Curve's* prose is in fact accessible to the lay reader who should not uncritically accept Herrnstein and Murray's evidence simply because it is "scientific" (Gould, *Mismeasure*, 31).

3. *The Bell Curve's* final chapter is devoted to an argument for this "place finding" solution (527–552).

4. In this vein, Herrnstein and Murray argue that "Government policy can do much to foster the vitality of neighborhoods by trying to do less for them" (540).

5. Nisbett, "Race, IQ, Scientism," 48–53.

6. Dorothy Nelkin and M. Susan Lindee offer a similar reading of the "disposable" status of groups thus defined by their genetic predispositons; see *The DNA Mystique*, 129.

7. See Troy Duster, *Backdoor to Eugenics*, 133–135.

8. For an overview of this eugenics history, see Marouf Arif Hasian, Jr., *The Rhetoric of Eugenics in Anglo-American Thought*.

9. See Arthur Jensen, "How Much Can We Boost IQ and Scholastic Achievement?" *Harvard Educational Review,* Winter 1969, 1–23; the passage is also cited by Nelkin and Lindee, *DNA Mystique*, 113.

10. Nelkin and Lindee, *DNA Mystique*, 113–14.

11. Hasian, *The Rhetoric of Eugenics*, 154.

12. Ibid., 153.

13. Nelkin and Lindee, *DNA Mystique*, 159.

14. Ibid., 11–18.

15. Ibid., 5.

16. Ibid., 6.

17. Ibid.

18. Ibid., 7.

19. Leon Jaroff, "The Gene Hunt," 62–67.

20. Christopher Wills, *Exons, Introns and Talking Genes*, 10.

21. Nelkin and Lindee, *DNA Mystique*, 9.

22. James Watson, "All For The Good: Why Genetic Engineering Must Soldier On," *Time* 153:1, January 11, 1999, 91.

23. Nelkin and Lindee, *DNA Mystique*, 9.

24. Nisbett, "Race, IQ, and Scientism," 45–48.

25. Howard Gardner, "Cracking Open the IQ Box," 27–32.

26. Gould proposes something similar at the beginning of his text when he

argues that "Impartiality (even if desirable) is unattainable by human beings with inevitable backgrounds, needs, beliefs, and desires. It is dangerous for a scholar even to imagine that (he or she) might attain complete neutrality, for then one stops being vigilant about personal preferences and their influences"(*Mismeasure*, 36).

27. Gould explores this distinction when he notes that "Sociobiologists work as if Galileo had really mounted the Leaning Tower (apparently he did not), dropped a set of diverse objects over the side, and sought a separate explanation for each behavior—the plunge of the cannonball as a result of something in the nature of cannonballness; the gentle descent of the feather as intrinsic to featherness. We know, instead, that the wide range of different falling behaviors arises from the interaction between two physical rules—gravity and frictional resistance. This interaction can generate a thousand different styles of descent. If we focus on the objects and seek an explanation for the behavior of each in its own terms, we are lost" (*Mismeasure*, 360).

28. See, for example, Elaine Hatfield, et al., "Equity Theory and Helping Relationships," 115–140.

29. Sasha Weitman, "Prosocial Behavior and Its Discontents," 229–248.

30. Ibid., 113.

31. Lauren Wispé, *Altruism, Sympathy and Helping*, 314–315.

32. Ibid.

33. Ibid., 304.

34. Wispé credits Smith with "economic" reduction (304–322), but this may well be an oversimplification of his writings. See Charles Bazerman, "Money Talks: The Rhetorical Project of Adam Smith's Wealth of Nations," in *Economics and Language,* ed. Willie Henderson et al., 173–199 (New York: Routledge, 1993).

35. For an example of the "selfish gene" theory, see Matt Ridley, *The Origins of Virtue*; on the limits of such approaches, see Gould, *The Mismeasure of Man,* 356; and Wispé, *Altruism,* 322.

36. Henry Louis Gates, Jr., "Why Now?" 95.

37. Wispé, *Altruism,* 323.

38. Sasha Weitman explores the "exclusionary dynamics" in "Prosocial Behavior and Its Discontents," 244–246.

39. Ibid.

40. Ibid.

41. Ibid., 238.

42. Caryl Emerson and Gary Saul Morson, *Mikhail Bakhtin: Creation of a Prosaics,* 226–227.

43. See Mikhail Bakhtin, *Rabelais and His World,* and *The Dialogic Imagination.* For an extended treatment of these themes in Bakhtin's work, see Emerson and Morson, *Mikhail Bakhtin,* in particular 433–472.

44. Mikhail Bakhtin, "Author and Character in Aesthetic Activity," 22.

Notes to the Conclusion

1. For newspaper stories treating the murder, see Eric Lichtblau and Nora Za-michow, "Guilty Plea in Casino Slaying," *Los Angeles Times,* September 9, 1998, A1; "Guilty Plea Is Made in Killing at Casino," *New York Times,* September 9, 1998, A14; and Michael Kelly, "Somebody Else's Problems," *Washington Post,* September 9, 1998, A19. For a summary of the media coverage, see Earl Ofari Hutchinson, "The Rehabilitation of Jeremy Strohmeyer," *Baltimore Times,* November 6, 1998.

2. See Jeremy Strohmeyer, "Defendant's Sentencing Statement," October 14, 1998, District Court, Clark County, Nevada, 1–24. The subsequent reporting on the case bore little resemblance to the coverage of the Polly Klaas and JonBenet Ramsey murders inasmuch as Sherrice Iverson was almost nonexistent, except for her age, a fact that has raised troubling questions about media representation of black victims; for an analysis, see Hutchinson, "The Rehabilitation of Jeremy Strohmeyer."

3. Greg Krikorian and Jeff Leeds, "Suspect in Girl's Slaying Enters Plea of Not Guilty," *Los Angeles Times,* June 4, 1997, A1.

4. Eric Lichtblau and Nora Zamichow, "U.S. Inquiry Targets Strohmeyer Friend," *Los Angeles Times,* December 18, 1998, A3.

5. Isabelle Gunning, "Two Forms of Justice," *Los Angeles Times,* September 21, 1998, B5.

6. For example, see "Troubling Questions in Murder," *Los Angeles Times,* September 17, 1998, B8; Kelly, "Somebody Else's Problems," A19.

7. Hugo Martin, "20,000 Sign Petition on Casino Slaying," *Los Angeles Times,* August 22, 1998, B1.

8. Anne-Marie O'Connor, "Protest Follows Accused Accomplice," *Los Angeles Times,* August 27, 1998, A3.

9. Robert M. Berdahl, "Statement from Robert M. Berdahl, Chancellor, University of California, Berkeley," Press Release, August 26, 1998, 1.

10. On April 13, 1998, the Nevada State Assembly unanimously passed AB267, a law which would require the reporting of crimes against juveniles; the U.S. Congress is also considering the "Sherrice Iverson Act," a bill that would apply criminal penalties to witnesses failing to report an individual 18 years old or older who sexually molests a child.

11. Vt. Stat. Ann., tit. 1 S 519 (Supp. 1971); Minn. Stat. 604A. 01 (1996).

12. "Witness," *Compact Edition of the Oxford English Dictionary,* 3803–3804.

13. Emile Durkheim, *Moral Education,* 179.

14. The instructions given to the jurors in the trial of the NYPD officers who killed Amadou Diallo is a case in point; see the analysis in the Introduction.

15. My summary of these events is drawn from Lindy Chamberlain's *Through My Eyes: An Autobiography,* and John Bryson's recounting of the trial, *Evil Angels.*

16. See John Kaplan, "A Legal Look at Prosocial Behavior," 293–297.

17. Ibid., 297–301.

18. See, for example, Vermont's 1971 statute that carries a fine of no more than $100.00; Vt. Stat. Ann., tit. 12 S 519 (Supp. 1971).

19. See Gunning, "Two Forms of Justice," B5; Maura Dolan, "Good Samaritan Laws Are Hard to Enact, Experts Say," *Los Angeles Times,* September 9, 1998, A1.

20. Kaplan, "A Legal Look at Prosocial Behavior," 291–301.

21. Consider the very significant resources that have been made available to Ward Connerly, Jr., the anti-affirmative action campaigner, and to Linda Chavez as a spokesperson against bilingual education and a variety of race-sensitive programs.

22. See Chapter 1 and the discussion of William Connolly's work on resentment.

23. See the discussion of Wendy Brown's work in Chapter 1.

24. Gary Orfield and Dean Whitla, 1–28.

25. Ibid., 2.

26. Ibid., 1.

WORKS CITED

Acuña, Rudolfo. *Occupied America: A History of Chicanos.* New York: Harper and Row, 1988.

Allen, Paula Gunn. *The Sacred Hoop: Recovering the Feminine in Native American Indian Traditions.* Boston: Beacon Press, 1986.

Alter, Robert. Recruitment Letter for Association of Literary Scholars and Critics. August 18, 1997.

Anderson, Annelise. "Immigration Good for U.S.?" *Stanford Magazine* (Winter 1988): 64.

Anzaldúa, Gloria. *Borderlands/La Frontera: The New Mestiza.* San Francisco: Spinsters/Aunt Lute Press, 1987.

Appiah, Anthony. "Identity, Authenticity Survival: Multicultural Societies and Social Reproduction." In *Multiculturalism and "The Politics of Recognition."* Ed. Amy Gutman. Princeton, NJ: Princeton University Press, 1992.

Arac, Jonathan. "American Pedagogies." Delivered at the Futures of American Studies Conference, Dartmouth College, August 14, 1997.

————, ed. *Postmodernism and Politics.* Minneapolis: University of Minnesota Press, 1979.

Ayau, Edward Halealoha. "Restoring the Ancestral Foundation of Native Hawaiians: Implementation of the Native American Graves Protection and Repatriation Act." *Arizona State Law Journal* 24 (1994): 193–216.

Bakhtin, Mikhail. "Author and Character in Aesthetic Activity." In *Mikhail Bakhtin: The Dialogical Principle.* Trans. Tzvetan Todorov and Wlad Godzich. Minneapolis: University of Minnesota Press, 1984.

————. *The Dialogic Imagination.* Ed. Michael Holquist. Trans. Caryl Emerson and Michael Holquist. Austin: University of Texas Press, 1981.

————. *Rabelais and His World.* Cambridge: MIT Press, 1968.

Baldwin, James. "The Price of the Ticket." In *James Baldwin: Collected Essays.* Ed. Toni Morrison, 830–844. New York: Penguin, 1998.

Bell, Derrick. *And We Are Not Saved: The Elusive Quest for Racial Justice.* New York: Basic Books, 1987.

Bird, Gloria. "Searching for Evidence of Colonialism at Work: A Reading of Louise Erdrich's 'Tracks.'" *Wicazo Sa Review* 8:2 (Rapid City, 1992): 40–47.

Boggess, Scott, and John Bounds. *Comparison Study of Uniform Crime Report, National Crime Survey and Imprisonment Rates*. National Bureau of Economic Research, University of Michigan, 1993.

Breitwieser, Mitchell. *American Puritanism and the Defense of Mourning: Religion, Grief, and Ethnology in Mary White Rowlandson's Captivity Narrative*. Madison: University of Wisconsin Press, 1990.

Bright, Charles. *The Powers That Punish: Prisons and Politics in the Era of the "Big House," 1920–1955*. Ann Arbor: University of Michigan Press, 1996.

Brinkley, Alan. "The Western Historians: Don't Fence Them In." *New York Times Book Review*, September 20, 1992.

Brooks, Peter, and Paul Gewirtz, eds. *Law's Stories: Narrative and Rhetoric in the Law*. New Haven: Yale University Press, 1996.

Brown, Dee. *Bury My Heart at Wounded Knee: An Indian History of the American West*. New York: Holt, 1991.

Brown, Wendy. "Injury, Identity, Politics." In *Mapping Multiculturalism*. Ed. Avery Gordon and Christopher Newfield. Minneapolis: University of Minnesota Press, 1996.

Bryson, John. *Evil Angels*. New York: Notable Trials Library, 1992.

Buck v. Bell, 274 U.S. 200 (1927).

Burger, Warren. "Isn't There a Better Way?" *American Bar Association Journal* 68 (1982): 274–277.

Butler, Judith. "Endangered/Endangering: Schematic Racism and White Paranoia." In *Reading Rodney King/Reading Urban Uprising*. Ed. Robert Gooding-Williams, 15–22. New York: Routledge, 1993.

———. *Excitable Speech: A Politics of the Performative*. New York: Routledge, 1997.

Calderón, Héctor, and José Saldívar, eds. *Criticism in the Borderlands: Studies in Chicano Literature, Culture, and Ideology*. Durham: Duke University Press, 1991.

Califa, Antonio J. "Declaring English the Official Language: Prejudice Spoken Here." *Harvard Civil Rights–Civil Liberties Law Review* 24 (1989): 294–348.

"Can the El Paso Experiment Work Here?" *Los Angeles Times*, Tuesday, October 5, 1993, B6.

Cannon, Lou. *Official Negligence: How Rodney King and the Riots Changed Los Angeles and the LAPD*. New York: Westview, 1999.

Carmichael, Stokely, and Charles Hamilton. *Black Power: The Politics of Liberation in America*. New York: Vintage, 1967.

Caruth, Cathy. *Trauma: Explorations in Memory*. Baltimore: Johns Hopkins University Press, 1995.

Castillo, Debra. "Double Zero Place: A Discourse on War." Delivered at the San Francisco MLA Meeting, December 30, 1987.

Castillo, Susan Pérez. "Postmodernism, Native American Literature and the Real: The Silko-Erdrich Controversy." *The Massachusetts Review* 32:1 (Summer 1991): 285–294.

Chamberlain, Lindy. *Through My Eyes: An Autobiography*. Port Melbourne, Victoria: W. Heinemann Australia, 1990.

Chavkin, Allan, and Nancy Feyl Chavkin, eds. *Conversations with Louise Erdrich and Michael Dorris*. Jackson: University Press of Mississippi, 1994.

Christie, Nils. *Crime Control as Industry: Towards Gulags Western Style?* New York: Routledge, 1993.

Cixous, Hélène. "Fiction and Its Phantoms." *New Literary History* 7 (1975): 525–548.

Clark, Rebecca, and Jeffrey Passel. *How Much Do Immigrants Pay in Taxes? Evidence from Los Angeles County*. Washington: The Urban Institute, 1993.

Coates, Robert B., Alden D. Miller, and Lloyd E. Ohlin. "Juvenile Detention and Its Consequences." *Center for Criminal Justice*. Cambridge: Harvard Law School, 1975.

Cohen, Carl. *Naked Racial Preference*. New York: Madison Books, 1995.

Compact Edition of the Oxford English Dictionary, The . Oxford: Oxford University Press, 1971.

Conelius, Wayne, and Ricardo Anzaldúa Montoya, eds. *International Inventory of Current Mexico-Related Research*, vols. 1–4. San Diego: Center for U.S.-Mexico Studies, 1982–84.

Connolly, William. *Identity/Difference: Democratic Negotiations of Political Paradox*. Ithaca: Cornell University Press, 1991.

Cox, Archibald. *The Court and the Constitution*. Boston: Houghton Mifflin, 1987.

Crenshaw, Kimberlé, Neil Gotanda, Gary Peller, and Kendall Thomas, eds. *Critical Race Theory: The Key Writings That Formed the Movement*. New York: The New Press, 1995.

Crenshaw, Kimberlé, and Gary Peller. "Reel Time/Real Justice." In *Reading Rodney King/Reading Urban Uprising*. Ed. Robert Gooding-Williams, 56–72. New York: Routledge, 1993.

Davis, Mike. *City of Quartz: Excavating the Future in Los Angeles*. New York: Vintage, 1990.

de Certeau, Michel. *Heterologies: Discourse on the Other*. Trans. Brian Massumi. Minneapolis: University of Minnesota Press, 1986.

———. *The Practice of Everyday Life*. Trans. Steven Rendall. Berkeley: University of California Press, 1984.

Delgado, Richard. *The Rodrigo Chronicles: Conversations about America and Race*. New York: New York University Press, 1995.

———. "Storytelling for Oppositionists and Others: A Plea for Narrative." *Michigan Law Review* 87:8 (August 1980): 2411–2441.

———, ed. *Critical Race Theory: The Cutting Edge*. Philadelphia: Temple University Press, 1995.

Delgado, Richard, and Jean Stefancic. *Must We Defend Nazis? Hate Speech, Pornography, and the New First Amendment*. New York: New York University Press, 1997.

Deloria, Vine, Jr. *Custer Died for Your Sins: An Indian Manifesto*. New York: Macmillan, 1969.

———. *Red Earth, White Lies: Native Americans and the Myth of Scientific Fact*. New York: Scribner, 1995.

Densmore, Frances. *Chippewa Customs*. Washington, DC: Smithsonian Institution (U.S. Bureau of American Ethnology, Bulletin 86), 1929.

Doherty, Tony. "Falling Down." *Cineaste* 20:1 (1993): 39.

D'Souza, Dinesh. *The End of Racism: Principles for a Multiracial Society*. New York: The Free Press, 1995.

Dumm, Thomas. "The New Enclosures: Racism in the Normalized Community." In *Reading Rodney King/Reading Urban Uprising*. Ed. Robert Gooding-Williams, 178–195. New York: Routledge, 1993.

Durkheim, Emile. *Moral Education: A Study in the Theory and Application of the Sociology of Education*. Trans. Everett K. Wilson and Herman Schnurer. New York: Crowell-Collier, 1961.

Duster, Troy. *Backdoor to Eugenics*. New York: Routledge, 1990.

Echo-Hawk, Walter. Preface. *American Indian Culture and Research Journal* 16:2 (1992): 1–8.

Emerson, Caryl, and Gary Saul Morson. *Mikhail Bakhtin: Creation of a Prosaics*. Stanford: Stanford University Press, 1990.

Erdrich, Louise. *Beet Queen*. New York: Holt, 1986.

———. *Conversations with Louise Erdrich and Michael Dorris*. Jackson: University Press of Mississippi, 1994.

———. *Love Medicine*. Holt, 1984.

———. *Tracks*. New York: Harper and Row, 1988.

Faulkner, William. *The Sound and the Fury*. New York: Random House, 1984.

Fellini, Federico, dir. *8 ½*. Cineriz (Italy), 1963.

Felman, Shoshana, and Dori Laub. *Testimony: Crises of Witnessing in Literature, Psychoanalysis, and History*. New York: Routledge, 1992.

Fincher, David, dir. *Alien 3*. CBS/Fox Video, 1992.

Fish, Stanley. *Doing What Comes Naturally: Change, Rhetoric, and the Practice of Theory in Literary and Legal Studies*. Durham: Duke University Press, 1989.

———. "Reverse Racism, or How the Pot Got to Call the Kettle Black." *New Crisis* 107:1 (January 2000): 14–19.

Friedlander, Saul. *Memory, History, and the Extermination of the Jews of Europe*. Bloomington: Indiana University Press, 1993.

Foucault, Michel. *Discipline and Punish: The Birth of the Prison*. Trans. Alan Sheridan. New York: Vintage, 1979.

———. *History of Sexuality*. Trans. Robert Hurley. New York: Pantheon Books, 1978.

Freeman, Alan. "Legitimizing Racial Discrimination through Anti-discrimination Law: A Critical Review of Supreme Court Doctrine." In *Critical Legal Studies*. Ed. Allan Hutchinson. Totowa, NJ: Rowman and Littlefield, 1989.

Freud, Sigmund. *Civilization and Its Discontents.* Trans. James Strachey. New York: Norton, 1961.

———. *Interpretation of Dreams.* Trans. James Strachey. New York: Norton. 1955.

———. *Standard Edition of the Complete Psychological Works of Sigmund Freud, The, Vol. XVII.* Trans. James Strachey, 217–253. London: Hogarth Press, 1955.

Frisk, Jerome. "The Theoretical (Re)Positions of the New Western History." In *The New Western History: The Territory Ahead.* Ed. Forrest G. Robinson. Tucson: University of Arizona Press, 1997.

Frisk, Jerome, and Forrest G. Robinson. "Introduction." In *The New Western History: The Territory Ahead.* Ed. Forrest G. Robinson. Tucson: University of Arizona Press, 1997.

Frontline. "Proposition 209." Aired January 18, 1996.

Gardner, Howard. "Cracking Open the IQ Box." In *The Bell Curve Wars: Race, Intelligence, and the Future of America.* Ed. Steven Fraser, 23–35. New York: Basic Books, 1995.

Gates, Henry Louis, Jr. "Editor's Introduction." *Critical Inquiry* 12:1 (Autumn 1985): 1–20.

———. *"Race," Writing, and Difference.* Chicago: University of Chicago Press, 1986.

———. "Why Now?" In *The Bell Curve Wars: Race, Intelligence and, the Future of America.* Ed. Steven Fraser, 94–96. New York: Basic Books, 1995.

Gewirtz, Paul. "Narrative and Rhetoric in the Law." In *Law's Stories: Narrative and Rhetoric in the Law.* Ed. Peter Brooks and Paul Gewirtz, 2–13. New Haven: Yale University Press, 1996.

Glassner, Barry. *The Culture of Fear: Why Americans Are Afraid of the Wrong Things.* New York: Basic Books, 1999.

Goldberg, David. *Multiculturalism: A Critical Reader.* Cambridge: Blackwell, 1994.

Goodchilds, Jacqueline, ed. *Psychological Perspectives on Human Diversity in America.* Washington, DC: American Psychological Association, 1991.

Gould, Stephen Jay. *The Mismeasure of Man.* New York: Norton, 1996.

Graff, Gerald. *Professing Literature: An Institutional History.* Chicago: University of Chicago Press, 1987.

Gramsci, Antonio. *Selections from the Prison Notebooks.* London: Lawrence and Wishart, 1973.

Gross, Alan G. *The Rhetoric of Science.* Cambridge: Harvard University Press, 1996.

Guillory, John. "Canonical and Non-Canonical: A Critique of the Current Debate." *English Literary History* 54.3 (Fall 1987): 483–527.

Gunn, Giles. "Review of *Our America: Nativism, Modernism and Pluralism,* by Walter Benn Michaels." *Journal of American History* (September 1996): 660.

Guthrie, Robert. *Even the Rat Was White: A Historical View of Psychology.* New York: Harper and Row, 1976.

Gutiérrez-Jones, Carl. "Legal Rhetoric and Cultural Critique: Notes Toward Guerrilla Writing." *diacritics* 20.4 (1995): 57–73.

Gutiérrez-Jones, Carl. "Resisting Cultural Dependency: The Manipulation of Surveillance and Paranoia in Alejandro Morales' *The Brick People.*" *The Américas Review* 22: 1–2 (Spring–Summer 1994): 230–243.

———. *Rethinking the Borderlands: Between Chicano Culture and Legal Discourse.* Berkeley: University of California Press, 1995.

Hall, Stuart. "Culture Studies: Two Paradigms." *Media, Culture and Society* 2 (1980): 55–72.

———. "Gramsci's Relevance for the Study of Race and Ethnicity." In *Stuart Hall: Critical Dialogues in Cultural Studies.* Ed. David Morley and Kuan-Hsing Chen. New York: Routledge, 1996.

Harris, Cheryl. "Whiteness as Property." In *Critical Race Theory: The Key Writings That Formed the Movement.* Ed. Kimberlé Crenshaw, Neil Gotanda, Gary Peller, and Kendall Thomas, 276–291. New York: The New Press, 1995.

Hasian, Marouf Arif, Jr. *The Rhetoric of Eugenics in Anglo-American Thought.* Athens: University of Georgia Press, 1996.

Hatfield, Elaine, G. William Walster, and Jane Allyn Piliavin. "Equity Theory and Helping Relationships." In *Altruism, Sympathy, and Helping: Psychological and Sociological Principles.* Ed. Lauren Wispé, 115–140. New York: Academic Press, 1978.

Henry, William, III. *In Defense of Elitism.* New York: Anchor, 1995.

Herrnstein, Richard, and Charles Murray. *The Bell Curve: Intelligence and Class Structure in American Life.* New York: The Free Press, 1994.

Hickerson, Harold. *Chippewa Indians: Ethnology of Mississippi Bands and Pillager and Winnibigoshish Bands of Chippewa.* New York: Garland, 1974.

Hirshman, Linda. "Angry Rewrite Man." *Extra!* May/June 1995, 11.

Hoffman, Abraham. "Stimulus to Repatriation: The 1931 Federal Deportation Drive and the Los Angeles Mexican Community." In *The Chicano.* Ed. Norris Hundley, Jr. Santa Barbara: Clio Press, 1975.

hooks, bell. *Black Looks: Race and Representation.* Boston: South End Press, 1992.

Houston, Lawrence. *Psychological Principles and the Black Experience.* New York: University Press of America, 1990.

Ignatieff, Michael. "Healing Nations: How Can Past Sins Be Absolved?" *World Press Review* 44.2 (February 1997): 6–9.

JanMohamed, Abdul R., and David Lloyd. Introduction. *Cultural Critique* 6 (Spring 1987): 5–12.

Jaroff, Leon. "The Gene Hunt." *Time* 20 March 1989: 62–67.

Jensen, A. R. "How Much Can We Boost IQ and Scholastic Achievement?" *Harvard Educational Review* 33 (1969): 1–123.

Johnson, Robert, and Jeffery Ostler. "The Politics and Anti-Politics of Western History." Unpublished paper delivered at the Western Historical Conference, Denver, 1995.

Kaplan, John. "A Legal Look at Prosocial Behavior." In *Altruism, Sympathy, and*

Helping: Psychological and Sociological Principles. Ed. Lauren Wispé, 291–302. New York: Academic Press, 1978.

Kelman, Mark. *A Guide to Critical Legal Studies.* Cambridge: Harvard University Press, 1987.

Kennedy, Duncan. "The Structure of Blackstone's Commentaries." In *Critical Legal Studies.* Ed. Allan Hutchinson. Totowa, NJ: Rowan and Littlefield, 1989.

Klinkner, Philip. "The 'Racial Realism' Hoax." *Nation* (December 14, 1998): 33–38.

Kull, Andrew. *The Color-Blind Constitution.* Cambridge: Harvard University Press, 1992.

LaCapra, Dominick. *History and Memory after Auschwitz.* Ithaca: Cornell University Press, 1998.

———. "History and Psychoanalysis." In *Soundings in Critical Theory.* Ithaca: Cornell University Press, 1989.

———. *Representing the Holocaust: History, Theory, Trauma.* Ithaca: Cornell University Press, 1994.

Laplanche, Jean, and J. B. Pontalis. *The Language of Psycho-Analysis.* New York: Norton, 1974.

Larson, Sidner. "The Fragmentation of a Tribal People in Louise Erdrich's *Tracks.*" *American Indian Culture and Research Journal* 17:2 (1993): 1–13.

Levinson, Barry, dir. *Disclosure.* Warner Bros., 1994.

Levinson, Sanford, and Steven Mailloux, eds. *Interpreting Law and Literature: A Hermeneutic Reader.* Evanston: Northwestern University Press, 1988.

Limerick, Patricia. *Legacy of Conquest: The Unbroken Past of the American West.* New York: Norton, 1987.

———. "Turnerians All: The Dream of a Helpful History in an Intelligible World." *American Historical Review* (June 1995): 697–716.

———. "What Raymond Chandler Knew and Western Historians Forgot." In *Old West—New West: Centennial Essays.* Ed. by Barbara Howard Meldrum, 28–42. Moscow: University of Idaho Press, 1993.

Lipsitz, George. *The Possessive Investment in Whiteness: How White People Profit from Identity Politics.* Philadelphia: Temple University Press, 1998.

Lloyd-Smith, Allan. *Uncanny American Fiction: Medusa's Face.* London: Macmillan, 1989.

Lopez, Gerald. *Rebellious Lawyering: One Chicano's Vision of Progressive Law Practice.* Boulder, CO: Westview Press, 1992.

Mailloux, Steven. *Rhetorical Power.* Ithaca: Cornell University Press, 1990.

Matsuda, Mari. "Looking to the Bottom: Critical Legal Studies and Reparations." In *Critical Race Theory: The Key Writings That Formed the Movement.* Ed. Kimberlé Crenshaw, Neil Gotanda, Gary Peller, and Kendall Thomas, 63–79. New York: The New Press, 1995.

Mauer, Mark. *Young Black Americans and the Criminal Justice System: Five Years Later.* Washington, DC: The Sentencing Project, 1995.

McDonnell, Patrick. "Light-Up-the-Border Drive Turned Off as Officials Pledge Action." *Los Angeles Times,* Saturday, June 23, 1990, A26.

———. "1000 Gather at Border, Protest Crossings." *Los Angeles Times,* Saturday, March 17, 1990, A27.

McGrory, Brian. "Clinton Sets a Dialogue about Race." *Boston Globe,* June 15, 1997, A1.

McGrory, Brian, and Jill Zuckman. "Talk of Apologizing for Slavery Sparks Debate on Efficacy." *Boston Globe,* June 17, 1997, A1.

McMurtry, Larry. "How the West Was Won or Lost." *New Republic,* October 22, 1990.

Michaels, Walter Benn. "Autobiography of an Ex-White Man: Why Race Is Not a Social Construction." *Transition: An International Review* 7:1 (1998): 122–43. Also delivered at the Futures of American Studies Conference, Dartmouth College, August 15, 1997.

———. "The Logic of Identity." Delivered at the School for Criticism and Theory, Dartmouth College, July 1996.

———. *Our America: Nativism, Modernism, and Pluralism.* Durham: Duke University Press, 1995.

———. "'You Who Never Was There': Slavery and the New Historicism, Deconstruction, and the Holocaust." *Narrative* 4:1 (January 1996): 1–16.

Miller, Jerome. *Search and Destroy: African American Males in the Criminal Justice System.* New York: Cambridge University Press, 1996.

Minow, Martha. *Making All the Difference: Inclusion, Exclusion, and American Law.* Ithaca: Cornell University Press, 1990.

Mirandé, Alfredo. *Gringo Justice.* Notre Dame: University of Notre Dame Press, 1987.

Momaday, N. Scott. *House Made of Dawn.* New York: Harper and Row, 1968.

Morales, Alejandro. *The Brick People.* Houston: Arte Público Press, 1988.

———. *The Rag Doll Plagues.* Houston: Arte Público Press, 1992.

Morrison, Toni. *Song of Solomon.* New York: Plume, 1987.

Nash Smith, Henry. *Virgin Land: The American West as Symbol and Myth.* Cambridge: Harvard University Press, 1965.

Nelkin, Dorothy, and M. Susan Lindee. *The DNA Mystique: The Gene as Cultural Icon.* New York: Freeman, 1995.

Nietzsche, Friedrich. *Thus Spoke Zarathustra.* In *The Portable Nietzsche.* Ed. and trans. Walter Kaufmann. New York: Penguin, 1954.

Nisbett, Richard. "Race, IQ, and Scientism." In *The Bell Curve Wars: Race, Intelligence, and the Future of America.* Ed. Steven Fraser, 36–57. New York: Basic Books, 1995.

Olmos, Edward, dir. *American Me.* MCA, 1992.

Omi, Michael, and Howard Winant. *Racial Formation in the United States from the 1960s to the 1990s,* 2d ed. New York: Routledge, 1994.

Orfield, Gary, and Dean Whitla. "Diversity and Legal Education: Student Experiences in the Leading Law Schools." Independent report, August 1999, Harvard University Civil Rights Project, 1–28.

———. "The Impact of Diversity on Educational Experiences of Law Students." Press release, August 3, 1999, Harvard University Civil Rights Project, 1–2.

Pascoe, Peggy. *Relations of Rescue: The Search for Female Moral Authority in the American West, 1874–1939.* New York: Oxford University Press, 1990.

Peller, Gary. "Race-Consciousness." In *Critical Race Theory: The Key Writings That Formed the Movement.* Ed. Kimberlé Crenshaw, Neil Gotanda, Gary Peller, and Kendall Thomas, 127–158. New York: The New Press, 1995.

Pisani, Donald. "The 'New Western History' Comes of Age." *Reviews in American History* 21 (1993): 166–171.

Plessy v. Ferguson, 163 U.S. 551 (1896).

Posner, Richard. "Legal Narratology." *University of Chicago Law Review* 64 (1997): 737–747.

Price, Marcus. *Disputing the Dead: U.S. Law on Aboriginal Remains and Grave Goods.* Columbia: University of Missouri Press, 1991.

Rechy, John. *The Miraculous Day of Amalia Gómez.* New York: Arcade, 1991.

Ridley, Matt. *The Origins of Virtue: Human Instincts and the Evolution of Cooperation.* London: Penguin, 1998.

Robbins, Brian, dir. *Gattaca.* Columbia Pictures, 1997.

Robinson, Forrest G., ed. *The New Western History: The Territory Ahead.* Tucson: University of Arizona Press, 1997.

Rosaldo, Renato. *Culture and Truth: The Remaking of Social Analysis.* Boston: Beacon Press, 1989.

———. "Imperialist Nostalgia." *Representations* 26 (Spring 1989): 107–122.

Rotella, Sebastian. "Light Brigade: First Segment of Border to Be Lit Up in Show of Force." *Los Angeles Times,* Wednesday, January 26, 1994, A3.

Russell, Katheryn. *The Color of Crime: Racial Hoaxes, White Fear, Black Protectionism, Police Harassment, and Other Macroagressions.* New York: New York University Press, 1998.

Saldívar, José. *Border Matters: The Multiple Routes of Cultural Studies.* Berkeley: University of California Press, 1997.

———. *The Dialectics of Our America.* Durham: Duke University Press, 1991.

Santner, Eric. *Stranded Objects: Mourning, Memory, and Film in Postwar Germany.* Ithaca: Cornell University Press, 1990.

Scales, Ann. "US Dialogue on Race May Lack Shared Language." *Boston Globe,* July 2, 1997, A1.

Schumacher, Joel, dir. *Falling Down.* Warner Bros., 1993.

Scott, Daryl Michael. *Contempt and Pity: Social Policy and the Image of the Damaged Black Psyche, 1880–1996.* Chapel Hill: University of North Carolina Press, 1997.

Scott, Ridley, dir. *Blade Runner.* Warner Brothers, 1982.

Sergi, Jennifer. "Storytelling: Tradition and Preservation in Louise Erdrich's *Tracks*." *World Literature Today* 66:2 (1992): 279–282.

Shaw, Clifford. *The Jack Roller: A Delinquent Boy's Own Story*. Chicago: University of Chicago Press, 1930.

Sheppard, R. Z. "Review of *Tracks*." *Time* 132:80 (September 12, 1988).

Silko, Leslie. *Ceremony*. New York: Viking, 1977.

———. "Here's an Odd Artifact for the Fairy Tale Shelf." *Studies in American Literature* 10 (1986): 177–184.

Singleton, John, dir. *Boyz N the Hood*. Columbia Pictures, 1991.

Slotkin, Richard. *Regeneration through Violence: The Mythology of the American Frontier, 1600–1960*. Middletown, CT: Wesleyan University Press, 1973.

Snake, Sam, et al. *The Adventures of Nanabush: Ojibway Indian Stories*. Comp. Emerson Coatsworth and David Coatsworth. Toronto: Doubleday Canada, 1979.

Spiegelman, Art. *Maus: A Survivor's Tale*. New York: Random House, 1986.

Stallybrass, Peter, and Allon White. *The Politics and Poetics of Transgression*. Ithaca: Cornell University Press, 1986.

Strousse, Jean. "Review of *Tracks*." *New York Times Book Review* (October 2, 1988).

Taylor, Charles. *Multiculturalism and "The Politics of Recognition."* Princeton, NJ: Princeton University Press, 1992.

Telotte, J. P. "Definitely *Falling Down*." *Journal of Popular Film and Television* 24:1 (Spring 1996): 19–25.

Thernstrom, Stephen, and Abigail Thernstrom. *America in Black and White: One Nation, Indivisible*. New York: Simon and Schuster, 1999.

Thomas, William Isaac. *The Child in America*. New York: Knopf, 1928.

Torres, Gerald, and Kathryn Milun. "Translating 'Yonnondio' by Precedent and Evidence: The Mashpee Indian Case." In *Critical Race Theory: The Key Writings That Formed the Movement*. Ed. Kimberlé Crenshaw, Neil Gotanda, Gary Peller, and Kendall Thomas, 177–190. New York: The New Press, 1995.

Turner, Frederick Jackson. "The Significance of the Frontier in American History." In *The Frontier in American History*. New York: Holt, 1920.

United Steelworkers of America v. Weber, 443 U.S. 193 (1979).

U.S. Congress: Senate Committee on Indian Affairs. *Native American Graves Protection and Repatriation Act: A Hearing before the Committee on Indian Affairs*. Washington, DC: U.S. Government Printing Office, 1993. Cited in the notes as *NAGPRA*.

Walker, Alice. *Meridian*. New York: Pocket Books, 1986.

Weber, Samuel. "The Sideshow, or: Remarks on a Canny Moment." *Modern Language Notes* 88 (1973): 1102–1133.

Weitman, Sasha. "Prosocial Behavior and Its Discontents." In *Altruism, Sympathy and Helping: Psychological and Sociological Principles*. Ed. Lauren Wispé, 229–248. New York: Academic Press, 1978.

Welch, James. *Fools Crow*. New York: Viking, 1986.

White, Richard. *It's Your Misfortune and None of My Own*. Norman: University of Oklahoma Press, 1991.

Wiegman, Robyn. *American Anatomies: Theorizing Race and Gender*. Durham: Duke University Press, 1995.

Williams, Patricia. *The Alchemy of Race and Rights*. Cambridge: Harvard University Press, 1991.

———. "*Metro Broadcasting, Inc. v. FCC*: Regrouping in Singular Times." In *Critical Race Theory: The Key Writings That Formed the Movement*. Ed. Kimberlé Crenshaw, Neil Gotanda, Gary Peller, and Kendall Thomas, 191–204. New York: The New Press, 1995.

———. *The Rooster's Egg: On the Persistence of Prejudice*. Cambridge: Harvard University Press, 1995.

Wills, Christopher. *Exons, Introns, and Talking Genes: The Science behind the Human Genome Project*. New York: Basic Books, 1991.

Wilson, James Q. *Crime and Human Nature*. New York: Simon and Schuster, 1985.

Wilson, Pete. "Closing the Door." *Spectrum* (Winter 1994): 14–15.

Wing, Adrien Katherine. *Critical Race Feminism: A Reader*. New York: New York University Press, 1997.

Winnicott, D.W. *Playing and Reality*. London: Tavistock, 1971.

Wispé, Lauren, ed. *Altruism, Sympathy, and Helping: Psychological and Sociological Principles*. New York: Academic Press, 1978.

Wolfe, Alan. "America in Black and White: One Nation Indivisible." Book Review. *New Republic* 217:13 (September 29, 1997): 27–33.

———. "Has There Been a Cognitive Revolution in America? The Flawed Sociology of *The Bell Curve*." In *The Bell Curve Wars: Race, Intelligence, and the Future of America*. Ed. Steven Fraser, 109–123. New York: Basic Books, 1995.

Worster, Donald. *Under Western Skies: Nature and History of the American West*. New York: Oxford University Press, 1992.

———. *Rivers of Empire: Water, Aridity, and the Growth of the American West*. New York: Pantheon, 1986.

White, Richard. *It's Your Misfortune and None of My Own: A New History of the American West.* Norman: University of Oklahoma Press, 1991.

Wolfe, Cary. *What Is Posthumanism?* Minneapolis: University of Minnesota Press, 2010.

INDEX

acting out: in *Falling Down,* 64; versus working through, 59, 180n. 73
Acuña, Rudolfo, 98
admissions policies, race-sensitive, 174–176
affirmative action: backlash against, 34, 39, 49, 61, 161; limitations and advantages, 14; racial injury in, 25; racial preferences, 39, 80; resentment and, 39, 174, 194n. 21
African Americans: as disposable group, 148, 191n. 6; genetic deficiency theories, 147–149; nonaggressive behavior, 120–121; notions about, 30, 181n. 9; representation of injury, 30, 182n. 10
agency, rethinking of, 78
Alchemy of Race and Rights, 15, 44, 72, 73, 84–86
Algonquin war, 46
Alien 3 (motion picture), 163
Allen, Paula Gunn, 109
altruism, 159–161, 163, 173
America in Black and White: One Nation Indivisible: bias of criminal justice system, 118–119; on black crime, 116–121; on black pessimism, 116; critique of, 122, 138; influence of, 15; method in, 114; narrative experimentation, 114; optimism in, 115; politics in, 115; racial progress since 1940s, 115; on welfare programs, 119
American Anatomies: Theorizing Race and Gender, 22
American Criminological Society, 189n. 14
American Me (motion picture), 30
American Puritanism and the Defense of Mourning, 45
American studies: debate on racism, 24; identity in, 185n. 6(ch. 2); skepticism toward inclusion, 21–22
Americans with Disabilities Act (1992), 152
And We Are Not Saved, 44, 72
angry white male: backlash against affirmative action, 49, 61, 161; in *Falling Down,* 61–65
Anishinabe tribe: mourning practices, 109–110; in *Tracks,* 104–108
anthropology, self-criticism in, 184n. 27
anti-Semitism, 85–86, 173
Arac, Jonathan, 185n. 6(ch. 2)
Arax, Mark, 190n. 20
Aryan Nation, 98

Association of Literary Scholars and Critics, 184n. 1
autobiography: back crime and racism, 120–121; in injury rhetoric, 44–45; naturalization of racism, 33; rhetorical enfranchisement, 87; as self-criticism, 85–86
Ayau, Edward Halealoha, 188n. 23

Bakhtin, Mikhail, 16, 162–163
Baldwin, James, 101, 181n. 9
Beet Queen, 104
behavior: genetics and, 153, 157–158, 192n. 27; nonaggressive, 120–121
Bell, Derrick, 44, 71, 89, 116
Bell Curve, The: Gould on, 154–159, 173; impact of, 15, 146–148; place finding solution, 147, 191n. 3; scientific framework, 147, 191n. 2
Berdahl, Robert, 169
bias, racial: in criminal justice system, 117–119, 189n. 14; in criminal penalties, 10, 117–118, 123–124; judicial attitudes, 124. *See also* discrimination
biodeterminism: in *Alien 3,* 163; genome and, 155; in racial injury, 159; social context in, 158–159
bioengineering, in *Gattaca,* 164
biology, evolutionary, 154
Bird, Gloria, 108, 188n. 22
Black Congressional Caucus, 117–118
black crime: acculturation and, 132; arrest rates, 117, 118–119; data trends, 122; drug-related offenses, 123–124; fear of, 116–117; genetics and, 149; incarceration rates, 122–123; informal processes involving, 124–125; racial labeling and, 125; racism as product of, 116, 120; rhetoric and, 126; social policy paradoxes, 136; welfare system and, 119
Black Looks, 30
blackness, identity and, 40–41
Black Power: The Politics of Liberation in America, 31
black power movement, 26, 70
blacks. *See* African Americans
Blade Runner (motion picture), 163–164
Blumer, Herbert, 125–126
Boggess, Scott, 122

ABOUT THE AUTHOR

Carl Gutiérrez-Jones is Professor of English at the University of California, Santa Barbara. He is also the author of *Rethinking the Borderlands: Between Chicano Culture and Legal Discourse* (University of California Press, 1995).